FREEDOM IN CHRIST

FOR YOUNG PEOPLE

A 13-session discipleship
course for 11-18s

LEADER'S GUIDE

First published in the UK in 2009 by Monarch Books
(a publishing imprint of Lion Hudson plc),
Wilkinson House, Jordan Hill Road, Oxford OX2 8DR.
Tel: +44 (0)1865 302750 Fax: +44 (0)1865 302757
Email: monarch@lionhudson.com
www.lionhudson.com

Published jointly with:
Freedom in Christ (www.ficm.org.uk) and British Youth for Christ (www.yfc.co.uk)

ISBN: 978-1-85424-923-4 (UK)
ISBN: 978-0-8254-6321-1 (USA)

Distributed by:
UK: Marston Book Services Ltd, PO Box 269, Abingdon, Oxon OX14 4YN;
USA: Kregel Publications, PO Box 2607, Grand Rapids, Michigan 49501

Unless otherwise stated, Scripture quotations are taken from the Holy Bible, New International Version,
© 1973, 1978, 1984 by the International Bible Society. Used by permission of Hodder & Stoughton Ltd. All
rights reserved.
This book has been printed on paper and board independently certified as having come from sustainable
forests.
British Library Cataloguing Data
A catalogue record for this book is available from the British Library.

Printed and bound in Hong Kong by Printplus Ltd.

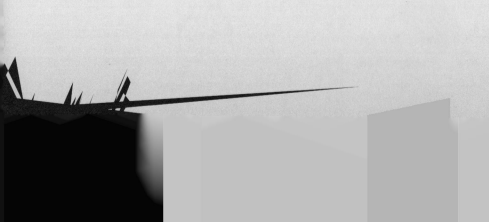

WHY USE THIS COURSE?

Freedom In Christ For Young People addresses three of the biggest issues facing Christian young people:

- **It helps them understand who they are in Christ**

  Young people are searching for identity and live in a media and peer culture that tells them that they have to look a certain way or achieve certain things in order to be loved. Knowing the truth of how God sees them will help them connect with the genuine unconditional security, significance and acceptance that they were always meant to have.

- **It gives them the tools to walk free from the rubbish that holds them back**

  There is so much temptation and pressure on young people to mess up in all kinds of ways. Learning what they are up against and how to stop, rethink and totally turn their back on sin will see them set free from all kinds of stuff from their past and in the present.

- **It empowers them to take hold of the authority they have in Christ**

  As children of God we have amazing authority in the spiritual world. We don't need to have to go to the 'right' event or respond to the 'right' message to be free. We can take full responsibility for our own freedom and relationship with God.

Jesus said, "You will know the truth, and the truth will set you free" (John 8:32). The aim of this course is to help young people connect with the truth of the Bible early in their Christian life so that they mature into fruitful disciples who live it out and change the world in Jesus' name. It is our prayer that whole youth groups, churches and communities are transformed by what God does through this course.

"There has never been a greater need for young people to find true freedom in Jesus. This incredible course provides churches with an innovative and user-friendly resource to help them in this. Freedom In Christ For Young People will transform the young people in your church and community. It is a real must have'"
Gavin Calver
National Director, British Youth For Christ

"The Freedom In Christ Discipleship Course (upon which Freedom In Christ For Young People is based) has been used by well over 100,000 Christians in the UK alone. We have received so many stories of changed lives - and even changed churches - that the prospect of young people getting hold of these life-changing principles relatively early in their Christian life is incredibly exciting."
Steve Goss
Executive Director, Freedom In Christ Ministries (UK)

THANKS!

Our grateful thanks go to Dr. Neil T. Anderson upon whose seminal teaching this course is based and who has encouraged us to create Freedom In Christ For Young People, and also to Sue Lea who worked on the prototype for three years without which this course could not have been created.

We are so grateful to those who contributed so generously to the production costs. Thank you - without your generosity, we could not have made this course.

A number of churches tested early versions of the course and gave us invaluable feedback that resulted in significant changes. Our thanks go to: City Church, Plymouth; Eternity Church, Warfield; Hillsborough Elim, N. Ireland; Otford Methodist Church; Viewpoint Community Church, Poole; St. Boniface, Quinton; Amblecote Christian Centre.

We really appreciate the great support we have received from Tony Collins and all at Monarch - you make it very easy for us.

And finally, what a great bunch of people we had working on this project! Their dedication to making this course absolutely as effective as it can be has been amazing.

Editors:

Steve Goss

Phil Knox

Sue Lea

Rich Miller

Contributors:

Anne Calver

Lorne Campbell

Sara Hargreaves

Rachael Heffer

Nathan Iles

Bethan Lawler

Lyn Morris

Tim Robinson

Simeon Whiting

DVD Presenters:

Nathan Iles

Kate John

Illustrations for Youth Guide:

Sue Lea

Overall Design Concepts:

Contrapositive Ltd, London

www.contrapositive.tv

Design Of Youth Guide Layouts:

Ezekiel Design, Manchester

www.ezekieldesign.co.uk

DVD Filming And Post-Production:

Blink Media, Lincoln

www.blinkmedia.org.uk

CONTENTS

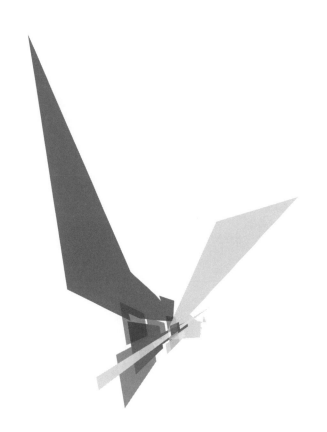

GETTING STARTED

WELCOME!

Welcome to Freedom In Christ for Young People! This is a course that has the potential to transform your youth group, church and community.

It is a partnership between Freedom In Christ Ministries and Youth for Christ and we hope and pray that God, through this material, radically changes the lives of countless young people.

Start by watching the short 'Leader's Introduction' on the DVD inside the back cover. Then please read through these 'Getting Started' pages for invaluable information on what to do next, what this course looks like and how to get the best out of it.

FIRST: PLEASE REGISTER

It costs nothing and you will receive:

- Access to the PowerPoint material for all the sessions
- Other additional resources to help you run the course
- Access to all updates to the course including illustrations from the latest DVD and music releases
- News of conferences and national Steps weekends
- Details of comprehensive youth resources from YFC
- A regular newsletter and full resource catalogue from Freedom in Christ

To register simply go to www.ficm.org.uk/youth and click on Register. (If you are in the USA, please see page 318).

HOW TO USE THE COURSE

HOW MANY WEEKS DO YOU NEED TO RUN THE COURSE?

There are four parts to Freedom In Christ For Young People each containing a number of sessions which are usually run weekly. In total there are 13 main sessions plus an optional launch evening. In addition, the third part of the course includes The Steps To Freedom In Christ which are designed to be run on an Away Day or Weekend.

If you ran the whole course including the Launch Session on consecutive weeks, you would need 14 weeks plus the Away Day/Weekend. That, however, is too long for most people to do in one go so the course has been designed with other options, the shortest of which is seven weeks.

The Launch Session (which we have called Session '0') is optional. It is useful in attracting young people to the course, facilitating the building of relationships and building anticipation but its main objective is to help young people with very little Christian background understand why it is perfectly reasonable to believe that the Bible is the inspired Word of God. Whether you run it or not depends largely on the make-up of your group. If it has people with very little Christian background or if it is a new group, you will want to include this session.

We strongly recommend running Sessions 1 - 10 (including The Steps To Freedom) in one consecutive block - these sessions form the key teaching. The final three sessions, however, can be used as a follow-up at a later date if desired.

If ten consecutive weekly sessions is still a little long for you, it is possible to run one or more of Sessions 8, 9 and 10 alongside The Steps To Freedom on your Away Day/Weekend. This means that you can, if desired, run the first ten sessions and Steps To Freedom in a seven week period, though ten weeks would be more comfortable.

WHAT IS THE STRUCTURE OF THE COURSE?

0. Launch

The Launch Session is a largely social event and we recommend you make every effort to make it as special as possible. The guide contains some suggestions as to how to do this. It includes teaching material on why we rely on the authority of the Bible. Amongst an increasingly Biblically illiterate culture, it is necessary to explain why it is reasonable to believe that God's Word is truth and is the authority on who God is, who we are and how to live life.

PART A – KEY TRUTHS

Jesus said you will know the truth and the truth will set you free. The truth about who we are now we are Christians is amazing. This first section of the course contains three sessions. They focus not so much about how to act as a follower of Jesus but on who we are.

1. Who was I?

When Adam and Eve were created, they had life in all its fullness. God met all their needs. They were perfectly accepted, secure and significant and this is a picture of how our relationship with God is meant to be. When they disobeyed God and turned their back on him, they lost their relationship with God. The result for us is that we were born physically alive but spiritually dead and with a huge need for acceptance, security and significance. Jesus came to restore to us the very same life, acceptance, security and significance that Adam and Eve had originally.

2. Who am I now?

The Bible is clear that when we become Christians, who we are and the way God sees us totally changes. This session explains that we should no longer regard ourselves as sinners but as new creations, children of God, saints! Furthermore, the way we see ourselves really matters. It is important to know that we can approach God with confidence, knowing we are not guilty in his eyes.

3. Where do I put my faith?

We all have faith in something. It is where we put that faith that decides whether or not it will be effective. If we want our Christian life to be fruitful and effective, we need to put our faith totally in God and the truth of the Bible. Our faith grows by putting it into practice.

PART B – WHAT ARE WE UP AGAINST?

Having considered the basic truths, the second part of the course (four sessions) looks at the things that try to deflect us from that truth, our enemies. Knowing what we are up against and how to fight against it can help us immensely to stand firm and not be held back in our relationship with God.

4. Worldview

We live in a world full of choices and 'mix and match' spirituality. The way that we see reality - our worldview - can vary massively based on where and when we were brought up. The world also tells us that there is no absolute unchangeable truth. When we become Christians we need to learn that, if we want to see reality as it is, we need to adopt the Biblical worldview.

5. Big choices

This session introduces something that the Bible calls 'the flesh', the unhelpful ways of thinking and coping that we developed as we grew up. These ways can still really affect us and hold us back, but we don't need to give in. We can choose every day and moment to live either according to our selfish 'flesh' or according to the guidance of the Holy Spirit.

6. Strongholds

The environment we grew up in, traumatic experiences and giving into temptation may have led to the development of what the Bible calls 'strongholds'. These are deeply-ingrained lies that we believe that affect the way we live. When we become a Christian, these lies were not deleted and we have to 'renew our minds' with the truth in the Bible.

7. Spiritual reality

It is important to realise that we are in a spiritual battle and the devil does exist and that he tells lies to us to affect what we believe and therefore how we live. Every day this battle between truth and lies takes place in our minds. This session looks at how the devil works and how to win the battle.

PART C – FREEDOM FROM THE PAST

Many young people have been hurt or affected by people or events that really affect their relationships with each other and with God. This third part of the course consists of two sessions plus the Steps To Freedom Away Day/Weekend. It is about resolving the negative effects of the past and dumping harmful spiritual 'baggage' that can hold us back.

8. Handling our emotions

Our emotions tell us if something is wrong and needs to be dealt with. Choosing to believe the truth about who we are and who God is makes sure that our feelings reflect reality. The best way to handle our emotions is to be totally honest with God.

9. Forgiveness

Nothing holds young people back more than an unwillingness to forgive. Forgiveness is not about setting the person who has hurt you free but about you being set free. Learning to forgive from the heart sets us free from the past and opens the door for God to heal our emotional pain.

The Steps to Freedom in Christ Away Day/Weekend

The Steps to Freedom in Christ is a key part of the course. It is a gentle repentance process, where young people look at seven different areas of their life, ask the Holy Spirit to bring to their mind stuff they need to deal with and then say sorry and turn their back on it. It is about reconnecting with God's love and getting back on track in our relationship with him.

PART D – GROWING AS CHRISTIANS

Having taken hold of our freedom In Christ, we need to keep learning, following and growing as a Christian. This final part of the Course looks at how to stand firm, relate to others and aim to become more like Jesus. It contains four sessions; Session 10 contains crucial teaching on how to renew our minds and should not be separated from the previous nine sessions. However, sessions 11 to 13 can stand on their own as a follow-up for those who do not want to run the whole Course in one go.

10. Truth = freedom

If we dealt honestly with everything the Holy Spirit showed us in the Steps to Freedom, we have taken hold of the freedom Jesus won for us. The key to growth now is staying free. This session looks at how we make truth part of our lives every day and regularly resist the devil and renew our mind.

11. Loving others

Jesus said that the most important command was to love God with all that we have and love our neighbour as ourselves. This session looks at the fact that relationships go wrong because people focus on their rights in a relationship rather than on their responsibilities. If we focus on how we are to treat others rather than what we feel we deserve our friendships will be stronger, more fruitful and reflect God more.

12. Where are you going?

It is important that we understand God's goal for our lives and bring our own goals into line with it. God's goal for us is that we become more like Jesus. We have all kinds of desires that other people or events can get in the way of but no one can stop us becoming more like Jesus.

13. Keeping going

The world tells us that we will only have real satisfaction, fulfilment and success if we achieve certain things and look the right way. This session looks at a number of aspects of our lives and how faith works in each of these areas as we aim to become more like Jesus.

WHAT IS THE BEST WAY TO PREPARE MYSELF TO LEAD?

We recommend that you start by watching the Leader's Introduction session on the enclosed DVD which will give you some excellent background understanding and advice.

The very best way of preparing yourself to lead Freedom In Christ For Young People is to attend the main Freedom In Christ Discipleship Course, ideally in your own church (Note: in the USA this is known as The Freedom In Christ Small Group Bible Study).

Failing that, we recommend that you read The Freedom In Christ Discipleship Series of books by Steve Goss which were specifically written to accompany the course and correspond to the four course sections. Details are on page 319. Alternatively, read The Bondage Breaker and Victory Over The Darkness, the foundational books written by Neil Anderson, founder of Freedom In Christ Ministries.

Freedom In Christ Ministries runs regular training days called "Making Fruitful Disciples - Getting Started With The Freedom In Christ Approach" which are designed to equip leaders to run the course. The day covers the main Biblical principles behind the course as well as hints and tips on how to run it. It is also available on DVD. Details of these can be found at www.ficm.org.uk.

A critical part of your own preparation is to experience The Steps To Freedom In Christ for yourself. You will get an opportunity to do this as part of the main course. Alternatively, you can simply go through it with a mature Christian in your own church.

WHAT ARE THE STEPS TO FREEDOM IN CHRIST?

The "Steps to Freedom In Christ" form the ministry component of the overall Freedom in Christ approach. They are simply a tool that provides an opportunity for the young person to put the whole of their life before God and deal with any rubbish that might be impeding their walk with him.

They start by asking God to show them any area in their life where an issue needs to be resolved. They then choose to repent of everything the Lord shows them which removes any ground the enemy may have had in their life. It is based on James 4:7, "Submit to God. Resist the devil and he will flee from you." Very simple and gentle - but amazingly effective!

HOW PRACTICALLY SHOULD THE STEPS TO FREEDOM BE RUN?

We recommend that this element of the course takes place as an Away Day or Weekend. It fits between sessions 9 and 10. One or more of sessions 8 to 10 can even be incorporated into the day/weekend. If done as part of a weekend, fun social activities can also be included, making the time even more memorable. For a sample weekend schedule and sample consent form please see 'Additional Resources' on the website.

The Steps themselves are integral to the whole course. Please do not be tempted to miss them out and make every effort to encourage all of your young people to be there. There are different versions of the Steps for 11-14 and 15-18. They can be found in the corresponding Youth Guide.

There are also national Freedom In Christ for Young People weekends taking place where the Freedom In Christ for Young People team will lead the weekend with groups from around the country. Please keep your eyes open on the website (www.ficm.org.uk/youth) for details.

There is a lot more information on running your Steps To Freedom session later in this Leader's Guide.

HOW THE COURSE WORKS

WHAT MATERIALS DO I NEED?

Leader's Guide

This Leader's Guide is your comprehensive guide to hosting and running Freedom In Christ For Young People.

DVD Material

At the back of this Leader's Guide, you will find the course DVD which contains video material for each session. Use the same material for both age groups. There are around 8 to 10 minutes of DVD material per session broken down into three chapters that we recommend are played separately. You will need to make preparations for showing the DVD. Projecting it onto a large screen is recommended if possible.

Downloadable Material

Once you register with us (free of charge) at www.ficm.org.uk/youth, you will be given access to a range of downloadable material including PowerPoint slides to complement each session.

Youth Guides

Although this Leader's Guide includes material for both 11-14s and 15-18s, there is a separate Youth Guide for each age range. We strongly recommend that everyone in your group should have their own copy of the Youth Guide. These contain not only the Steps To Freedom In Christ but a load of additional material for each session of the course including summaries of the key points, Bible verses, challenges, games and an opportunity to journal how the course is impacting their lives. They are available for the 11-14s and 15-18s age streams.

Biblical Truths Postcards

The first three sessions contain core lists of truth from the Bible. It is great to encourage people to make real connections with these truths so they are available on a set of 3 postcards that your young people can stick on their wall, use as a bookmark or carry around with them. The postcards are available for both 11-14s and 15-18s age streams.

HOW IS EACH SESSION STRUCTURED?

In this Leader's Guide, you will see that each session has three distinct sections: The Core; 11-14; and 15-18.

The Core

This section is for you, the leader of the course. If you haven't first got your own mind around the principles being taught, you won't be able to pass them on to your young people.

That's an obvious point to make, we know, but you would be amazed how many mature Christian people who have been through the main adult course (including church leaders) tell us that, although they have been Christians for decades, they had never before really understood the key truths taught.

The Core is the heart of each session and contains the key teaching and questions to think about as you prepare. Take particular note of the objective of each session.

The Core is laid out in such a way that you can easily incorporate sections from it into the main session itself as you teach it.

Session Guides For 11-14 And 15-18 Age Ranges

Freedom In Christ for Young People is presented in two age streams, designed to meet the specific needs and tastes of younger and older teenagers. Communicating this message to a 12 year old is, of course, very different to communicating it to a 17 year old.

The other two sections in the Leader's Guide contain age appropriate material for 11-14s and 15-18s. You will see that there are different games, illustrations, worship activities etc. which are tailored to the general interests and learning styles of the different age groups.

WHAT DIFFERENCES ARE THERE IN LEADING THE DIFFERENT AGES?

Younger teens (11-14s) are often quite high energy and need lots of activities to keep them entertained and busy. Things may have to be done in a very creative way to hold their attention and keep them sitting still!

The 11-14s material is written with their energy and need to interact in mind. It is fast-paced, fun, but thought-provoking and filled with enough ideas to present and reinforce the teaching points from each session.

Older teens (15-18s) may find it easier to get involved when there is room for discussion. They will want to be engaged and challenged physically and mentally, but they may have their own opinions about things. Some may have already formed quite definite opinions while others may be just working things through, needing space to explore.

The 15-18s material is written for this age group's ability to discuss ideas and think them through in more depth. The sessions will challenge them on misconceptions and encourage them to put what they learn into practice.

FORMAT OF SESSIONS

Each session (apart from the Launch Session which is much shorter) follows the same basic framework:

PREPARATION

There is a section at the beginning for those leading. We strongly recommend that you have a team around you when delivering this course and that you pray together as a team before each session. There is a prayer to guide you and your team as you prepare spiritually before the meeting.

There is also a list of the resources you may need for the session. Some will need more preparation than others so do look at this list well in advance of the session.

PRAYER AND DECLARATION

We recommend that you start each session with a prayer and a declaration. You may well be wondering at this point what a 'declaration' actually is.... Whereas a prayer is directed to God specifically, a declaration is spoken out to the spiritual world generally. This may be something that you and your young people are unfamiliar with but it is a really powerful tool to clear the spiritual atmosphere and introduce young people to the authority they have in Christ as a child of God. Encourage them to make the declaration confidently, shouting it out - with appropriate actions perhaps - because they (not the enemy) are the ones who have power and authority in Christ. It can be a lot of fun as well as spiritually powerful.

The words for the prayer and declaration are available on the downloadable PowerPoint file and can be projected or printed out.

STARTING POINT

As you get underway with the teaching content of the each session, we suggest you start with a brief summary of what was covered in the previous session, especially if there are some young people who missed it. This is also your opportunity to ask for one or two thoughts on the closing question from the previous session. Keep it short, however, and use the responses to prepare people for the current session during which the answer to the question should emerge.

You will then start to break new ground. Sessions start gently, usually with an icebreaker such as a game that will help introduce the theme.

THE MAIN POINT

The session proceeds with a mix of activities designed to make delivery of the teaching as easy and effective as possible. You will find illustrations, stories, Bible references and, of course, the accompanying DVD. There are three DVD clips for each session and they are designed to be played one at a time with other material in between.

When you reach the banner saying "The Main Point", it is flagging up to you that you have reached the point where the main teaching point will be covered.

Do remember to use the Core section to supplement what is written in The Main Point as you lead. Also, do encourage the young people to bring their Bibles and get used to using them.

RESPONSE

At the end of each session there is time for the young people to respond. It will often be in an active, creative way that should leave the young people with a practical way of letting the subject affect their lives. There will be opportunity to get the young people talking about the issues raised in the session.

AND THERE'S MORE

The material in the Youth Guide is generally aimed at engaging the young people in the periods between sessions rather than in the sessions themselves. Towards the end of the session, the Leader's Guide will remind you to direct their attention to the material in the Youth Guide and encourage them to use it during the coming week.

CLOSING QUESTION

To continue a sense of journey, a question relating to the following week's topic is asked at the end of the Session. It is also in the Youth Guide.

There are various other elements that you will encounter. Just a note on a couple of them:

Soapbox (15-18s sessions)

Soapbox is the young people's opportunity to share what they think. There are generally a few discussion questions to get some of their reflections on the videos and the topics covered so far. Sometimes you as the leader are invited to 'get on your soapbox'. In some situations feedback and questions are invited. Sometimes it is just a moment to share. Use it as fits your group. The core material may be especially helpful to help you answer questions from the young people in this part of the session.

Movie Clip

Sometimes we may recommend a short clip from a movie to illustrate a truth from the session material. If you want to use it, you will need to get hold of a DVD of the movie and ensure you abide by any copyright restrictions.

It doesn't take long, of course, for clips to become outdated. Please check our website for fresh suggestions. Perhaps you have a great idea for a clip that would work - do let us know via the website and we will spread the word to others.

Worship Activity

Young people express their worship to God in different ways. In each session there is a creative way of focusing the group on God and praising, thanking Him for the freedom He brings and recognising who he is as we look at who we are in him. The activity will often be linked to the theme of the session and is a great way of setting God in the right place in our hearts.

PRACTICAL TIPS FOR LEADERS

USING THE MATERIAL EFFECTIVELY

Freedom In Christ for Young People helps you develop a place where young people feel secure to express what they are thinking. The resources provide many opportunities to challenge and increase their knowledge and experience. However, the sessions should not be regarded as simply 'ready to use' meetings. You should:

- **Adapt the material for your group**. Groups of young people can vary greatly. We suggest that you look to adapt individual activities to suit the taste and setting of your group. Try to keep to the core teaching material, but use the material flexibly and creatively to make it appropriate for your own group. Think carefully about the age group you are working with. Some activities may need to be adapted so that everyone enjoys taking part. Let us know through the website what you find works and what doesn't.

- **Make it your own.** Rather than repeating the written talks word for word, each leader should present in his/her own unique style, using their own examples and personal experiences where appropriate. Elements such as extra gimmicks will go down well with your own group and help to keep the weekly meetings fresh.

- **Leave some stuff out.** We'd like to think that you'll be able to cram in all the items in each week's session, but this might not always be that beneficial. More often than not, there will be more material than you can fit in. This means you'll need to decide what you're going to include or leave out well in advance of the meeting.

- **Take time to prepare each session.** Especially make sure you are well acquainted with the Core section of each session.

- **Foster friendships**. Experience shows that developing positive friendships can be crucial to young people attending the whole course and getting the most from it.

VENUE

Think carefully about your venue, since this makes a big difference to the atmosphere. Consider size, acoustics, temperature, how it feels, and think about a place where everyone will feel comfortable and relaxed. If you have a good sitting room available, take up the offer. If you have a big group, think about whether you will need a video screen or sound system. If you don't have a huge choice of venue, remember you can always make it feel inviting, with relaxed seating and comfortable room temperature.

SET A DATE FOR THE STEPS TO FREEDOM IN CHRIST IN GOOD TIME

For most people, going through the Steps To Freedom is a life-changing experience. It would be such a shame for any of your young people to miss it. For that reason, plan how and where you are going to do it well ahead of time. Ideally let people know the date at the first meeting (if not before) and remind them every week after that.

REFRESHMENTS

In each weekly meeting plan we recommend setting aside around 10 minutes for refreshments before the session starts, which you should adapt according to your own needs. This will help to create a setting for the young people to relate informally. As has already been mentioned, young people meeting up with their friends will be a major factor in Freedom In Christ for Young People being a winner. The refreshments don't have to be elaborate, but there should be drinks and something to eat that everyone will enjoy.

FINANCE

Work out how much money you may need to buy refreshments and materials and to cover other expenses.

CHILD PROTECTION

Freedom In Christ For Young People is designed to be run in the context of a local church. Make sure you are well acquainted with the appropriate child protection guidelines that should already have been set up by your church. If you are in any doubt, ask your church leader, or contact Youth For Christ. We strongly recommend using a parental consent form for taking children through the Steps To Freedom - there is more information on this in the Steps To Freedom section and a downloadable sample consent form in the Additional Resources section of the website.

LEADERSHIP

'No no – not me! I don't do the talky bits!' Maybe that's how you are feeling right now about talking in front of a group. Alternatively, you may be longing for the chance to explore your alter ego as a public speaker! Here are some tips:

Keep it simple. Remember who you are communicating with. Avoid jargon, explain difficult terms and keep things simple, especially with young people who are new and may not understand.

Be confident. Don't be intimidated, and don't worry about the odd mistake (it shows you are human). Speaking with humour and authority will support what you say, so just jump on in.

Stay relevant... to the subject, and the audience. Spend time with the group, get to know what they're in to, what they struggle with, and recognise their individual gifts. If you're prone to going off at a tangent, keep yourself in check.

Be creative. Each session should have "light and shade" including quiet and noise, times of activity and times of reflection. Encourage these; they will allow different individuals time to share in their own way. Think through how to make what you say more interesting – use images, humour, stories and keep it interactive. Involve the group as much as possible in ideas, preparation and the sessions themselves. Encourage them to own the sessions.

Be yourself. No-one is expecting you to be up on the latest tunes if that's not your thing. (Trying too hard to be cool will inevitably backfire, so beware!) Remember, in this setting what they need most is for you to be a friend.

Be a model. You are trying to encourage your young people to show acceptance, respect and grace to each other, even if they hold different views. So make sure you demonstrate this in what you do and say.

Don't let your body language give you away. Remember, your words only communicate part of the message. How you hold your arms, how far or near you are from your group, whether you sit or stand, whether you fiddle about and look nervous – all these communicate how you feel about the subject and the young people you are working with. Think about what you are communicating, not just what you are saying.

Don't forget to look people in the eye. Eye contact shows you are interested, and that you care. And don't just focus on the one person who finds you funny. Engage with all members of your group. This involves them and draws them into the group dynamics and discussion.

Remember your own relationship with God. Get right with God before you speak. Ensure that you make extra time for your own personal reflection and prayer each week. Pray for the course, that God will use you and guide your heart in all you do to serve him.

Come only expecting that God will move. Our role as leaders is simply to make space so that God can move, touching hearts and minds. Do all you can to facilitate this.

And finally.... Keep it moving, keep it relevant and HAVE FUN!

LEADING A DISCUSSION GROUP

Many of the sessions have a few discussion questions. These are also listed on the downloadable PowerPoint slides so groups can see them as they talk. Discussion groups are great places for young people to learn from each other and express their views. They provide a fantastic opportunity for encouragement and fellowship. Your role in leading the small group is to facilitate this process. Here are some tips to help this happen:

- Don't preach at the group.

- Try to involve everyone, especially the quieter ones.

- Create an environment where young people feel safe to express themselves, and disagree with each other, without putting each other down.

- Avoid questions that are vague, manipulative, or only require one-word answers.

- Use the prepared list of questions, but don't be tied to this. Use answers from previous questions to spawn new questions.

- Keep to the subject.

- Keep it moving.

- Don't allow groups to sit in silence for too long!

DISCIPLINE MATTERS

Young people respect and look up to those leaders who set fair, acceptable standards of behaviour. They feel more secure when they have stated boundaries. So, it's important to deal with undesirable behaviour. However you choose to do this, there are some principles you should keep in mind:

- Don't make threats unless you can carry them out and are prepared to do so.

- Don't overreact.

- Set clear and definite boundaries and try to stick to them.

- Be consistent: fair but firm.

- Don't give unjust punishment.

- Don't shout – use a calm voice.

- Discipline should be positive (as much as possible) and not negative.

- Give praise often.

- Never use sarcasm.

- Show that you have a sense of humour.

USING TECHNOLOGY

DVDs, CDs or MP3s and other media are great to use as part of a session, but make sure you've set it all up beforehand. Even if you're a technical genius, preparation is important.

Before each session:

- Cue any DVD or music you're going to use to the right point, and set the volume.

- View any movie or other clip beforehand to check that it's relevant and that it doesn't contain any 'undesirable' content.

- Make sure everyone will be able to see the screen.

- Check that there is not too much light on the screen. Close curtains and turn lights off if necessary.

SUPPORT

Make sure that your church know what you are doing, and are supporting you throughout the course. Meet your church leader and ask for advice, support and prayer. If you get the opportunity, share with the congregation during a meeting or service: inspire them with your work and ask them to pray for your group.

Find others around you who will pray for you, your team and your young people, before, during and after the Freedom In Christ for Young People course. You could communicate by email, text or a regular phone call to update those who are supporting you in prayer.

It is the heart of the partnership that we support you in whatever way we can. Please do get in touch with us if there is anything we can do.

SESSION ZERO:
LAUNCH EVENING

'For the word of God is living and active.
Sharper than any double-edged sword, it
penetrates even to dividing soul and spirit,
joints and marrow; it judges the thoughts and
attitudes of the heart.'

Hebrews 4:12

LAUNCH EVENING CORE

OBJECTIVE

This optional session is designed to introduce the course to your young people and create a sense of expectation but there is one overriding thing we want to achieve:

- to help the young people understand that it is perfectly reasonable to trust the Bible.

If you have a number of young people who have very little Christian background, as the course progresses they may struggle to understand why we put so much emphasis on the truth in God's Word, the Bible. They will legitimately have questions and in this session we want to pre-empt those.

If you are doing the course with a group of young people who have a good background and are already convinced that the Bible is trustworthy, there is no need to do this session, though you may still want to have a fun evening together to kick it off.

There is deliberately only a small amount of teaching in this session. Most of the time should be taken up with fun activities but do make sure that you cover the basic message.

Note that, although we imply that this will take place in an evening, it can, of course, take place at any time.

PREPARATION

Prepare some appropriate activities. There are suggestions below.

Make sure you have a personal testimony to share during the session. Ideally this will focus on a time where you experienced the truth in the Bible. You might also want to ask some of the young people in advance to come prepared to share a testimony.

Although we do not want this session to turn into a long discussion, be prepared for questions on the historical accuracy of the Bible and so on. We are assuming you have resolved this question for yourself but you could always have a book to hand such as Josh McDowell's 'Evidence That Demands A Verdict'.

Have you watched the Leader's Introduction on the enclosed DVD yet? If not, we recommend you do before you lead the session.

Here are some suggestions to make your session fun!

FOOD & DRINK:

- Have a pizza party with lots of different types of pizza. Alternatively, buy pizza bases and lots of different toppings (eg. Pepperoni, chicken, ham, peppers, onion and loads of cheese!) and let each young person make their own pizza.

- Set up a non-alcoholic cocktail bar. Get transparent plastic cups, umbrellas, lots of ice, slices of lemon and lime and ingredients for some tasty cocktails (eg. Cranberry Sunrise (cranberry juice - first - and orange juice), Pina Colada (pineapple juice, coconut milk) etc.

- Have a gorgeous-looking cake buffet by asking lots of willing bakers to provide a cake each. Make sure you have enough to fill a whole, big table.

- If you're optimistic about the weather, get a few barbecues together and stick on loads of burgers, sausages etc. For a tasty end to the meal, cut a slice in a banana, fill with chunks of chocolate and wrap the whole thing up with aluminium foil. Make one for each guest, chuck on the barbecue when finished with the main course, and enjoy plain or with some ice cream 30 minutes later.

- Organise an unexpected picnic. Make old-school picnic food like sandwiches, snacks, pies, cake etc. and pack nicely in a few baskets. Invite the guests to join you somewhere unexpected, eg. on your town square, an unused corner of your church etc.

- Have an ice cream extravaganza. Get lots of different types of ice cream (not just the cheapest stuff...), and plenty of toppings!

- Especially if you have a small group, you can invite everyone to a fancy sit-down, three course meal. Set the table with a proper, white linen cloth, cloth napkins, cutlery for each course and a printed menu. Get some friends or leaders to dress up in stylish waiter / waitress clothes to serve at the tables.

OTHER IDEAS & ACTIVITIES:

- Have a luau. Most party shops will sell luau 'props' – all palm trees and pineapples themed! Encourage visitors to come dressed in summer clothes, crank up the heating (if it's winter), play Hawaiian music, put up lots of lanterns and serve drinks with cocktail umbrellas.

- Organise a fancy-dress party! Add an interesting theme to the dress code, eg. Biblical characters, countries of the world, celebrity or anything that suits your context.

- Hire lots of inflatables and either use an open space or put it all inside if you have a large church.

- Have a tournament night with competitions in everything you can think of or have access to; Playstation / Wii, dance mat, karaoke, table tennis, pool, darts, snap, thumb wrestling etc. etc.

- Create the atmosphere of a chilled hang-out. Put up lots of fairy lights and candles, and turn the main lights off. Put out lots of low seating or cushions on the floor and put on some slow drum 'n' bass.

- Or, create the atmosphere of a high-energy disco / club. Get a DJ in to play the latest dance tunes, clear space to create a dance floor and borrow or hire some proper disco lights and / or a smoke machine.

- Organise a 'treasure hunt' where clues take the young people (in smaller groups / pairs if you have a large group) from a starting point (eg. your church) to someone's house where there's some nice food and drink waiting. You could have a list of things they need to find / take photos of along the way.

ESPECIALLY FOR GROUPS OF 10 OR LESS:

- Get everyone together for an evening/night bike ride where you plan a route through your town, maybe taking you past friends' (who don't mind staying up late) houses where you can drop in for competitions, food, the 'Main Point' section etc. If you plan to do something noisy, don't forget to check with neighbours first.

- Go for an outing. Travel together to eg. a theme park, and plan to do the 'word' section over lunch or in some other quiet corner.

- Meet for a nice meal out, and do the 'Main Point' section between courses. Book a restaurant where you know that you can get a separate room or quiet section.

- If you live near each other, separate out different responsibilities (eg. snacks and drinks, starters, mains, dessert, games etc.) and walk from house to house.

- Have a board games night. Everyone gets to bring their favourite game and try to get through as many as possible (avoid games like Risk and Monopoly if you want to get through more than one...).

GAMES IDEAS:

- **The Animal Game**. Sit in a circle. Everyone needs to choose an animal that they want to be (eg. elephant) and an action to go with it (eg. making a trunk with one arm). One person says, for example, 'elephant to tiger' whilst making the actions as well, the tiger then continues by saying, for example, 'tiger to pig' etc. All this must be done without showing any teeth; after a couple of practise runs, anyone showing their teeth is out of the game.

- **The Malteser Game.** Divide the group into two teams. Put two bowls full of Maltesers one end of the room and two empty bowls on the other end. Hand out a straw to each person. Appoint a leader dice-master. Whilst the dice-master rolls the dice, one person in each team must transport Maltesers to the empty bowl by using the straw. When the dice-master rolls a 1 or a 6, it's the next person's term. The team that manages to transport their Maltesers first wins.

- **Elk Elk Elk.** Sit in a circle. The person who is 'it' must say 'elk elk elk elk' whilst holding their hands like big elk's horns to the sides of their head. The person to the left of 'it' must also hold up their right hand in the same way, and the person to the right of 'it' must hold of their left hand in the same way. Then 'it' might pass this task onto someone else in the circle by bringing their hands together in a big pointing clap. The idea is to get a good rhythm of 'elk elk elk' going. Anyone who put the wrong hand up at the wrong time is out.

- **Mad Rounders.** Play an ordinary game of rounders, but with the following additions: By every base, put something that the player must get through (eg. a paddling pool of chocolate mousse, just plain water, or bath-bubbles, a tunnel with saw-dust, a washing up bowl of tapioca, a limbo stick with spaghetti hanging down etc. – use your gross imagination!). The fielding team must get the ball to the base where the batter is but must at that point sing a song all together ('Jerusalem' would sound great, for example!) before they can stop the batter. Don't play this game without giving people a chance to bring a change of clothes.

LAUNCH EVENING 11-14

🔍 INTRODUCTION TO SESSION

Have some Bibles (maybe different looking ones and different translations) mixed with lots of different magazines, newspapers, popular science books, novels and school text books in a large pile next to you.

I don't know about you, but I sometimes find it hard to know whose advice to take. There are so many voices around me telling me what to do: my parents, teachers, friends, TV, magazines and so on – who's telling the truth? Who should we listen to?

For example, of these different publications here [point to your pile of books], which do you think is the most trustworthy source of guidance?

Ask the whole group, or if your group is large, a couple of volunteers, to line the books and papers up in order of trustworthiness.

People think all kinds of things about the Bible. Some think it is a load of rubbish and not to be trusted at all. Some think it used to be useful but is now totally out of date. Others think some of it is good advice on how to live your life. Others still have given their whole lives to following it and doing what it says.

No matter what you think of the Bible, the important thing is that you read it and find out what it says for yourself and then make up your own mind about whether you trust it or not.

As Christians we believe that the Bible is totally to be trusted and this is not just because we have to or because we feel like it. It is based on really good evidence and the experience of millions of people who have put it into practice and found that it works and has a massive impact on them.

This session is all about why believing what it says in the Bible is reasonable and how it can change your life. I wonder if you know what the Bible says...

INTRODUCTORY ACTIVITIES

'TRUE OR FALSE BIBLE QUIZ'
Appoint one side of the room the 'true' side and one the 'false' side. As you read a statement, the young people must choose whether it's true or false by moving to one side or the other.

Statements:

- The Bible says that we shouldn't lie (true, Deuteronomy 5:20)

- The Bible says that ball sports are dangerous (false)

- The Bible says that Christians are always happy (false)

- The Bible says that it's OK to dance in an embarrassing way (true, 2 Samuel 6:21)

- Luke was a converted thief (false, he was a doctor).

- Noah got really drunk and embarrassed himself (true, Genesis 9:20ff)

- There were two of each kind of animal on Noah's Ark (false, of the ritually clean animals, there were seven of each kind (Genesis 7:2))

- Jesus said that it's wrong to dress like a goth (false)

- The Bible says that money is the root of all evil (false, it says that the love of money is the root of all kinds of evil, 1 Timothy 6:10).

- Adam lived for 930 years (true, Genesis 5:5).

THE MAIN POINT

If other people tell you that you're mad to trust in the Bible, I'm here to tell you that you're not. I'm going to give you five good reasons why the Bible can be trusted:

1. Because the people who wrote the book were there when it happened! In around AD 40 when people started writing down the stories of Jesus and his life, death and resurrection, there were plenty of people still alive who would have put a stop to the whole thing, had it been lies. But they didn't because they had seen Jesus with their own eyes. And many of them went on to die rather than give up believing what they had seen.

2. The claims of the Bible have been backed up by archaeology where experts dig up the ground and examine evidence to find out what happened in history. Archaeology has confirmed many facts from the Bible, like names of cities, kings and other people, the destruction of places, historical and political events and so on.

3. The Bible has survived! Although it has been attacked and worked against during hundreds of years by philosophers, regimes and individuals; it has survived and flourished.

4. Jesus says so. When we become a Christian, we choose to follow Jesus who is the star of the Bible. This book is all about him – the first 39 books build up to him and the last 27 books are about him and how he transforms lives! And Jesus tells us in Matthew 5:17-19 that he has come to fulfil, to completely make true, the Bible. So the Bible is to be trusted because Jesus, the king of the world and king of our lives, backs it up.

5. It works. Millions of people across the world and throughout history have read the Bible, and experienced the Jesus that they have read about. They have known the truth of the Bible in their hearts and their lives have been changed.

Insert your own testimony here, or invite another leader up to give theirs. Here's one from one of our contributors:

A friend of mine had a really hard time once. Her husband had passed away with cancer and she was alone with two small children. She struggled to keep up with her rent payments, and the day came when she was told that she would be evicted. As she opened her Bible that day, her eyes fell on John 14:2 – 'In my Father's house there are many rooms…'. My friend felt in her spirit that this was a promise for her for this time; God wouldn't let her go homeless.

The days passed and as the eviction date got nearer my friend started to worry that maybe she had imagined this particular verse speaking to her. The miracle happened the day before the eviction day, when her local church decided to buy a neighbouring house and offered it to her to live rent-free.

Hebrews 4:12 says that '…the word of God is living and active.' It's not just a dusty, old book – it changes our lives!

The apostle Peter wrote 'We did not follow cleverly invented stories when we told you about the power and coming of our Lord Jesus Christ, but we were eye-witnesses of his majesty.' (2 Peter 1:16)

We believe that Peter was telling the truth and that the Bible is the ultimate authority for our lives. That's why in this course is founded on the Bible. If we want to know who we are, what it means to be a Christian and how we should live, we have to look in the Bible. You will find that throughout the Freedom in Christ for Young People course, we will keep referring to God's Word as the authority and the truth. And it is perfectly logical and reasonable to do that.

INTRODUCTION TO THE REST OF THE COURSE

This course will take you through some really important and life-changing stuff, things like our identity: who we are and what that means. We're going to dig deep into some tricky topics like truth and evil, and make sure that we all understand them. Towards the second half of the course, we're going to get more practical, going through the Steps To The Freedom In Christ, and learning about how to handle our emotions and how to have good relationships, among other things.

There are certain elements that will return in each session. We'll start with some icebreakers and games every time, to have some fun and get to know each other. Then there will be a video clip to introduce the topic, and we'll use different, creative ways to worship in each session. The 'word' section is where you'll get some input on the topics I mentioned, and we will have plenty of time to discuss it all and also respond to God.

This course is an opportunity for you to become the best person you could become, it's a chance to find out God's plan for your life.

At this point you could hand out the Youth Guides and remind the young people to bring them next week.

LAUNCH EVENING 15-18

🔍 INTRODUCTION TO SESSION

Have some Bibles (maybe different looking ones and different translations) mixed with lots of different magazines, newspapers, popular science books, novels and school text books in a large pile next to you.

I don't know about you, but I sometimes find it hard to know whose advice to take. There are so many voices around me telling me what to do: my parents, teachers, friends, TV, magazines and so on – who's telling the truth? Whom should we listen to?

For example, of these different publications here [point to your pile of books], which do you think is the most trustworthy source of guidance?

Ask the whole group, or if your group is large, a couple of volunteers, to line the books and papers up in order of trustworthiness.

People think all kinds of things about the Bible. Some think it is a load of rubbish and not to be trusted at all. Some think it used to be useful but is now totally out of date. Others think some of it is good advice on how to live your life. Others still have given their whole lives to following it and doing what it says.

No matter what you think of the Bible, the important thing is that you read it and find out what it says for yourself and then make up your own mind about whether you trust it or not.

As Christians we believe that the Bible is totally to be trusted and this is not just because we have to or because we feel like it. It is based on really good evidence and the experience of millions of people who have put it into practice and found that it works and has a massive impact on them.

This session is all about why believing what it says in the Bible is reasonable and how it can change your life.

☰ THE MAIN POINT

If you do read the Bible, if you do use it to guide your life, you may have come across people - perhaps friends, or maybe teachers - who think that this makes you a nutcase. Let's have a look at some good reasons why the Bible can be trusted:

1. Because it's an eyewitness account of something that really happened.

In around AD 40 when people started writing down the stories of Jesus and his life, death and resurrection, there were plenty of people still alive who would have put a stop to the whole thing, had it been lies. But they didn't because they had seen Jesus with their own eyes. What's more, many of them went on to die for that belief. They were clearly completely convinced of what they had seen.

Read 1 Corinthians 15:3-8 and explain that, when Jesus rose from the dead, he appeared to over 500 disciples and here they are talking about it.

Did you know that pretty much everyone believes that Julius Caesar came to Britain in 55 BC? What do we base this belief on? Well, there are some good sources, 9 or 10 manuscripts that tell us about it, the earliest one written around 900 years after the event. In contrast, we have around 2,000 manuscripts that support the events of the gospels, and the earliest copy that has been found so far, dates from AD 130 – only a few decades after the original was written! The gospels are the first four books of the New Testament and were written by Matthew, Mark, Luke and John.

2. The claims of the Bible have been backed up by archaeology.

Archaeology - where experts dig up the ground and examine evidence to find out what happened in history - has confirmed many facts from the Bible, like names of cities, kings and other people, the destruction of places, historical and political events and so on. In fact, professor Donald Wiseman of University of London has said that there have been no archaeological finds up to this day that contradict the Bible. Take, for example, the account of the Bethesda pool in John 5. Some researchers had called John's description of the Bethesda pool 'poetic licence'. Recently, however, archaeologists have examined the whole area and discovered all five colonnades and inscriptions which tell of the pool's healing powers - just as John described it (see John 5:2).

3. It backs itself up!

The Old Testament is full of prophecies of things that hadn't happened yet but then amazingly took place hundreds of years later in the New Testament.

Ensure that everyone has Bibles and give them the list below (available on the PowerPoint - you could put it up on a screen).

Ask the young people to work out what the Old Testament passage refers to in the New Testament, and possibly even to find the reference (provide concordances or biblegateway.com). Let the young people work in groups where they are seated.

Old Testament prophecies: Micah 5:1, Isaiah 7:14, Jeremiah 31:15, Psalm 41:10, Zechariah 11:12-13, Psalm 22:17 and Zechariah 12:10, Exodus 12:46 and Psalm 34:21, Psalm 22:19. All these things and hundreds more actually take place hundreds of years later in the New Testament.

4. The Bible has survived!

Although it has been attacked and worked against during hundreds of years by philosophers, regimes and individuals, it has survived and flourished.

All this is great, but the most compelling argument for the authority and trustworthiness of the Bible has to be the fact that it works! Millions of people across the world, and throughout history has read the Bible, and experienced the Jesus that they have read about. The truth of the Bible has been confirmed in their hearts and their lives have been changed.

Insert your own testimony here, or even better; ask some of the young people beforehand to share their testimonies of how the Bible has helped them. Here's one from one of our contributors:

A friend of mine had a really hard time once. Her husband had passed away with cancer and she was alone with two small children. She struggled to keep up with her rent payments, and the day came when she was told that she would be evicted. As she opened her Bible that day, her eyes fell on John 14:2 - 'In my Father's house there are many rooms...'. My friend felt in her spirit that this was a promise for her for this time; God wouldn't let her go homeless.

The days passed and as the eviction date got nearer my friend started to worry that maybe she had imagined this particular verse speaking to her. The miracle happened the day before the eviction day, when her local church decided to buy a neighbouring house and offered it to her to live rent-free.

5. Jesus says so.

When we become a Christian, we choose to follow Jesus and give our everything to him. The whole Bible is centred on Jesus - the first 39 books build up to him and the last 27 books are about him and how his first followers worked out what being a Christian was about. The whole book is about who God is, who we are and how we can live a life to the max centred on Jesus. And Jesus tells us in Matthew 5:17-19 that he has come to fulfil, to completely make true, the Bible. So the Bible is to be trusted because Jesus, the king of the world and king of our lives, backs it up.

Hebrews 4:12 says that '...the word of God is living and active.' It's not just a dusty, old book – it changes our lives!

The apostle Peter wrote 'We did not follow cleverly invented stories when we told you about the power and coming of our Lord Jesus Christ, but we were eye-witnesses of his majesty.' (2 Peter 1:16)

We believe that Peter was telling the truth and that the Bible is the ultimate authority for our lives. That's why this course is founded on the Bible. If we want to know who we are, what it means to be a Christian and how we should live, we have to look in the Bible. You will find that throughout the Freedom in Christ for Young People course, we will keep referring to God's Word as the authority and the truth. And, as I hope you can see, it is a perfectly logical and rational thing to do.

INTRODUCTION TO THE REST OF THE COURSE

This course will take you through some really important and life-changing stuff, things like our identity; who we are and what that means. We're going to dig deep into some tricky topics like truth and evil, and make sure that we all understand them. Towards the second half of the course, we're going to get more practical, going through the Steps To The Freedom In Christ, and learning about how to handle our emotions and how to have good relationships, among other things.

There are certain elements that we will return in each session. We'll start with some icebreakers and games every time, to have some fun and get to know each other. Then there will be a video clip to introduce the topic, and we'll use different, creative ways to worship in each session. We'll get some input from the Bible on the topics I mentioned, and we will have plenty of time to discuss it all and also respond to God.

This course is an opportunity for you to become the best person you could become, it's a chance to find out God's plan for your life.

You might like to hand out the Youth Guides at this point and remind the young people to bring them next week.

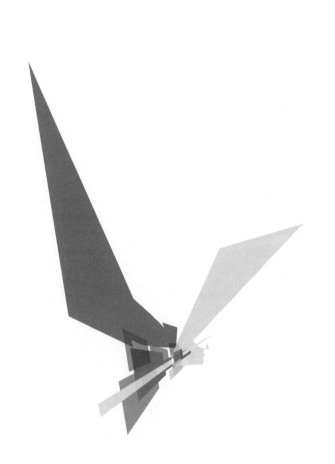

SESSION ONE:
WHO WAS I?

'I have come that they may have life, and have it to the full.'

John 10:10

WHO WAS I? CORE

PREPARATION

This is the first of three sessions in Part A of Freedom In Christ For Young People in which we are looking at basic truths. Even though we are calling them 'basic', we find that many Christians can go for decades without really grasping them. You will be doing your young people a huge service in helping them get hold of them at a relatively young age. However, if you don't first 'get it' yourself, you can't pass it on! That's why this "Core" section is so important. It summarises the principles you need to have at your fingertips. Please make sure you are familiar with them before leading the session. It is written in such a way that you could take sections of it and teach them at appropriate points in the session.

The best way of making sure you yourself have got hold of the principles before trying to teach them is to go through the adult version of this course or to read some of Freedom In Christ's main books. Steve Goss has written four short books, collectively known as The Freedom In Christ Discipleship Series, that correspond to the four parts of the course (see page 319). The first in the series, Free To Be Yourself (Monarch 2008), corresponds to Part A (the first four sessions). Read up to page 35 in the book for the material that relates to this session.

KEY VERSE

John 10:10: 'I have come that they may have life, and have it to the full.'

AIM

To understand how Adam and Eve's disobedience in the garden led to humanity being born spiritually dead; with every one of us having a deep need for significance, security and acceptance.

KEY TRUTH

Before we became Christians we were driven by the need to be accepted, secure and significant. Now, in Christ, we are spiritually alive children of God who are accepted, secure and significant.

OVERVIEW

When Adam and Eve were created, they had life in all its fullness. They had legitimate needs - to be accepted, secure and significant - which were completely fulfilled in their relationship with God. However, when Adam and Eve disobeyed God (sinned), the deep connection they had with him was lost. Subsequently all of humanity has inherited this loss of relationship and we were all born separate from God, 'spiritually dead', yet still had that huge need for acceptance, security and significance. Thankfully and amazingly, Jesus came to give back to us the spiritual life that was lost so that we can have the acceptance, security and significance that Adam and Eve had with God, through the restoration of our relationship with him.

WHO ARE YOU?

This course is all about learning to live in the freedom that Christ has won for us. But how are we freed?

Jesus said in John 8:32: 'You will know the truth and the truth will set you free.'

Jesus means that we need to know truth like we know a person, not just head-knowledge like we know about a subject at school like chemistry or English literature.

The first truth we need to find out about is where we have come from and who we really are.

So, who are you? You might think that's an easy question to answer!

If I say, 'Well, I'm John', you might say 'No, that's just your name. Who are you?'

'I go to such and such school/college.'

'No, that's what you do.'

'I'm British/American/African.'

'No, that's where you live or where you were born.'

Does the fact that I have dark hair, freckles and a wonky nose make me me?

You could try to put me on an operating table to find out who I really am.

If you chopped off one of my arms, would I still be me?

If you chopped off one of my legs as well, would I still be me?

What if you transplanted my heart, kidneys and liver, would I still be me?

Where am I then? If you keep chopping, will you eventually find me in there, somewhere?

What makes up the real 'me', the real 'you'? Is it my body? What I have? What I do? What I think?

Often, we tend to identify ourselves and others by the way we look, by how well or badly we do in school or if we're popular or not.

What does the Bible say?

In Genesis 1:26 we read that we are made in God's image. And God is spirit. That means that we're not just bodies that look a certain way or are popular or not, but we are spiritual beings – there's more to us than just bones, blood and skin.

So to answer the question of who we are properly we would need to say that fundamentally deep down inside we are spiritual. The bit of us deep down inside us that makes us who we are is referred to in the Bible as our 'soul' or our 'spirit'. When my body dies, this is the bit of me that will live for ever.

HOW YOU WERE DESIGNED TO BE

When God created Adam, Adam was physically alive. We too are physically alive:

* we have a body in which our spirit/soul lives

* we can taste, touch, smell, feel, see

But Adam was also spiritually alive which meant that the 'real him' (his spirit/soul) was connected to God. We were created to be spiritually alive too, not just with our soul/spirit connected to our bodies, but also connected to God.

For Adam, being spiritually alive meant that he was:

1.   Significant

God asked Adam to give names to the animals and rule over creation. He didn't have to search for the meaning of life or be worried about his own importance – he already knew it!

2.   Secure

Adam didn't know what it meant to have a need that wasn't met – everything was taken care of by God, including his need for human companionship, provided by Eve. Adam was completely safe and secure in God's presence.

3.   Accepted

Adam had a close relationship with God, he could talk to him at any time - Adam knew that he was accepted by God. Once Eve was created, Adam and Eve also experienced acceptance from one another.

This is how God created you to be – significant, secure and accepted. You were specifically designed for this kind of life: complete security; a real purpose; no need to worry about anything; and a sense of belonging to God and to other people. God loves you and originally designed you for this purpose.

ADAM AND EVE MESSED UP

When Adam and Eve were tricked by Satan into eating the fruit, and disobeying God – what the Bible calls sin – God said they would die. They didn't die physically (at least not immediately). So how did they die? Spiritually.

The spiritual connection between God and the core of their being was lost. Everyone born after Adam and Eve has inherited this disconnectedness. Even though we were designed to be spiritually alive we were all born spiritually dead, separated from God.

The effect of this spiritual death was enormous, both for Adam and Eve and for us.

These are two of the symptoms:

1.   Lost knowledge of God

People who are spiritually dead don't know who they are and they don't know God. They have to work out the meaning of their life and their identity without God's input.

Knowing God was never meant to be a brain exercise. Imagine that you met someone over the internet. Romance blossomed and after a few years of intense web-based flirting, you decide to get married. Imagine that you got married and then kept just chatting and meeting online, never seeing each other in person – what kind of relationship would that be? In the same way, knowing God needs to be a close heart relationship, not just head knowledge.

Paul in the New Testament is a good example of this. Before he met Jesus on the road to Damascus, he knew a lot about God, but afterwards he knew God for real. Paul himself claimed that this relationship was the most important thing in his life and that everything else was 'rubbish' in comparison (Philippians 3:8).

2.   Negative Emotions

At their spiritual death, for the first time in their lives, Adam and Eve started experiencing negative emotions. They started feeling scared (Genesis 3:10), guilty and ashamed. They felt rejected, weak, depressed and angry.

- Do you ever experience any of these feelings?

- Do you ever feel the desire to be accepted?

- Shame over something you've done?

- Anger over how someone has treated you?

Like Adam and Eve we instinctively do everything we can to get back to how things were before they messed up. We want significance, so we try and prove ourselves with good grades, by winning a TV talent show or becoming a pro footballer. We want security, so we try and make lots of money and get a good career. We want to be accepted, so we try and look our best and hope to be admired by those around us.

But we can't get back to how things were by trying harder, because the problem is that we were born separated from God.

In the Old Testament we see how God's people worked really hard to follow lots of rules and laws, and so get back in touch with God. But if you read about it, you'll see that it didn't work. God set up the Law specifically to show that on our own we cannot reconnect ourselves to God.

So God sent Jesus, to undo the work that Satan had done when he tricked Adam and Eve. Jesus was like Adam – he was both physically and spiritually alive – but unlike Adam, Jesus didn't sin.

Because of this, Jesus could both model spiritual life to us and give that spiritual life to us. Why did Jesus come? Yes, he came to forgive our sins but that was just the beginning. He himself put it like this, "I have come that they may have life, and have it to the full" (John 10:10). What did Adam lose? Life. What did Jesus come to give us? Life!

1 John 5:12 says: 'He who has the Son has life; he who does not have the Son does not have life.'

When we become Christians we receive life.

Real life.

Life to the full right now.

And life forever in heaven when we die.

When we get that spiritual life back, the real us – our soul/spirit – is reconnected to God, and we can have the same relationship with God that Adam and Eve did before they messed up.

As a result we are instantly significant, secure and accepted. This is an amazing truth! Even if it doesn't feel like it, when we decided to follow Jesus we became completely secure, significant and accepted. On page 46 there is a whole list of truths from the Bible that demonstrate clearly that we are indeed secure, significant and accepted. These are key things that young people really need to know are absolutely true about them if they know Jesus.

Throughout the course we are going to look at these truths and others and make sure we really know them, not just in our heads but in our hearts. Jesus said it is when we know the truth - not just know about it - that we will experience true freedom (John 8:32). Jesus himself is the Truth (John 14:6) and his Spirit will guide us into all truth (John 16:13).

QUESTIONS TO THINK ABOUT AS YOU PREPARE

1. Imagine what life must have been like for Adam and Eve before they messed up.

2. How would it have been different from yours?

3. What do you think they thought about as they dropped off to sleep each night?

4. How did the fact that Adam disobeyed God affect us?

5. Do you ever experience those emotions that Adam and Eve experienced for the first time after they sinned (fear, guilt, shame, depression and anger)?

6. What did Adam lose and what did Jesus come to give us? What would it look like and feel like?

7. Thinking about out list of truths on page 46 if God says something about you, does that mean that it's true even if it doesn't feel true?

WHO WAS I? 11-14

LEADER'S PREPARATION

Read through the truths on page 46 with your team. Pick the one that most stands out to you and share it with the rest of the team.

Then pray together as a group:

 Father God, thank you for sending Jesus to give us life. Please, share this life with us as we meet, as we worship and as we hear your word. Please help each young person to choose to believe the truth about who you are. Amen.

YOU MAY NEED

Pens and Paper

CD of worship music

Post-its

Bibles

Blu-tac

Card

The first Biblical Truth postcard to hand out (optional)

🎤 PRAYER AND DECLARATION

Start by encouraging everyone to join together in saying the following prayer and declaration. You can download the PowerPoint slides with the words for these from the website.

It would be good to suggest that the young people stand up and speak out the declaration clearly and confidently to the heavenly realms. They could shout it out and use appropriate actions!

PRAYER

Father God, I want to thank you for sending Jesus to give me life. Please, share this life with me by your Holy Spirit as we all meet, worship and hear your word. Amen

DECLARATION: IN A CLEAR, CONFIDENT TONE!

As a Child of God I speak to any and all evil and tell you that you have no right or authority to be here. I command! I don't suggest! I command you to leave this place now! You are not going to annoy or distract me. Go now in Jesus' name. My mind will be a quiet place just for the Lord Jesus and me to talk.

STARTING POINT

INTRODUCTORY ACTIVITIES

DEFINE ME

Divide the group into teams of 4 to 8 people. The objective of the game is to line themselves up in the right order as quickly as possible. The teams get a point per win, and the team with the most points at the end wins the game.

Sample categories:

- height
- age
- house number (no number counts as zero)

- length of hair
- length of name (first, middle and surname combined)
- number of brothers and sisters

GETTING TO KNOW YOU

Ask the young people to pair up with someone they don't know very well. Get them to try to find out as much as possible about each other in two minutes.

Either: Give each young person pen and paper, and ask them to write down the answers to the questions below. Ask the partner to check the answers. The pair with most correct answers win.

Or: If your group is small enough, you can ask everyone in turn a question about their partner and eliminate the people that answer incorrectly. You can obviously repeat the questions for different people.

Sample questions. What is your partner's...

- name?
- date of birth?
- best-loved food?
- parents' name?
- best movie ever seen?
- school?

- most detested food?
- best subject in school?
- home address?
- ambition in life?
- preferred style of music?
- email address?

DVD CHAPTER 1

Play Session 1, Chapter 1 - 'Who am I?' - of the accompanying DVD.

The game/s we just played got us to share information about ourselves but do we really know what makes us, us?

In this session we will try to understand where we have come from and who we are. We will look at how God designed us to be, but how sin has messed this up. By the end of this time together, we will know how God has made a way to reconnect us with himself.

ILLUSTRATION

[Before the session starts prepare a white card on which you have written with lemon juice: 'The invisible things are as real as the stuff that's visible'.]

Show the white card to the young people, then light a candle and gently heat the card up as you speak, until they can see what is written: 'The invisible things are as real as the stuff that's visible'. Then explain that you will come back to that later.

Leader's Warning: Please assess the risk of using the above illustration, bearing in mind your group and the surroundings / environment you are in. Can matches / lighter and a candle be safely used / stored?

WHO ARE YOU?

Go around the group asking this question - 'Who are you?' - and noting down answers (explain there are no right or wrong answers).

- Did you think that was an easy question to answer?
- Some of you said your names, but that's not who you are, it's just your name.
- You might answer with what you do: 'I'm a student' or 'I'm a skater' – but those are just activities you do, not who you are!
- Or you might tell me your nationality – but that's just where you were born, not who you are!

WHAT MAKES ME ME?

- Is it my freckles and wonky nose [describe your own appearance]?
- Or what I do?
- Or what I have?

You and I often give ourselves an identity – deciding who we are – based on how we look, if we do well in school or not, if we're popular or not.

This is not how God identifies us!

In Genesis 1:26 it says that we were made in God's image – that means that we are spiritual beings. And do you know what...?

Leader's Note: It is really good actually to get a Bible out and turn to the reading. You set the example that your young people will follow, so when quoting from the Bible try actually to read from it as it then becomes a resource book that can be accessed and used.

Pick up the white card with the now visible 'The invisible things are as real as the stuff that's visible'

In this course we will talk about things inside us, things that we can't see, but that doesn't mean they are not real!

▤ THE MAIN POINT

◉ DVD CHAPTER 2

At this point play Session 1 Chapter 2 – 'Created by God' – of the accompanying DVD.

Now lead straight into the Graffiti activity.

GRAFFITI
Hand out pieces of paper and pens to each group member and divide them into three groups. Ask one group to write 'Accepted', another to write 'Secure' and the final group to write 'Significant' in as cool a graffiti style as they can.

Display the words somewhere around the room with blu-tac and then ask the group what they mean.

- Significant: to be important and worthy of attention
- Secure: feeling safe, stable, and free from fear or anxiety
- Accepted: to be approved of and welcomed; to belong

EXPLAIN
These words are really important because they describe how God designed us to be.

But do you always feel like that?

GAME - CAN I COME TO YOUR PARTY...?
Now explain that you are going to play a game that explains what you mean.

Sit your group down in a circle and explain that you are going to have a party but people have to bring certain things if they want to be invited and accepted into the party. Tell the group that there is a logical reason why you will accept people and they must try to figure it out.

Each person has to say: 'Can I come to your party if I bring a........?' They then have to suggest something to bring.

'Can I come to your party if I bring a sweet?' The answer to the first question is always 'yes'.

Subsequent questions must use the last letter of the thing that the person before is going to bring. For example the first person asked if they could bring a sweet. If the next person asks, 'Can I come to your party if I play the trumpet?' or 'Can I come to your party if I give you a tooth?', the answer will be 'yes'.

If they ask, 'Can I come to your party if I give you money?', the answer in this case will be 'no'. As they have used an 'M' instead of a 'T'.

For an added twist have crisps or sweets that only the ones accepted to the party can eat. You may need to control how many your 'guests' have so that everyone gets some by the end.

Keep going until everyone has been accepted or the group gets bored.

Leader's Note: Make sure that the leaders, or a couple of other people in the group, know the rules of this game before starting. Also explain that once you have understood the rule you have to keep it a secret and not give it away. If necessary double check with your existing 'guest' to make sure they understand how they got accepted by asking them to answer the question again following on from the last question. If they don't answer correctly throw them out of your party.

EXPLAIN

- How did it feel to be rejected?

- How did it feel to be accepted?

- How did it feel to be thrown out?

During our life we can often feel insignificant, insecure and unaccepted – just like during that game.

- If you didn't understand how to get into the party you were left out, rejected and insignificant.
- If you managed to get in but didn't really know how you managed it you could feel nervous about being found out, you could feel insecure.
- But once you were in and you knew why you may have felt confident – significant, secure and accepted.

But what about real life? Don't we all want to feel significant, secure and accepted? Why is that? The answer can be found thousands of years ago in a garden.

◉ DVD CHAPTER 3

At this point play Session 1, chapter 3 – 'Significant, Secure, Accepted' – of the accompanying DVD.

Now lead straight into the overview.

OVERVIEW
It was in a garden that Adam and Eve – the first humans – stopped trusting in God and decided to disobey him. They broke the one rule designed to keep them safe. It changed the future for all human beings! Because of their actions they died, not physically but spiritually. They lost their relationship and their knowledge of God and because of them so have we.

Instead of feeling good they felt all these negative emotions - fear, anxiety, guilt, shame, rejection, powerlessness, weakness, depression and anger.

Can you think when you've had any of those feelings?

The result?

We attempt to get back to what God intended for us by trying really hard in our own strength. We try to be popular, attractive, hard-working and nice, all to feel significant, secure and accepted.

In TV talent shows we see hundreds of people searching for significance, security and acceptance in fame and stardom.

- We want to be accepted, so we try to look our best, get lots of boyfriends or girlfriends and to be admired by the people around us.
- We want to feel secure, so we try to make lots of money or become really popular.

- We want to feel significant, so we try to prove our worth by getting good grades in school or by trying to win a TV talent show.
- No matter how hard we try all too often we feel negative emotions instead of feeling good about ourselves.

But can we ever get back to how we were created to be just by trying harder, hoping that it will make us feel better?

Something had to happen in the invisible – which, as you'll remember – is just as real as the stuff that's visible. What Adam lost was **life**. So God sent Jesus to give us **life**

When we become Christians, God gives us back the eternal life that Adam messed up and lost for us. If you thought that you got eternal life just when you die you are going to be pleased to hear that it's much more than that, it's a whole different quality of life **right now**.

You and I can have the same relationship with God that Adam and Eve had before they disobeyed him. We can know God. And our needs to be accepted, secure and significant can be completely met because Jesus came to give us the spiritual life we were always meant to have.

RESPONSE

Try to think of three things that struck you personally as you watched the DVD or read the overview. Can you form them into questions for your group? If they were challenging or thought-provoking to you, they will be to your group too and through this shared experience you can connect with your group and really get to the root of feelings and thoughts. Then go on to explore what your group feels about the truths (below).

THE TRUTH ABOUT WHO I AM IN CHRIST
Read aloud as a group the list of things that God says about us if we are alive in Christ (pages 8 and 9 in the Youth Guide 11-14). If appropriate to your group, use this as a declaration of truth over their life. Be confident and sure, and be willing to repeat them as a reminder.

If young people have difficulty reading they could repeat them after the leader.

Ask the young people to pick out the truth that they find hardest to believe and copy it onto a piece of card. Encourage them to put this card somewhere where they will see it every day, maybe on a mirror, or in their pocket.

Emphasise: all these things are true about you if you are a Christian even if they don't feel true, and throughout this course we will understand these truths more and more.

Note that the lists of key truths from the first three sessions are also available on cool postcards that young people can take home and stick on their wall etc. You may like to order these before running the session. This would be an appropriate time to hand them out.

AND THERE'S MORE!

Draw the young people's attention to the 'Challenge' and 'Think' sections on page 7 of the Youth Guide.

Challenge: Learn at least one of the truths about who you are in Christ. Keep saying it over and over again to yourself until you remember it without looking.

You could ask them to pick one now that means the most to them.

Think: What do you do to try and feel significant, secure or accepted? Know that you are significant, secure and accepted just because of what God has done for you and your relationship with him.

Use this to emphasise the main point. Suggest they focus on this every day this coming week.

WORSHIP ACTIVITY

Get hold of a copy of some contemporary worship music – preferably a song containing plenty of words that describe God's character.

Hand out pens and a number of post-its to each group member.

Ask the young people to listen to the song and think of words or phrases from the song that stand out to them when they think of God. Ask each member to write them down on individual post-it notes and to stick them around the room. Alternatively ask for feedback after the song and write up the post-its yourself.

Then pray something like this:

Father God, we worship you for who you are. You are... [fill in with the words and phrases picked by the young people]. Amen

If possible, display the post-its in your meeting room for the rest of this course, as a reminder of who God is.

NB: You know your group so be aware of 'Christian' experience, choose your song carefully especially if some of your young people have limited worship experience. Make sure you explain simply and even give an example of a couple of words that stood out to you, once you have played the song.

? CLOSING QUESTION

Draw the young people's attention to the question on page 9 of the Youth Guide 11-14: 'Imagine that you're talking to someone who is not a Christian. Can you think of a short way to share your faith in a few sentences?' Ask them to come prepared to share their thoughts on this next session.

This would be a good time to let the young people know the date for the Steps To Freedom Away Day/Weekend.

WHO I AM IN CHRIST
11-14

I AM SIGNIFICANT

I am no longer worthless, inadequate, helpless or hopeless. In Christ I am deeply significant and special. God says:

- I am a temple of God where God's Holy Spirit lives (1 Corinthians 3:16).
- I am God's workmanship, created for good works (Ephesians 2:10).
- I may approach God with freedom and confidence (Ephesians 3:12).
- I can do all things through Christ who strengthens me (Philippians 4:13).

I AM SECURE

I am no longer guilty, unprotected, alone or abandoned. In Christ I am totally secure. God says:

- I am free from any guilty charges against me from God (Romans 8:31-34).
- I cannot be separated from the love of God (Romans 8:35-39).
- I am sure that the good work God has begun in me will be perfected (Philippians 1:6).
- I am kept safe with Christ in God (Colossians 3:3).
- I am a child of God and I am safe from any evil (1 John 5:18).

I AM ACCEPTED

I am no longer rejected, unloved or dirty. In Christ I am completely accepted. God says:

I am God's child (John 1:12).

I am Jesus' chosen friend (John 15:15).

I am a saint, a holy person (Ephesians 1:1).

I have been forgiven for all the things I've done wrong (Colossians 1:14).

WHO WAS I? 15-18

LEADERS' PREPARATION
Read through the truths on page 46 with your team. Pick the one that most stands out to you and share it with the rest of the team.

Then pray together as a group:

❝ **Father God, thank you for sending Jesus to give us life. Please, share this life with us as we meet, as we worship and as we hear your word. Please help each young person to choose to believe the truth about who you are. Amen.**

YOU MAY NEED
Large Mirror

Large sheet / flipchart paper & Pens

Accompanying DVD / DVD player / TV / projector

CD / MP-3 / worship music

Bibles

The first Biblical Truth postcard to hand out (optional)

PRAYER AND DECLARATION

Start by encouraging everyone to join together in saying the following prayer and declaration. You can download the PowerPoint slides with the words for these from the website).

It would be good to suggest that the young people stand up and speak out the declaration clearly and confidently to the heavenly realms. They could shout it out and use appropriate actions!

PRAYER:

❝ **Lord thank you for sending Jesus so that we can be re-connected with 'you' and know that we are truly significant, secure and accepted because we are in relationship with the Living God. Amen.**

DECLARATION: IN A CLEAR, CONFIDENT TONE!

❝ **I belong to Jesus and therefore no enemy of his has authority over me. They must leave now in Jesus' name. Get out of here!**

🔍 STARTING POINT

Have a large mirror centrally located in the room that you meet in. Make no comment about it but make a mental note of how the young people interact with it (e.g. checking hair / make up, pulling a funny face, avoid) when they enter the room.

◉ DVD CHAPTER 1

Play Session 1, Chapter 1 – 'Who am I?' – of the accompanying DVD.

SALESPERSON OF THE YEAR

Stand in front of the mirror as you start to speak as if checking / admiring yourself, then explain this activity.

- Divide your young people into teams of threes or fours and give them four sheets of large paper/ flipchart paper.

- On one sheet ask them to write down all they know about you.

- On the second sheet get them to prepare, and then present, a promotional poster about you.

- On the third sheet ask them to write up a 50 word advert describing and promoting you as an amazing person.

- Host presentations, asking the teams to use the fourth sheet to make comments about what they thought.

Standing in front of the mirror, pass comment to the effect that, 'Many of us find it difficult to talk about ourselves and prefer to stay in the back ground, whilst there are others of us who are happiest (it would seem) when we are in the spotlight.'

But we need to discover where we have come from and who we really are.

So, who am I? Was it an easy question to answer?

- Reflect back on some of the comments that they made trying to promote you

- Refer back to the Core section to help you unpack this line of thought.

Ask the group how they would like other people to sum them up/promote them.

What makes up the real 'me', the real 'you'?

- Is it my body?

- What I have?

- What I do?

- What I think?

Often, we identify ourselves and others by the way we look, by how well or badly we do in school, or how popular we are.

In this session we will try to understand where we have come from and who we are. We will look at how God designed us to be, but how sin has messed this up. By the end of this time together, we will know how God has reconnected us with himself.

SOAP BOX
MY OPINION - WHAT DO YOU THINK?

In Genesis 1:26 we read that we are made in God's image – that means that we're not just bodies that look a certain way or are popular or not, but we are spiritual beings – there's more to us than just bones, blood and skin. Because fundamentally God is spirit.

Who we really are is deep down inside. It is the spiritual part of us that makes us who we are – the Bible refers to it as our 'soul' or our 'spirit.' Even though my body will die one day, my spirit will live forever.

Divide the young people into pairs, and ask them these questions. Then either encourage them to write down their responses or give them a few moments to discuss and feed back their thoughts.

- How do I know I am physically alive?

- What does it mean?

- How do I know I am spiritually alive?

- What does it mean?

When God created Adam, Adam was both physically and spiritually alive. We too are physically alive; our soul/spirit is connected to our body and we can taste, touch, smell, feel and see.

The fact that Adam was spiritually alive, meant that the real him - the spiritual bit - was connected to God. We were created to live like that too, connected to our bodies but also to God.

 ACTIVITY

Stick three large sheets / flipchart paper around the room,

Write the word SIGNIFICANT across the top of one sheet, SECURITY on another, and ACCEPTANCE on the third sheet.

Then hand out marker pens and ask the group to go round each sheet and write on them what they feel that particular word means generally and/or what it means to them.

Go through this exercise yourself first so you can share your own thoughts as well as reflecting much better on what they have written. Remember to consider the thickness of the paper and the type of pens – will the ink go through onto the wall?! Also if wall space is difficult simply use the floor space.

After about five minutes reflect with the group on what they have written under each of the three words.

Discussion

What do you think about these three words?

Do you feel you are searching for significance, security, acceptance?

MAKES ME MAD

Do you ever get annoyed that someone thinks they know you and what you are going to do/say?

Do you ever feel boxed or labelled?

Do you ever do that to someone else?

What about that old man at church who always moans about young people not helping?

◉ DVD CHAPTER 2

Play Session 1, Chapter 2 – 'Created by God' – of the accompanying DVD.

Genesis 1 & 2 – the creation story right at the beginning of the Bible, really helps us to understand how God went about designing the whole world, including you and me.

It describes humanity – that's us. And it says that we were created in the very image of God. And God says that He saw it all and it was good.

How do you imagine God?

What does he look like? Happy? Sad? Big beard? Wearing sandals?

Do you agree?

- God is spirit. And if we are made in his image then we too are fundamentally spiritual beings.

- The ultimate statistic is death. Unless Jesus returns first, 100% of us will one day die.

- That means that one day our body, what you can see, our outer physical person will stop working and die.

- So is that it? Is that the end?

- No because our inner spiritual person - 'the real us' - goes on living.

So who are you?

You are not just what others see, or think they see on the outside. Deep down inside you are a spiritual person.

God made the most beautiful garden in the history of time with all kinds of trees, rivers, animals and birds. And into this garden God placed this couple; Adam and Eve. He said to them, 'this is just for you. Enjoy.'

They were physically alive. But they were also spiritually alive: they were connected to God. And that spiritual life, that connection to God, meant that they would have felt so significant, so loved, so secure, so accepted.

That's how God created us to be.

⬆ WORSHIP ACTIVITY

Get hold of a copy of some contemporary worship music – preferably a song containing plenty of words that describe God's character.

Hand out pens and a number of post-its to each group member.

Ask the young people to listen to the song and think of words or phrases from it that stand out to them when they think of God. Ask each member to write them down on individual post-it notes, and then, as the song plays again, ask them to stick them around the room. Alternatively ask for feedback after the song and write up the post-its yourself.

Then pray something like this:

Father God, we worship you for who you are. You are... [fill in with the words and phrases picked by the young people]. Amen

If possible, display the post-its in your meeting room for the rest of this course, as a reminder of who God is.

NB: You know your group so be aware of 'Christian' experience, choose your song carefully especially if some of your young people have limited worship experience. Make sure you explain simply and once you have played the song give an example of a couple of words that stood out to you.

THE MAIN POINT

Refer to page 6 of the Youth Guide15-18.

God designed us to be secure, significant and accepted and we often search for these things in the wrong places. When Adam and Eve messed up they lost spiritual life which had given them security, significance and acceptance. Jesus, through his life, death and resurrection, came to restore this to us by giving us back spiritual life. When we become Christians we automatically become secure, significant and accepted in Jesus even if sometimes it doesn't feel like it.

What difference does it make?

For Adam, being spiritually alive meant that he knew his...

1.   Significance

God asked Adam to give names to the animals and rule over creation. He didn't have to search for the meaning of life or be worried about his own importance – he already knew it!

2.   Security

Adam didn't know what it meant to have a need that wasn't met – everything was taken care of by God, including his need for human companionship, provided by Eve. Adam was completely safe and secure in God's presence.

3.   Acceptance

Adam had a close relationship with God, he could talk to him at any time - Adam knew that he was accepted by God. Once Eve was created, Adam and Eve also experienced acceptance from one another.

This is how God created you to be – significant, secure and accepted – you were specifically designed for this kind of life. Complete security, a real purpose, no need to worry about anything and a sense of belonging to God and to other people. God loves you and originally designed you for this purpose.

Ask the group to be really honest and to turn to the person next to them and finish these sentences

- 'One day I will...'

- 'One day I hope to see...'

- 'One day I will be...'

- 'One day there will be...'

- 'One day I hope...'

- 'One day I'm going to...'

There is so much more to us than we can imagine and today we will be trying to understand a little more how we can tap into the potential we have.

◉ DVD CHAPTER 3

Play Session 1, Chapter 3 – 'Significant, Secure, Accepted' – of the accompanying DVD.

Discussion

Think about what was said in the DVD. Can you imagine what it must have been like for Adam and Eve?

Text from DVD: 'Adam and Eve died. Not physically. But spiritually. Deep down inside they died. They were still physically alive. They looked the same. But they were cut off from God. For Adam and Eve, suddenly all these new feelings started appearing. Like fear, and guilt, and shame, and emptiness, and loneliness. Things they had never, ever felt before.'

- How did they feel?

- What did they think?

- What did they say to each other?

As a result, all of their descendants from that time on – that's you and me – would be born physically alive but spiritually dead. Without the amazing spiritual life we were meant to have.

What do you think?

Do you agree / disagree that:

- we were designed to be born into an amazing spiritual life, connected to God?

- we were designed to be spiritually alive knowing we are are absolutely significant, where we always feel secure, and we always know that we are accepted?

- we find ourselves born without that spiritual life?

- we all still have those deep-rooted needs to feel significant, secure and accepted?

- everyone goes looking for the answers in different places, relationships, drugs, sex, alcohol, stardom, money, career.

- we can look there, but we won't find the answer there.

Do you believe there was only one way for God to restore the real relationship with us and that it was through sending his son Jesus to die a terrible death on the cross and then rising from the dead?

Adam and Eve died when they ate the fruit and lost their spiritual life but Jesus said "I have come so that they might have life". Spiritual life!

Because of Jesus, you can become the person God always intended you to be. When you become a Christian, you become spiritually alive as you were always meant to be. You become completely new deep down inside.

ALTERNATIVE DISCUSSION QUESTIONS:

1. Imagine what life must have been like for Adam and Eve before the Fall. How would it have been different from yours? What do you think they thought about as they dropped off to sleep each night?

2. How did the fact that Adam disobeyed God affect us?

3. Do you ever experience those emotions that Adam and Eve experienced for the first time after the fall (fear, guilt, shame, depressed and angry)? What situations make you feel like this?

4. What was it that Jesus came to give us?

5. Look at the list of truths on pages 8 and 9 of the youth guide. If God says something about you, does that mean that it's true even if it doesn't feel true? Why? Why not?

RESPONSE

Leader's Note: Try to think of three things that struck you as you watched the DVD or read the overview. Can you form them into questions for your group? Perhaps ask them to discuss how they feel about the different truths outlined. If they were challenging or thought-provoking to you, they probably will be to your group and through this shared experience you can connect with them on a deeper level, really getting to the root of their feelings and thoughts.

Read aloud as a group the list of things that God says about us if we are alive in Christ (on pages 8 and 9 in the Youth Guide 15-18).

If it works with your group use the list as a declaration of truth over their life. Be confident and sure, and be willing to repeat them as a reminder

Leader's Note: If young people have difficulty reading they could repeat them after the leader.

Note that the lists of key truths from the first three sessions are also available on cool postcards that young people can take home and stick on their wall etc. You may like to order these before running the session. This would be an appropriate time to hand them out.

AND THERE'S MORE!

Draw attention to the journal activity on page 7 of the Youth Guide 15-18:

'What the Bible says about who we are in Christ is amazing. What are the truths on the next two pages that particularly stand out to you? Spend this week's journal page writing down the truths that mean the most and how they make you feel.'

? CLOSING QUESTION

Ask them to consider the question on page 9 of their guide before the next session:

Imagine that you're talking to someone who is not a Christian. Can you think of a short way to share your faith in a few sentences? Come prepared to share your sentences next week.

This would be a good time to let the young people know the date for the Steps To Freedom Away Day/Weekend.

WHO I AM IN CHRIST
15-18

I AM SIGNIFICANT
I am no longer worthless, inadequate, helpless or hopeless. In Christ I am deeply significant and special. God says:

- I have been chosen and appointed by God to change the world around me. (John 15:16)

- I am a temple of God where God's Holy Spirit lives. (1 Corinthians 3:16)

- I am a minister of 'making peace' for God. (2 Corinthians 5:17-21)

- I am God's workmanship, created for good works. (Ephesians 2:10)

- I may approach God with freedom and confidence. (Ephesians 3:12)

- I can do all things through Christ who strengthens me! (Philippians 4:13)

- I am part of God's family and I have my role to play. (1 Corinthians 12:27)

I AM SECURE
I am no longer guilty, unprotected, alone or abandoned. In Christ I am totally secure. God says:

- I am assured that in every circumstance God works for my good. (Romans 8:28)

- I am free from any guilty charges against me from God. (Romans 8:31-34)

- I cannot be separated from the love of God. (Romans 8:35-39)

- I am sure that the good work God has begun in me will be perfected. (Philippians 1:6)

- I am a citizen of heaven. (Philippians 3:20)

- I am kept safe with Christ in God. (Colossians 3:3)

- I am a child of God and I am safe from any evil. (1 John 5:18)

I AM SECURE
I am no longer rejected, unloved or dirty. In Christ I am completely accepted. God says:

- I am God's child. (John 1:12)

- I am Jesus' chosen friend. (John 15:15)

- I am holy and acceptable to God. (Romans 5:1)

- I am a saint, a holy person. (Ephesians 1:1)

- I have been forgiven for all the things I've done wrong. (Colossians 1:14)

- I am complete in Christ. (Colossians 2:10)

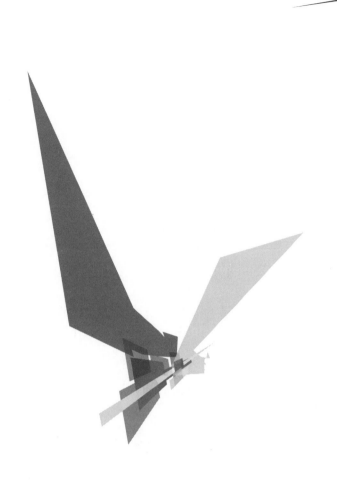

SESSION TWO:
WHO AM I NOW?

'If anyone is in Christ, he is a new creation; the
old has gone, the new has come!'

2 Corinthians 5:17

WHO AM I NOW? CORE

PREPARATION

This is the second of three sessions in Part A of Freedom In Christ For Young People in which we are looking at basic truths. Even though we calling them 'basic', we find that many Christians can go for decades without really grasping them. You will be doing your young people a huge service in helping them get hold of them at a relatively young age. However, if you don't first 'get it' yourself, you can't pass it on! That's why this "Core" section is so important. It summarises the principles you need to have at your fingertips. Please make sure you are familiar with them before leading the session. It is written in such a way that you could take sections of it and teach them at appropriate points in the session.

The best way of making sure you yourself have got hold of the principles before trying to teach them is to go through the adult version of this course or to read some of Freedom In Christ's main books. Steve Goss has written four short books, collectively known as The Freedom In Christ Discipleship Series, that correspond to the four parts of the course (see page 319). The first book, Free To Be Yourself (Monarch 2008), corresponds to Part A (the first four sessions). Read pages 36 - 59 in the book for the material for this session.

KEY VERSE

2 Corinthians 5:17 – 'If anyone is in Christ, he is a new creation; the old has gone, the new has come!'

AIM

To realise that deep down inside we are now completely new creations in Christ.

KEY TRUTH

Your decision to follow Christ was the defining moment in your life and led to a complete change in who you are.

OVERVIEW

Many Christians think of themselves as simply 'forgiven sinners', but in fact the Bible makes it clear that, because of what Jesus has done for us, we are new creations in Christ. The fact that we can know the truth that we are children of God who can come boldly into God's presence without condemnation ultimately changes everything in our life; our perspective, our approach and our confidence.

WHO AM I NOW?

Last session we started to explore who we really are by looking at how God designed us to be. We learned that Jesus came to give us back life. One thing is certain; when you became a Christian you changed radically – even if you didn't feel anything!

The Bible puts it in dramatic language; it says that you are a 'new creation' (2 Cor. 5:17) and that, although you were once 'darkness', now you are light (Ephesians 5:8). It's clear that to God there's no half-way point – you either are in his kingdom (and these things apply to you) or you're not (see Colossians 1:13).

ALL SAINTS

Do you think of yourself as a 'holy person'? Or are you more comfortable thinking of yourself as a 'sinner'? The Bible says this: 'While we were still sinners, Christ died for us' (Romans 5:8). Note the past tense! It seems that God doesn't call us sinners any more and in fact the New Testament refers to Christians not as sinners but as 'saints' more than 300 times.

That doesn't mean that you walk around with a halo! But it does mean that you really are a 'holy one'. You really are a new creation, someone completely new. You have changed from someone who was unholy and sinful, to someone who is accepted, secure and significant in Christ (as we saw last time). Deep down inside 'the real you' has changed from someone who could not help but be displeasing to God ('an object of wrath' - Ephesians 2:3) to someone who is now holy through and through and actually shares the nature of God himself (2 Peter 1:4)!

You don't have to be a mature or old Christian to be a saint – it's simply what you now are, whether you became a Christian 10 years ago or yesterday!

A NEW PERSON IN CHRIST

The reason we can be called 'saints' is because of our new identity 'in Christ'. In the book of Ephesians alone, the phrase 'in Christ' is used around 40 times. That must make it kind of important! Being 'in Christ' means that we now share in God's nature (2 Peter 1:4). We are saints because of Jesus.

If you think of yourself as a sinner who's been lucky enough to get to know Jesus, has had their sins forgiven and is therefore going to heaven when they die, you're likely to keep sinning – because you see your identity as a sinner. And what do sinners do? Sin!

If you play football, you will know how easy it is to make mistakes, give the ball away or simply fall over. Coaches will often say, 'You're better than that! Come on!' God probably thinks the same of us and says, 'Come on! You're better than that – you're a saint! My child!' Knowing that you are not a sinner any longer but are now a holy person is your hope for living a righteous life. You behave according to what you believe.

Now, the fact that you're a saint doesn't give you the right to boast – you know that it was nothing that you earned. It was a free gift. And it's an offer open to everyone.

LIVING AS SOMEONE WE'RE NOT

Satan can't take away your status as a saint. It's a fact – simple as that. His aim is instead to deceive you into believing lies about who you are. If you, for example, believe the lie that you are inferior or useless, that's how you'll start to behave. Or if Satan deceives you into believing that you're dirty and abandoned – which is not true for any child of God – that's how you will act.

You are not saved by how you behave, but by how you believe. This course isn't about learning to behave differently, but to believe differently - in line with what God says is true which, of course, is how things are.

LIVING AS NEW CREATIONS

We often struggle to see ourselves as saints rather than sinners, because there is a huge problem: we know that we sometimes sin. So, we conclude that we must be sinners.

I sometimes burp – but that doesn't mean that I identify myself as a 'burper'! I don't introduce myself to other people saying 'Hi, I'm Bob and I'm a burper.' What we **do** does not define who we **are**. Rather it's the other way around. What we **are** should define what we **do**.

If we have become Christians, we share God's nature – we have become someone completely new. We are not God or a god, but we can now become godly and like Jesus. Being a saint means that we can choose not to sin, but that does not mean our behaviour will always be perfect. 1 John 1:8 says 'If we claim to be without sin, we deceive ourselves and the truth is not in us'.

The reality is that, despite the fact that deep down inside where it really matters we are holy through and through, we still have our old ways of thinking constantly pushing us towards sin. And from time to time we will mess up.

So, what should we do when we sin?

- Remember that it doesn't change who we are. Can anything change the fact that you are your parents' child? No – you can disown them, never see them, they might be dead; but the DNA evidence remains. When you became a Christian you became a child of God, and in a way God's DNA is now in you – he sent his own Spirit to live in you (Romans 8:9). There is nothing you can do to change this (Romans 8:39, John 10:28).

- We need to restore the harmony in our relationship with God by agreeing with him that we were wrong (confess) and then turn away from our sin (repent). We can know that because of Christ's death, we are already forgiven.

- Remember that God doesn't condemn us. Romans 8:1 says 'Therefore, there is no condemnation for those who are in Christ Jesus.' We don't need to earn our way back into God's favour by having really good and long quiet times or going to church several Sundays in a row – we are already in his favour because of Jesus. Knowing that we can come straight back to God in confession and repentance when we have done something wrong – no extra punishments or work needed – is important if we want to grow as Christians.

It's so important that we realise that there is nothing we can do to make God love us any more or any less. Often when we read the Bible, we skip the bits where it talks about who we are, and go straight to the practical application: what we should do. So, we end up with lists of how to behave (which is important) but not as important as what to believe.

What is even more exciting is that being a saint, a completely new person, means that we can know that God sees us that way too. We need to know who we are so we can have a friendship with God and can come into His presence knowing that he sees us as his children whom he just loves.

GIVING OPPORTUNITY TO BECOME A CHRISTIAN
Of course, the answer to, 'Who am I now?' is only "spiritually alive, in relationship with God, secure, significant and accepted" if someone has chosen to follow Jesus and has become a Christian.

This session also offers an opportunity for young people to accept Jesus and the new life he offers. In each stream there is a challenge and a prayer for young people to choose to follow God if they are not doing that already and want to at this point.

QUESTIONS TO THINK ABOUT AS YOU PREPARE
1. Think back to the question we sent the young people home with last week: can you summarise your own faith in a few sentences?

2. Has preparing for this session helped you understand what happened when you became a Christian? Put into your own words what actually happened.

3. Do you find it difficult not to think of yourself as a sinner? Why? Why not?

4. Why is it important to know that you are a saint?

5. Which truth from the 'My Father God' list (see page 69) is the most important one for you personally?

As a really helpful exercise for yourself this week, why not look up the Bible references in the 'My Father God' list on page 69 in your own times with the Lord and make sure you know for yourself the wonderful truth about who God is.

WHO AM I NOW? 11-14

LEADER'S PREPARATION

In this session we are going to find out something amazing that happened when we became Christians. We didn't just get a ticket to heaven and a relationship with God. We became someone completely new deep down.

'If anyone is in Christ, he is a new creation; the old has gone, the new has come!'
2 Corinthians 5:17

This truth is SO important because if we don't really know deep down who we are as Christians then we'll never be really free to live the way God wants us to.

Pray together:

" **Father God, I thank you that I am a saint and a new creation. Help me teach and model what it means to be 'in Christ.' Amen.**

YOU MAY NEED

List of celebrity names

List of cartoon characters

Face paints / make-up

Plasticine / pipe cleaners (one for each group member)

Accompanying DVD / DVD player / TV / projector

Enough Bibles for the group

Pen & paper

Large paper / flipchart paper & marker pens

The second Biblical Truth postcard to hand out (optional)

 ## PRAYER AND DECLARATION

Encourage everyone to join together in saying the following prayer and declaration. You can download the PowerPoint slides with the words for these from the website.

It would be good to suggest that the young people stand up and speak out the declaration clearly and confidently to the heavenly realms. They could shout it out and use appropriate actions!

PRAYER

" Heavenly Father, I want to thank you that I am a new creation. Please help me really understand what it means to be 'in Christ'. Amen.

DECLARATION: IN A CLEAR, CONFIDENT TONE!

" I am a Child of God, I am a new creation.

I am not here to be distracted or bothered by enemies of the Lord Jesus. So, I'm telling every enemy of the Lord Jesus Christ to leave my presence now.

This is an instruction, this is not an option. You must leave now in Jesus name.

God's holy angels will show you the door. Go! GO! GO!

🔍 STARTING POINT

Start by giving a short summary of the previous session. A good resource for this is the Overview found in the Core of the previous session.

Also invite one or two responses to the Closing Question from last time:

'Imagine that you're talking to someone who is not a Christian. Can you think of a short way to share your faith in a few sentences?'

Do not dwell on this too long but take note of what is said for later. It will be interesting to see whether anyone mentions the fundamental fact that we become new creations or whether the focus is simply on being a 'forgiven sinner'.

🎮 INTRODUCTORY ACTIVITIES

CELEBRITY CHARADES

Divide your group into two teams and pick 3-5 players from each team. Give each player the name of a celebrity whom they need to act out without making any noise or doing any writing. If the player's team can guess the celebrity within 2 minutes, the team gains 2 points. If the player's team guesses incorrectly, the opposing team may guess and gains 1 point for a correct answer.

CARTOON BEAUTY CONTEST

Divide the group into pairs, and give each pair the name of a cartoon figure which they must keep secret (you might want to print out small pictures of the figures to help).

Provide each pair with face paints and / or make-up. The aim of the game is to make one person in each pair look like the cartoon figure. At the end (say 5 minutes), people may guess who each other is (and so gain points according to how many are able to guess correctly), and / or you may take a vote to see who's the most gorgeous cartoon figure. Ideas for figures:

*   Mickey Mouse

- Garfield

- Sponge-Bob Square-Pants

- Spiderman

- Donald Duck

A variation could be to divide into as many groups as you have leaders and the leader is the one who is 'transformed' into the cartoon character.

⬆ WORSHIP ACTIVITY

Hand out a small lump of plasticine or a pipe cleaner to each group member. Ask them to make a model of themselves out of it. Explain while they are doing it that it says in Psalm 139 that God knitted us together. As they make their models ask them to think about the care and attention God put into making them and ask what that means to them.

Leave a moment's silence, then say:

'Ephesians 2:10 says that you are God's workmanship and Romans 15:7 says that you are accepted by Jesus. Let's spend a moment in silence thanking God for making us as we are and loving and accepting us.'

Leave a moment's silence.

Finally read out loud together Psalm 139:14:

'I praise you because I am fearfully and wonderfully made; your works are wonderful, I know that full well.'

Ask:

Do you think that you're a saint or a sinner?

◉ DVD CHAPTER 1

Play Session 2, Chapter 1 - 'Change' - of the accompanying DVD.

Did you know that when you became a Christian, you were completely changed? It might not have felt any different or it might have felt totally different – people respond in different ways – but you were transformed.

Illustration: Make two models of yourself out of the material, one in, say, blue and the other in, say, red. Explain that when you became a Christian, the change was so fundamental that, instead of being blue all the way through, you are now red all the way through. It's not as though the blue bit was simply covered by a red outer coat - it was completely changed!

Illustration: it's a bit like on our birthday. We don't feel a big change, but we're actually a year older. Give a personal example, possibly when you turned 13 and became a teenager. Detail the preparation and possibly the anticlimax of the day.

AND / OR
When you go up to secondary/high school, you may not feel different, but you've actually changed.

You're now a secondary/high schooler. Again tell a personal story about your first day at your new school, getting up and getting ready, what you wore, what you took with you etc. – you were still you but something different was going on and you were not sure what.

Leader's Note: If you find thinking of a memory difficult, try closing your eyes for a moment and think back to that time; picture your school, the building the playground, the classrooms, the main hall, your teacher, the person who sat next to you. Now imagine the smells, the way things were done, how you were split into classes, what books you were given. Open your eyes and now try to note down that memory adding in all that detail.

COMPLETELY CHANGED

In the same way, becoming a Christian means that we're completely changed. The Bible says that we are new creations (2 Corinthians 5:17) and that we were darkness, but are now light (Ephesians 5:8). You can't be both at the same time - and you're not, even though it may feel like you are.

So, in actual fact – you are completely new!

God doesn't call us sinners any more (Romans 5:8) but says that we're saints over 300 times in the Bible!

Being a saint doesn't mean walking around with a halo on your head or having constant mystical experiences. It just means that you're a 'holy one'. It means that you have changed from someone who was unholy and sinful to someone who is – (do you remember the words from last time?)

- Accepted

- Secure

- Significant

You don't have to be a mature or old Christian to be a saint – it's simply what you are, whether you became a Christian 10 years ago or yesterday!

◉ DVD CHAPTER 2

Play Session 2, Chapter 2 - 'Changing Minds' of the accompanying DVD.

OVERVIEW – IN CHRIST

The Bible has an expression, 'in Christ', that is mentioned lots of times. Display this expression somewhere, on PowerPoint, overhead projector, whiteboard or flipchart.

Explain that you are going to set a challenge to the group.

Make sure that everyone has a Bible

- You have 1 minute to complete this challenge

- You must find the book of Ephesians

- Then you have to count how many times you can find 'in Christ', or 'in him' in this book

Let the young people guess and award a prize to whoever gets closest to 40.

Leader's Note: If you have young people in your group who struggle with literacy it may be a good idea to have the group pair up.

 THE MAIN POINT

What does it mean to be 'in Christ'?

It doesn't mean that we are physically swallowed up into Jesus' body, but it means that when God looks at us, we look like Jesus. There is now nothing inherently displeasing in us. Like Jesus we are now holy. That's why we are called saints, not sinners.

A NEW PERSON

Hand out a sheet of paper to everyone, including leaders.

Ask them to turn the sheet so that it is in a landscape orientation, and then to draw a line down the middle. Ask them to draw a matchstick person on each side of the sheet.

Around the drawing on the right ask them to write down what they think a saint is like.

- How do they behave?

- What do they think about?

- What do they do?

- How are they with other people?

- What sort of things do they say?

- How do they react when bad things happen?

Around the drawing on the left ask them to write or draw what they think of themselves.

- How do you behave?

- What do you think about?

- What do you do?

- How are you with other people?

- What sort of things do you say?

- How do you react when bad things happen?

Leader's Note: some variations might be to divide the young people into: two or three groups; age appropriate groups; girls and boys.

Try doing this exercise for yourself first with a larger sheet of paper. That will help when you come to explain what to do / when you explain what differences you found. Hopefully your honesty will encourage them to share their findings too.

Ask a few willing volunteers to talk about what they wrote down. An idea to get things going is to ask a young leader to start. If possible warn them beforehand so they know that it's coming and have an opportunity to decline.

Allow space for discussion and comments. Encourage the group to understand that God sees them differently from how they see themselves. But how God sees them, of course, is how they really are.

◉ DVD CHAPTER 3

Play Session 2, Chapter 3 - 'Changing For Good' - of the accompanying DVD.

Ask the group:

- What did you think/feel about the caterpillar and butterfly illustration?

- Which stage do you most identify with: the caterpillar; the chrysalis; or the butterfly?

- So who are you?

How you act depends on how you think of yourself. If you keep thinking of yourself as a sinner, you are likely to keep sinning. But if you think of yourself as you really are, as a saint, a Christian, a follower of Jesus, a son or daughter of the King then this will help you live like one.

DOES THIS MEAN I WON'T EVER MESS UP?
Of course not – but it does mean you are less likely to if you think of yourself as a saint. And when you do mess up, it's as simple as coming back to God and doing the following:

- Remember that who you are hasn't changed. You are still a saint in Christ.

- Quickly tell God you were wrong (confess) and turn away from what you have done (this is called 'to repent'). You can know that you are forgiven because Jesus died for all of your sins.

- Remember that God does not condemn you.

What is even more exciting is that being a saint, a completely new person, means that God sees us that way too. We need to know who we are so we can have a friendship with God and can come into his presence knowing that he sees us as his children whom he just loves – isn't that amazing?

 RESPONSE

Say to the group:

In this session we have looked at what an amazing difference being a Christian makes to someone. Obviously these things only apply to you if you have made that decision to become one. We would love to offer an opportunity to anyone who has not yet made that decision - or is not sure they have - and wants to do so.

There is a simple prayer that you can pray that just says sorry to God for the things you have done wrong and tells him that you want to follow him and go his way from now on.

Invite any who want to take that step to pray this simple prayer after you committing to follow Jesus:

Dear God, thank you that you love me just the way I am, no matter what. I am sorry for the things that I have done wrong that get in the way of my relationship with you. Thank you Jesus for dying on the cross to get rid of these things and for rising from the dead to give me the chance to have life to the max and life in heaven forever. I give up the selfish bit of me that wants to go my way and I choose to follow you forever. Please help me to do this God. Amen

In a way that is appropriate to your group find out who, if anyone, prayed this prayer – getting young people to put their hands up, tell the leader nearest them, tell the leader at the end of the session etc.

If anyone in your group commits their life to Jesus in the session, do affirm them that they are now in Christ, a whole new person and totally forgiven – all the stuff that we have been talking about in the session.

Say:

We've spent some time getting straight in our minds that, despite how we may feel or what we may have done, we have become completely new people. We also need to make sure that we have our minds straight about what God is like. It's really easy to get the wrong idea about God, especially if we base it on our experience of people.

Sometimes, without even thinking about it, we base our idea of God on authority figures such as our own father, mother, teacher or church leader. No matter how good they may be, they still don't measure up to God's goodness. And sometimes we've had bad experiences of other people and can easily think God is the same as they are.

We're going to read out together some truths about God and turn our back on lies about him that we might have believed.

Read out loud together the 'My Father God' list on page 12 of the Youth Guide 11-14 as a way of turning our back on the lies that we may believe about who God is and joyfully accepting the truth of who God is and our relationship with him as a result of who we are in Christ.

Pray:

Father God, forgive us for believing lies about you. We choose to not believe them any more, and we throw these lies away. Thank you for your grace and forgiveness. Help us to live this week in the light of the truth of who you are. Amen.

👥 SMALL GROUPS & PRAYER FOCUS

1. Think back to the question we sent you home with last week: can you summarise your faith in a few sentences? [Let a few more young people present their efforts, and then fill in for each other where there is truth missing or get the group to come up with a new answer based on what they have learned today]. It would be helpful to praise particularly any emphasis on how becoming a Christian is to become someone new or to get back the spiritual life we were always meant to have.

2. Has the session today helped you understand what happened when you became a Christian? Put in your own words what actually happened.

3. Do you still think of yourself as a sinner? Why? Why not?

4. Why is it important to think of yourself as a saint?

5. Which truth from the 'My Father God' list is the most important one for you?

⭐ AND THERE'S MORE!

If you are using the Biblical truth postcards, this is a good time to hand the second one out.

Draw the young people's attention to the 'Just For Fun', 'Challenge' and 'Think' sections on page 11 of their Youth Guide 11-14.

Just For Fun: 'Draw a sketch of yourself in a mirror. Then write around the outside some of the things that you now are because you know Jesus (eg "forgiven").'

Challenge: 'Take one of the truths from the 'Truths Section' on pages 8&9, write it down and pin it up above your bed or somewhere that you can see it. At the beginning of every day, thank God for the fact that it really is true of you.'

They should have picked the truth that meant most to them and memorised it last week. You could ask some to share that. This week ask them to pick a different truth or, if they prefer, a truth about God from this week's list.

Think: Remember what to do when you sin:

*   Know that it hasn't changed who you are; you are still a loved child of God

*   Say sorry for it and totally turn your back on it.

*   Remember that God doesn't condemn you or find you guilty because Jesus has already paid for it.

❓ CLOSING QUESTION

Ask the group to think about this question (on page 12 of the Youth Guide 11-14) during the week:

Do you believe that a person who doesn't believe in God has more or less faith than a Christian? What about a Hindu or a Muslim? Or someone who just doesn't know?

My Father God

I turn my back on the lie that my Father God is:

I joyfully accept the truth that my Father God is:

distant and uninterested in me

close and involved in my life (see Psalm 139:1-18)

stern and demanding

kind and caring (see Psalm 103:8-14)

too busy for me or not there

accepting and filled with joy and love (see Romans 15:7; Zephaniah 3:17)

impatient, angry or never satisfied with what I do

patient and slow to get angry and delights in those who put their hope in his unfailing love (see Exodus 34:6; 2 Peter 3:9, Psalm 147:11)

mean, cruel or abusive

loving and gentle and protects me (see Jeremiah 31:3; Isaiah 42:3; Psalm 18:2)

trying to take all the fun out of life

to be trusted and wants to give me the best possible life! (see Lamentations 3:22, 23; John 10:10; Rom 12:1-2)

condemning or not forgiving

kind and forgiving; his heart and arms are always open to me (see Psalm 130:1-4; Luke 15:17-24)

looking for faults or expecting me to be perfect

wants me to grow and is proud of me (see Romans 8:28; Hebrews 12:5-11; 2 Cor 5:17)

WHO AM I NOW? 15-18

LEADER'S PREPARATION

In this session we are going to find out something amazing that happened when we became Christians. We didn't just get a ticket to heaven and a relationship with God. We became someone completely new deep down.

'If anyone is in Christ, he is a new creation; the old has gone, the new has come!'
2 Corinthians 5:17

This truth is SO important because if we don't really know deep down who we are as Christians then we'll never be really free to live the way God wants us to.

Pray together:

❝ Father God, I thank you that I am a saint and a new creation. Help me teach and model what it means to be 'in Christ.' Amen.

YOU MAY NEED

Photos of when you and other leaders were younger

Accompanying DVD / DVD player / TV / projector

Modelling clay/pipe cleaners (one for each group member)

Paper and pens

Bibles

The second Biblical Truth postcard to hand out (optional)

 ## PRAYER AND DECLARATION

Encourage everyone to join together in saying the following prayer and declaration. You can download the PowerPoint slides with the words for these from the website.

It would be good to suggest that the young people stand up and speak out the declaration clearly and confidently to the heavenly realms. They could shout it out and use appropriate actions!

PRAYER:

❝ Heavenly Father, I want to thank you that I am a new creation. Please help me to really understand what it means to be 'in Christ'. Amen.

DECLARATION:

I am a child of God, I am a new creation. I refuse to be bothered by the enemy because I belong to Jesus. Every enemy of the Lord must leave now in Jesus name: Get lost!

 STARTING POINT

Over the welcome drinks, hand out photos of you and other leaders when you were younger. Discuss what has changed: hair, clothes, styles etc.

Give a short summary of the previous session. A good resource for this is the Overview found in the Core of the previous session.

Also invite one or two responses to the Closing Question from last time:

'Imagine that you're talking to someone who is not a Christian. Can you think of a short way to share your faith in a few sentences?'

Do not dwell on this too long but take note of what is said for later. It will be interesting to see whether anyone mentions the fundamental fact that we become new creations or whether the focus is simply on being a 'forgiven sinner'.

 DVD CHAPTER 1

Play Session 2, Chapter 1 – 'Change' – of the accompanying DVD.

Ask the group:

Did you know that when you became a Christian, you were completely changed?

I don't know how you felt - some people don't feel instantly different, others sense something shift immediately (everyone responds differently) - but the fact is that you were transformed.

ILLUSTRATION

It's a bit like on our birthday, we don't feel a big change, but we're actually a year older. Give a personal example, possibly when you turned 13 and became a teenager. Talk about what happened that day and whether it was a milestone in your life or not.

⬆ WORSHIP ACTIVITY

Hand out a small lump of modelling clay or a pipe cleaner to each group member. Ask them to make a model of themselves out of it. Explain while they are doing it that it says in Psalm 139 that God knitted us together. As they make their models ask them to think about the care and attention God put into making them and ask what that means to them.

Leave a moment's silence, then say:

'Ephesians 2:10 says that you are God's workmanship and Romans 15:7 says that you are accepted by Jesus. Let's spend a moment in silence thanking God for making us as we are and loving and accepting us.'

Leave a moment's silence.

Finally read out loud together Psalm 139:14:

'I praise you because I am fearfully and wonderfully made; your works are wonderful, I know that full well.'

DVD CHAPTER 2

Play Session 2, Chapter 2 – 'Changing Minds' – of the accompanying DVD.

Getting changed can sometimes take a long time right?

The amazing thing about this change on the inside is that it takes no effort on our part. God does it all. As soon as we choose to accept him into our lives and make him our Lord we **are** changed.

◢ SOAPBOX

A NEW PERSON

Hand out a sheet of paper to everyone, including leaders.

Ask them to turn the sheet so that it is in landscape orientation, to draw a line down the middle. and to draw a matchstick person on each side.

Around the drawing on the right ask them to write down what they think of when they think of a saint.

- How do they behave?
- What do they think about?
- What do they do?
- How are they with other people?
- What sort of things do they say?
- How do they react when bad things happen?

Around the drawing on the left ask them to write or draw what they think of themselves.

- How do you behave?
- What do you think about?
- What do you do?
- How are you with other people?
- What sort of things do you say?
- How do you react when bad things happen?

When God looks at you now, he thinks you are amazing. He delights in you.

The thing is, although we are completely new inside, no one ever hits the delete button in our heads. We are still stuck with our old habits, our old ways of thinking and behaving.

And let's be honest, we sometimes go wrong.

When we do, it's easy to think we haven't changed inside at all; that because we have sinned, we must be sinners.

The Bible doesn't say that.

In God's eyes we have become this completely new person. He sees us as holy people, saints, because we're now in Christ. And if that's how he sees us, that's how we really are!

⊙ DVD CHAPTER 3

Play Session 2, Chapter 3 – 'Changing for Good' – of the accompanying DVD.

Ask the group what they thought about the illustration of the caterpillar. What did they agree/disagree with about that comparison?

What is the hardest thing to understand and believe?

- The lowly crawling start?

- The odd looking nature of a caterpillar?

- The length of time (compared to its whole life) it spends at that initial stage?

- The process of becoming a chrysalis?

- The wrapping itself up and focusing on itself?

- The concept that it could suddenly burst out in glorious technicolour and start to fly?

- That it chooses to fly not crawl?

In the same way, what we need to see as Christians is that when we chose to follow Jesus our old self died and we became someone completely new inside.

Draw the group's attention to What's The Point? on page 10 of the Youth Guide which says:

- We used to be sinners but when we became Christians, Jesus transformed us into saints, children of God.

- Every child of God has a brand new identity and heart but if we believe our old identity of a 'sinner' still exists, that's how we will act.

- We are more than just forgiven by God; we also have his Spirit in us and can live in freedom.

What difference does it make? Ask the group if they agree with this line of logic:

- If we sin, we're just going back to behaving like the person we used to be. But we're not that person any more.

- We are now saints. Deep down inside we are pure and holy because of Jesus.

- We don't have to live as sinners any more, because we are **not** sinners.

- But if you think of yourself as a sinner what will you do? Sin! Because that's what sinners do.

- If you realise the truth - that you are a saint, a brand new person - then why would you ever want to go back to living how you used to live?

No Christian is useless, inferior or dirty. But if you think you are, that's how you will behave.

SESSION TWO: WHO AM I NOW?

When we are in Christ, it's not about the external: the new hair, new clothes, or the tan. It's all about the internal changes: because what happens inside affects everything that goes on outside.

If you are a Christian, you have been made clean and new and good inside. Because of what Jesus did. He loves you so much, not because of anything you have or haven't done; he loves us because of who **he** is.

We can often forget that it isn't about us, but it is all about God. There is nothing you could do that would make God love you more. There is nothing you could do that could make God love you less.

So, who are you?

- You are a saint. Plain and simple. A saint is a holy person.

- You are not someone that is trying hard to 'get there' one day.

- Right now deep down inside you are holy. Whether it feels like it or not.

- You are already someone completely different.

- The old has gone and the new has come.

 # RESPONSE

Say:

During this session when we were talking about **when** you became a Christian, did any of you think you had not actually made that step or you weren't completely sure? Do you want to know what it is to be 'In Christ' and be significant, secure and accepted and in an amazing, life changing relationship with God?

Invite any who want to take that step to pray this simple prayer after you:

Dear God, thank you that you love me just the way I am, no matter what. I am sorry for the things that I have done wrong that get in the way of my relationship with you. Thank you Jesus for dying on the cross to get rid of these things and for rising from the dead to give me the chance to have life to the max and life in heaven forever. I give up the selfish bit of me that wants to go my way and I choose to follow you forever. Please help me to do this God. Amen

In a way that is appropriate to your group find out who, if anyone, prayed this prayer – getting young people to put their hands up, tell the leader nearest them, tell the leader at the end of the session etc.

If anyone in your group commits their life to Jesus in the session, do affirm them that they are now in Christ, a whole new person and totally forgiven – all the stuff that we have been talking about in the session.

Point out that it isn't just our own identity that we can be deceived about. We can also be deceived about what God is like.

Read out loud together the 'My Father God' list (on pages 12 & 13 of the Youth Guide 15-18) as a way of turning our back on the lies that we may believe about who God is and joyfully accepting the truth of who he is.

The truth of who we are in him and the relationship that we can have with Jesus will be cemented by reading the list and reflecting on it.

If you are using the Biblical truth postcards, this would be an appropriate time to hand the second one out.

DISCUSSION

1. Think back to the question we sent you home with last week: can you summarise your faith in a few sentences? [Let a few more young people present their efforts, and then fill in for each other where there is truth missing or get the group to come up with a new answer based on what they have learned today]. It would be helpful to praise particularly any emphasis on how becoming a Christian is to become someone new or to get back the spiritual life we were always meant to have.

2. Has the session today helped you understand what happened when you became a Christian? Put in your own words what actually happened.

3. Do you still think of yourself as a sinner?

4. Why is it important to think of yourself as a saint?

5. Which truth from the 'My Father God' list is the most important one for you?

PRAYER

Father God, forgive us for believing lies about you. We choose not to believe them any more, and we throw these lies away. Thank you for your grace and forgiveness. Help us to live this week in the light of the truth of who you are. Amen.

? CLOSING QUESTION

Question for next week - see page 13 of the Youth Guide 15-18:

Do you believe that a person who doesn't believe in God has more or less faith than a Christian? What about a Hindu or Muslim? Or someone who just doesn't know?

SESSION THREE:
CHOOSING TO BELIEVE THE TRUTH

'Without faith it is impossible to please God,
because anyone who comes to him must
believe that he exists and that he rewards those
who earnestly seek him.'

Hebrews 11:6

CHOOSING TO BELIEVE THE TRUTH CORE

PREPARATION

This is the final session in Part A of Freedom In Christ For Young People in which we are looking at basic truths.

If you are reading The Freedom In Christ Discipleship Series books to help in your preparation, read pages 60 - 93 of Free To Be Yourself for the material that corresponds to this session.

KEY VERSE

Hebrews 11: 6 – 'Without faith it is impossible to please God, because anyone who comes to him must believe that he exists and that he rewards those who earnestly seek him.'

AIM

To understand that everyone lives by faith in something or someone and that faith in God is simply finding out what is already true and choosing to believe and act on it.

KEY TRUTH

God is truth: find out what he has said and choose to believe it, whether it feels true or not, and your Christian life will be transformed.

OVERVIEW

Everyone lives by faith, even those who are not Christians. It's who or what we put our faith in that determines whether or not it will be effective. As Christians, it's essential that what we believe is in agreement with what God has revealed in His Word.

INTRODUCTION

In this session we'll find out about how important it is to have faith and we're going to think about who we put our faith in.

THE IMPORTANCE OF FAITH

There is nothing you can do that will make God love you any more or any less. That's a fact! But how much you grow as a Christian will depend on how much you trust in God's word and act on it.

'It's impossible to please God apart from faith. And why? Because anyone who wants to approach God must believe both that he exists and that he cares enough to respond to those who seek him.' (Hebrews 11:6, The Message).

When we hear of amazing Christians, maybe speakers we've heard at conferences or a worship leader who inspires us, what do we do? Well, we might get their book, CD or DVD. We might learn something through these resources, but they are not the most important thing.

Hebrews 13:7 says: 'Remember your leaders who spoke the word of God to you. Consider the outcome of their way of life and imitate their faith.' Imitate their what? Not so much what they **do** but what they **believe**. What we do will grow out of our faith.

Faith is so important. It's through faith that we are saved! All through the Bible we can read that we should walk by faith. A real, living faith is the secret to a successful Christian life.

Faith is not about gritting your teeth and trying really hard to believe something that you are not sure about. It is not about relying on your feelings all the time and quitting when things get tough. Faith is believing that God is the truth and choosing to follow him. For a Christian faith is simply finding out in God's Word what is already true and making a decision to believe it.

Actually everyone exercises faith in something practically all the time. Faith is actually part of our everyday lives. Almost every decision you make involves faith.

When you cross the road at a pedestrian crossing with traffic lights, you press the button, and the signal indicates that it's safe to cross. You may see a car coming down the road towards you, but you cross anyway, because you know that the approaching car has a red light. This is an action taken completely by faith! There is no way that you can know for sure that the driver will definitely stop at the lights, rather than drive straight over you.

Some people believe that the human race is just some sort of accidental mutation, and there is no such thing as a God. That is faith just as much as Christian faith is – you have to believe that part that science can't prove. And even with science, you have to believe that the instruments are telling the truth, and that the lab assistant didn't make any mistakes.

THE DIFFERENCE IS WHAT WE BELIEVE IN

The fact that we believe doesn't make that faith work – it's what or whom we put our faith in that matters!

There's a story about Elijah in the Bible (1 Kings 18), where he has a big faith show-down with the so-called 'prophets' of a false god, Baal. As the people were watching, he encouraged the prophets of Baal to ask their god to throw down fire on their pile of sacrificed bull. The prophets shouted, danced, engaged in some self-harming; they did everything to make Baal hear them. After a few hours of this, Elijah started teasing them a bit, 'Maybe Baal has gone away on a trip? Or maybe he's tired out and asleep?'

When evening came, Elijah took to the stage. He built an altar for his sacrifice, and then soaked the whole thing in water, three times over – just to be sure that an expected miracle couldn't be explained away. Then, he prayed a simple prayer, and God threw down fire that consumed the entire altar.

It wasn't necessarily that Elijah had a stronger faith than the prophets of Baal – the difference was who he had put his faith in. Baal couldn't answer, because he is not real, but the Living God proved how real and powerful he really is.

Read Matthew 17:20-21.

Get hold of a mustard seed and hold it in the palm of your hand.

Why does Jesus say we only need faith as small as a mustard seed?

Because the size of our faith doesn't matter so much as who we put our faith in. A mountain won't move because we're trying really hard, or because we're powerful, but because God is powerful. You may choose to use this mustard seed illustration in your session.

Out of everything, or everyone, we can put our faith in, Christ is the only one who won't fail us. Traffic lights can break and parents, friends, teachers, youth leaders (!) can let us down, but 'Jesus Christ is the same yesterday and today and forever' (Hebrews 13:8). He is the truth, he is eternally faithful and trustworthy.

GROWING IN FAITH

Do you want your faith to grow? How strong your faith is, depends on just one thing: how well you know the one you put your faith in. It's all about relationship.

EXERCISE!

You are in control of how much your faith grows. It can grow every time you memorise a Bible verse, take part in a Bible study and so on. But most of all it grows when you act on what God says is true. For example, the Bible says that God will give us what we need, and that we don't need to worry (Matthew 6:25). If you act on this, by not worrying or by giving money to the poor, and you discover that God still gives you all that you need, your faith will grow.

When we experience God being faithful, our faith grows. If we take little steps of faith with God, we will learn by experience pretty soon that he can be trusted. And then we will start trusting him with bigger and bigger things.

Don't try to start by 'feeling' lots of faith. Just go with what you know is true: choose to believe it and act on it no matter what feelings tell you. If you trust your feelings, you end up all over the place, and your faith will not grow.

You don't feel your way into good behaviour- you behave your way into good feelings!

You also can't push your faith beyond what you know is true from the Bible. That's why it's important to know the truths that are in there.

FAITH GROWS IN DIFFICULT TIMES

Because faith is so important, God wants to help us grow it. That's why we often find ourselves in situations where we can choose whether we will put our faith in God or in something else.

It could be health problems, family or relationship issues or worries about the future.

God's role is to be truth. Our role and responsibility is to believe and act according to that truth.

FAITH LEADS TO ACTION

Real faith isn't just some kind of mental agreement with something, just believing something in our heads. You only know that faith is real, when it shows up in your actions. We can say all the right things, but it's your actions that show whether you really believe it or not.

James 2:17-18 says 'Faith by itself, if it is not accompanied by action, is dead. But someone will say, "You have faith: I have deeds." Show me your faith without deeds, and I will show you my faith by what I do.'

Faith without deeds is a bit like standing at the train station, wanting to go somewhere, and knowing everything about the trains, their technical detail, the timetables and so on – but never actually getting on a train.

The good news is that there is no one in your group of young people who can't have faith that really works. There's no one who cannot resist temptation, no one who could not become a mature Christian. They don't need some special prayer from a famous Christian, their youth leader or church leader or to have read all the right books. They just need to know what is already true, choose to believe it and act on it.

The Bible says this about God: 'There is no-one holy like the Lord; there is no-one besides you; there is no Rock like our God.' (1 Samuel 2:2). Rock can not easily be broken. It is solid. God is our rock – he can be trusted, we can put our faith in him.

QUESTIONS TO THINK ABOUT AS YOU PREPARE

1. Have you ever taken a step of faith – believed what God says is true and acted on it? What happened?

2. Do you agree that whether your faith really works is more about who you put your faith in, than how much you try really hard to believe something? Why? Why not?

3. How can you help your faith to grow?

4. What would the difference be in your life if you started acting on what you believe, rather than just keeping your faith in your head?

5. Think back to the question the young people were sent home with last week. What is your answer? Who has the most faith? What do atheists put their faith in? Think about your friends – what do they put their faith in?

CHOOSING TO BELIEVE THE TRUTH 11-14

PRAYER AND DECLARATION

Encourage everyone to join together in saying the following prayer and declaration. You can download the PowerPoint slides with the words for these from the website.

It would be good to suggest that the young people stand up and speak out the declaration clearly and confidently to the heavenly realms. They could shout it out and use appropriate actions!

PRAYER

❝ Father, I ask you to talk to me and show me how I can grow in faith today as I hear your word. I don't want to lean on my own understanding, so I ask you, Holy Spirit, to teach me how to walk by faith in you. Amen

DECLARATION: IN A CLEAR, CONFIDENT TONE!

❝ I am a treasured child of the Lord God Almighty so I speak to all evil, and tell you that you have no right to be here distracting me. I command you to leave now in Jesus' name. This time is only for me and God.

🔍 STARTING POINT

Start by giving a short summary of the previous session. A good resource for this is the Overview found in the Core of the previous session.

INTRODUCTORY ACTIVITIES

TRUE OR FALSE
Read the list of crazy facts below and ask if they are true or false. Spice things up by asking the young people to go to one side of the room or the other depending on their answer.

- If you broke wind consistently for 6 years and 9 months, enough gas would be produced to create the energy of an atomic bomb. TRUE

- A cockroach can live up to 2 weeks without its head before it starves to death. FALSE

- Butterflies can taste with their feet. TRUE

- 40,000 Americans are injured by toilets each year. TRUE

- The strongest muscle in the body is your heart. FALSE (it's the tongue!)

- It is impossible to lick your elbow. TRUE

- Coca Cola was originally red. FALSE

- Men can hear better than women. FALSE

- Bullet proof vests were designed by a woman. TRUE

BLIND AGILITY TRACK
Set up an agility course in your meeting room (it can be as big or small as you like, eg. two chairs to walk between, a box to step over, a table to avoid etc). Pair up some or all of the young people. One in the pair must wear a blind-fold and the other one must direct their blind-folded partner through the course without touching their partner.

DISCUSSION
You had to put your faith in your friend, and trust that they were leading you the right way.

Who do you put your faith in?

INTRODUCTION TO SESSION
Today we'll find out about how important it is to have faith – we're going to think about what faith really is and where we put our faith.

⊕ MOVIE CLIP

DVD clip: Evan Almighty (PG)

Start clip: 00:50:00

End clip: 00:53:47

Evan is a politician who is asked by God to build an ark. He thinks it sounds ridiculous but in the end he takes a step of faith and has a go. In this clip he tries to do his job, but God makes things a little more difficult so that Evan is forced to stand up for the truth.

↑ WORSHIP ACTIVITY

Get lots of medium-sized (tennis ball size) stones together – at least as many as you have members of your group. Give each person a stone.

Explain:

In the Old Testament, the people of God often gathered stones into a pile as worship to him. Sometimes they made altars to offer sacrifices on and sometimes they made huge piles just to be a sign of something God had done. For example: Noah built an altar when he left the Ark and walked onto dry land; Jacob build a pillar of stones when he had a vision of heaven during the night; and Joshua built a pile to remind Israel how God had led them across Jordan into their promised land.

Today we are going to use stones to build a symbol of worship to God together.

Encourage the young people to think of just one reason to worship God. It could be because of who he is ('I worship God because he is faithful') or because of something he has done in our lives ('I worship God because he healed my mother').

After a moment's thinking time (if your group doesn't cope well with silence you could play quiet music here), ask each person to put their stone in a central place (one on top of another), one at a time, and at the same time say their worship out loud.

Finish by praying something like this:

'Great God, we've build this monument as a symbol of our worship to you. You are wonderful and you have done great things – you deserve our worship. Amen'

⊕ MOVIE CLIP

DVD Clip: Evan Almighty (PG)

Start clip: 01:17:50   End clip: 01:20:25

This is the scene where Evan is commandeering the ark. Sometimes, we think that having faith is always this bizarre, supernatural affair...

Leader's Note: Watch the clip before hand so that you can draw out Evan's view on faith with the group and then can blend it in with the illustration.

◉ DVD CHAPTER 1

Play Session 3, chapter 1 – 'Everyday Faith' – of the accompanying DVD.

Explain:

Faith is actually part of our everyday lives – everyone exercises faith! Almost every decision you make involves faith.

Say that you're crossing the road at a pedestrian crossing with traffic lights.

You press the button, and the signal indicates that it's safe to cross.

You may see a car coming down the road towards you, but you cross anyway, because you know that the approaching car has a red light.

This is an action taken completely by faith!

There is no way you can know for sure that the driver will stop at the lights, rather than drive straight over you.

WHO HAS THE MOST FAITH?

Last week I asked you to think about who has the most faith; Christians, atheists, Hindus, Muslims, people who 'just don't know'?

Discuss what everyone thinks. It may be wise to text this question between sessions to the group and to ask some to come prepared to share their thoughts with the group.

Some people believe that the human race is just some sort of accidental mutation, and there is no such thing as a God. That is faith as just as much as Christian faith is – you have to believe that part that science can't prove. And even with science, you have to believe that the instruments are telling the truth, and that the lab assistant didn't make any mistakes.

THE DIFFERENCE IS WHAT WE BELIEVE IN

The fact that we believe doesn't make that faith powerful – it's what or whom we put our faith in that matters!

Leader's Note: Try to paraphrase this yourself or ask another leader/someone from your church that is good at telling a story to share this Bible story - 1 Kings 18.

There's a story about Elijah in the Bible (1 Kings 18), where he has a big faith show-down with the so-called 'prophets' of the false god, Baal. As the people were watching, he encouraged the prophets of Baal to ask their god to throw down fire on their pile of sacrificed bull. The prophets shouted, danced, engaged in some self-harming. They did everything to make Baal hear them. After a few hours of this, Elijah started teasing them a bit, 'Maybe Baal has gone away on a trip? Or maybe he's tired out and asleep?'

When evening came, Elijah took to the stage. He built an altar for his sacrifice, and then soaked the whole thing in water, three times over – just to be sure that the expected miracle couldn't be explained away. Then, he prayed a simple prayer, and God threw down fire that burned up the entire altar.

It wasn't necessarily that Elijah had a stronger faith than the prophets of Baal – the difference was who he had put his faith in.

SESSION THREE: CHOOSING TO BELIEVE THE TRUTH

⦿ DVD CHAPTER 2

Play Session 3, Chapter 2 – 'Foundations' – of the accompanying DVD.

Ask the group

- What do you put your faith in?

- Has it ever let you down?

- Has it ever stood firm?

- What do you think / feel about what was said in this clip?

Explain:

Out of everything, or everyone, we can put our faith in, Jesus is the only one who won't fail us. Traffic lights can break and parents, friends, teachers, even youth workers (!) can let us down, but 'Jesus Christ is the same yesterday and today and forever' (Hebrews 13:8).

Having faith isn't about trying really hard to believe things that you're not all that sure about.

It's actually the opposite!

Faith is just believing what is already true. God is truth, and all we need to do is to believe what he says, whether it feels true or not.

THE MAIN POINT

⦿ DVD CHAPTER 3

Play Session 3, Chapter 3 – 'Making A Choice' – of the accompanying DVD.

Ask the group:

- What do you think about what you have just heard?

- Do you agree / disagree?

- What do you think they mean about Jesus talking about a mustard seed being no accident?

- Are you willing to grow your faith?

GROWING FAITH – CHOOSE TO BELIEVE IT AND THEN ACT ON IT!

Faith can only grow when we put it into action. If you take some steps of faith, and see that God is trustworthy, your faith will grow.

Bring up a brave volunteer, blind-fold them and challenge them to fall straight backwards, trusting that the rest of the group will catch them.

Afterwards, ask them how it felt ('scary' perhaps). Ask if it would feel less scary to do it a second time, knowing that they can trust the group.

Say something like:

Bob's [insert correct name] faith in us grew when he dared trusting us in the first place. We need to dare taking risks for God, only then will our faith grow.

The good news is that there is no one here who can't grow in their faith. All we need to do is to know what's already true (read the Bible!), choose to believe it and then act on it!

Leader's Note: Risk assess this activity. Make sure you choose the right volunteer and the right people directly behind them to catch them. We would recommend that you practise it with another leader first to find the safest and easiest way to catch someone. You can then explain it to the group easier. You could even use this process as an illustration of how faith works – little steps that turn into big leaps.

RESPONSE

Ask the young people to read through the 'What Can I Do?' list on page 16 of the Youth Guide 11-14, and choose the one that they find most helpful at the moment. Let each young person pick a stone from the worship activity pile and give them a marker pen (or nice acrylic paints and brushes if you're feeling artistic).

The Bible says this about God:

'There is no-one holy like the Lord; there is no-one besides you; there is no Rock like our God.' (1 Samuel 2:2).

Rock – stone – can not easily be broken. It is solid. God is our rock – he can be trusted, we can put our faith in him.

Ask the young people to write their chosen point from the list on their stone.

Declaration:

Read out the 'What Can I Do?' section (on page 16 of the Youth Guide 11-14) all together again. If some young people struggle to read, ask the group to repeat it after the leader.

Pray:

Father God, we choose to put our faith in you – because you are our rock, trustworthy and solid. Remind us with these stones to act on our faith. Amen

SMALL GROUPS & PRAYER FOCUS

Think back to the question we sent you home with last week: Who has most faith? What do atheists put their faith in? Think about your friends – what kinds of other stuff do they put their faith in?

1. Have you ever taken a step of faith – believed anything God said was true and done something about it? What happened?

2. Why do you think God is a good place to put your faith?

3. How can you help your faith to grow?

4. When is it difficult to put your faith in God?

Spend some time in prayer and help the members of your group make this kind of commitment to God.

AND THERE'S MORE!

If you are using the Biblical truth postcards, this would be an appropriate time to hand the third one out.

Draw the young people's attention to the activities in their Youth Guide 11-14, particularly the Mustard Seed exercise and Challenge on page 15.

? CLOSING QUESTION

Imagine you were born in a completely different country - you can pick which.

How would that change the way you look at the world and what you believe?

NEXT WEEK
Ask each young person to bring a torch (flashlight) to next week's session.

WHAT CAN I DO?
11-14

1. Why should I say I can't when the Bible says I can do all things through Christ who gives me strength (Philippians 4:13)?

2. Why should I be afraid when the Bible says God has not given me a spirit of fear, but one of power, love and a sound mind (2 Timothy 1:7)?

3. Why should I be weak when the Bible says that the Lord is the strength of my life and that I will display strength and take action because I know God (Psalm 27:1; Daniel 11:32)?

4. Why should I worry and fret when I can cast all my anxiety on Christ who cares for me (1 Peter 5:7)?

5. Why should I feel judged guilty when the Bible says I am not judged guilty because I am in Christ (Romans 8:1)?

6. Why should I feel alone when Jesus said he is with me always and he will never leave me (Matthew 28:20; Hebrews 13:5)?

7. Why should I feel worthless when Jesus thought I was worth dying for (2 Corinthians 5:21)?

8. Why should I be confused when God is the author of peace and helps me understand him (1 Corinthians 14:33; 1 Corinthians 2:12)?

9. Why should I feel like a failure when I am a conqueror in all things through Christ (Romans 8:37)?

10. Why should I let the pressures of life bother me when I can take courage knowing that Jesus has overcome the world and its problems (John 16:33)?

CHOOSING TO BELIEVE THE TRUTH 15-18

 ## PRAYER AND DECLARATION

Encourage everyone to join together in saying the following prayer and declaration. You can download the PowerPoint slides with the words for these from the website.

It would be good to suggest that the young people stand up and speak out the declaration clearly and confidently to the heavenly realms. They could shout it out and use appropriate actions!

PRAYER:

❝ Father, as I hear your word today please talk to me through it and increase my faith in you. I don't want to lean on my own understanding, so I ask you, Holy Spirit, to teach me how to walk by faith in you. Amen

DECLARATION:

❝ I am a treasured child of the Lord God Almighty so I speak to all evil, and tell you that you have no right to be here distracting me. I command you to leave now in Jesus' name. This time is only for me and God.

🔍 STARTING POINT

Over the welcome drinks start asking what the young people put their faith in. Do they see faith as part of their everyday life?

Give a short summary of the previous session. A good resource for this is the Overview found in the Core of the previous session.

◎ DVD CHAPTER 1

Play Session 3, Chapter 1 – 'Everyday Faith' – of the accompanying DVD.

Explain:

Faith is actually part of our everyday lives – everyone exercises faith!

Almost every decision you make involves faith. Say that you're crossing the road at a pedestrian crossing with traffic lights.

You press the button and the little man turns green. You can see that there's a car coming further down the road but you cross anyway, because the lights have gone red for the car.

This is an action taken completely by faith!

There is no way you can know for sure that the driver will stop at the lights, rather than drive straight over you.

⌃ SOAPBOX

WHO HAS THE MOST FAITH?

Last week I asked you to think about who has the most faith; Christians, atheists, Hindus, Muslims, people who 'just don't know'?

Discuss what everyone thinks. It may be wise to text this question between sessions to the group and ask some to come prepared to share their thoughts with the group.

Leader's note: Make a mental note of some of the reasons that they give – jot them down on a flip chart or on a pad so that you can read them back to them when thoughts have been shared. This will help conclude the comments but also clarify in their minds (and yours) what qualifies having 'a lot of faith.'

▤ THE MAIN POINT

◎ DVD CHAPTER 2

Play Session 3, Chapter 2 – 'Foundations' – of the accompanying DVD.

Ask the group:

- What do you put your faith in?

- Has it ever let you down?

- Has it ever stood firm?

- What do you think / feel about what was said in this clip?

Review the story with your group.

In Matthew 7 Jesus says a wise man will build his house upon the rock. With the rock as a solid, firm, unmovable foundation, the rains might come, the floods might hit, the winds might blow, but the house will never fall down.

Jesus then goes on to speak about a guy who builds his house on the sand.

Sand is not that great for building anything on, because when the rains come, the floods hit and the winds blow, the house will crumble. All because the foundations are poor.

So was Jesus really referring to building a house? Was he really meaning to focus on constructing a great piece of architecture? No. He's talking about our lives.

Would the foolish man have built on the sand, if he thought his house would collapse?

Of course not. He had faith that it would stand, but it didn't. The foolish man put his faith in the wrong thing. His plan was not based on truth.

Both men had faith that their houses were going to stand, but they put their faith in different things.

Jesus is saying we need to put our faith in something that won't crumble beneath us. We need to put our faith in something that will stand – that will really work.

DISCUSSION
Turn to the person next to you and discuss what you think of these statements:

'Find out what is really true and choose to believe it, then your life will work out. Your house will stand. Choose to put your faith in something that isn't true and it won't work.'

'It is not as if some people live by faith and others don't. Absolutely everyone lives by faith in someone or something. But only those who put their faith in the truth will find that their houses stand.'

Explain:

Out of everything, or everyone, we can put our faith in, Jesus is the only one who won't fail us. Traffic lights can break and parents, friends, teachers, even youth workers (!) can let us down, but 'Jesus Christ is the same yesterday and today and forever' (Hebrews 13:8).

Having faith isn't about trying really hard to believe things that you're not all that sure about. It's actually the opposite!

Faith is just believing what is already true. God is truth, and all we need to do is to believe what he says, whether it feels true or not.

Do you agree / disagree?

⬆ WORSHIP ACTIVITY

Get lots of medium-sized (tennis ball size) stones together – at least as many as you have members of your group. Give each person a stone.

Explain:

In the Old Testament, the people of God often gathered stones into a pile as worship to him; sometimes they made altars to offer sacrifices on and sometimes they made huge piles just to be a sign of something God had done. For example; Noah built an altar when he left the Ark and walked onto dry land, Jacob build a pillar of stones when he had a vision of heaven during the night and Joshua built a pile to remind Israel how God had led them across Jordan into their promised land. Today we are going to use stones to build a symbol of worship to God together.

Encourage the young people to think of just one reason to worship God. It could be because of who he is ('I worship God because he is faithful') or because of something he has done in our lives ('I worship God because he healed my mother').

After a moment's thinking time (if your group doesn't cope well with silence you could play quiet music here), ask each person to put their stone in a central place (one on top of another) one at a time. As they lay their stone down encourage them to say their worship out loud.

Finish by praying something like this:

'Great God, we've build this monument as a symbol of our worship to you. You are wonderful and you have done great things – you deserve our worship. Amen.'

WHAT'S THE POINT?
Draw the young people's attention to page 14 of the Youth Guide 15-18 where it says:

- Everyone has faith in something. It's part of everyday life.

- It's not the fact that we have faith. What's important is what or whom we put our faith in.

- We can see from our actions what we really believe. If we trust God, then people will see it in our actions.

What difference would a deeper faith in God make to your life?

⊙ DVD CHAPTER 3

Play Session 3, Chapter 3 – 'Making A Choice' – of the accompanying DVD.

Ask the group

- What do you think about what you have just heard?

- Do you agree / disagree?

- What do you think they mean about Jesus talking about a mustard seed being no accident?

- Are you willing to grow your faith?

GROWING FAITH – CHOOSE TO BELIEVE IT AND THEN ACT ON IT!
Faith can only grow when we put it into action. If you take some steps of faith, and see that God is trustworthy, your faith will grow.

FAITH LEADS TO ACTION

Real faith isn't just believing something in our heads. If you really believe it, it will show up in your actions. We can say all the right things, but it's your actions that show whether you really believe it or not.

Ask one of your group to read James 2:17-18:

'Faith by itself, if it is not accompanied by action, is dead. But someone will say, "You have faith: I have deeds." Show me your faith without deeds, and I will show you my faith by what I do.'

Share this:

'Faith without deeds is a bit like standing on the train station, wanting to go somewhere, and knowing everything about the trains, their technical detail, the timetables and so on – but never actually getting on a train.'

Ask if anyone can come up with another way of illustrating faith without deeds.

'The good news is that there is no one here who can't have faith – no one who cannot resist temptation, no one who could not become a mature Christian. You don't need some special prayer from a famous Christian, your youth leader or church leader or to have read all the right books. You just need to know what is already true, choose to believe it and act on it.'

Turn to the person next to you and discuss this. Do you agree? Why should you care?

 # RESPONSE

DISCUSSION AS A GROUP

Think back to the question we sent you home with last week: Who has most faith? What do atheists put their faith in? Think about your friends – what kind of stuff do they put their faith in?

1. Have you ever taken a step of faith – made a decision to believe something God says is true – and done something about it? What happened?

2. Why do you think God is a good place to put your faith?

3. How can you help your faith to grow?

4. When is it difficult to put your faith in God?

Spend some time in prayer and help the members of your group to make a commitment to step out in faith.

ACTIVITY

Ask the young people to read through the 'What Can I Do?' list on page 16 of the Youth Guide 15-18 and choose the one that they find most helpful at the moment. Let each young person pick a stone from the worship activity pile and give them a marker pen (or nice acrylic paints and brushes if you're feeling artistic).

The Bible says this about God:

'There is no-one holy like the Lord; there is no-one besides you; there is no Rock like our God.' (1 Samuel 2:2).

Rock – stone – can not easily be broken. It is solid. God is our rock – he can be trusted, we can put our faith in him.

Ask the young people to write their chosen point from the list on their stone.

Declaration:

Read out the 'What Can I Do?' list (page 16 Youth Guide 15-18) all together. If some young people struggle to read, ask the group to repeat it after the leader.

Pray:

Father God, we choose to put our faith in you – because you are our rock, trustworthy and solid. Please use these stones as a reminder to us to act on our faith. Amen

If you are using the Biblical truth postcards, this would be an appropriate time to hand the third one out.

★ AND THERE'S MORE!

Draw attention to the Challenge on page 17 of the Youth Guide 15-18:

Pick one verse from the 'What Can I Do' list that particularly stands out to you. Write it in the Journal section and say it out loud to yourself every day this week as a reminder of what you can do with God.

? CLOSING QUESTION

Question for next week - page 17 Youth Guide 15-18:

Imagine you were born in another country; do you think the way you look at the world and your beliefs would be different?

NEXT WEEK
Ask each young person to bring a torch (flashlight) to next week's session.

WHAT CAN I DO?
15-18

1. Why should I say 'I can't' when the Bible says I can do all things through Christ who gives me strength (Philippians 4:13)?

2. Why should I lack when I know that God will supply all my needs according to his riches in glory in Christ Jesus (Philippians 4:19)?

3. Why should I be afraid when the Bible says God has not given me a spirit of fear, but one of power, love and a sound mind (2 Timothy 1:7)?

4. Why should I be weak when the Bible says that the Lord is the strength of my life and that I will display strength and take action because I know God (Psalm 27:1; Daniel 11:32)?

5. Why should I allow Satan supremacy over my life when he that is in me is greater than he that is in the world (1 John 4:4)?

6. Why should I be depressed when I can recall to mind God's loving kindness, compassion and faithfulness and have hope (Lamentations 3:21-23)?

7. Why should I worry and fret when I can cast all my anxiety on Christ who cares for me (1 Peter 5:7)?

8. Why should I ever not be free from stuff that holds me back knowing that, where the Spirit of the Lord is, there is freedom (2 Corinthians 3:17; Galatians 5:1)?

9. Why should I feel condemned when the Bible says I am not condemned because I am in Christ (Romans 8:1)?

10. Why should I feel alone when Jesus said he is with me always and he will never leave me nor forsake me (Matthew 28:20; Hebrews 13:5)?

11. Why should I be discontented when I, like Paul, can learn to be content in all my circumstances (Philippians 4:11)?

12. Why should I feel worthless when Christ became sin on my behalf that I might become the righteousness of God in him (2 Corinthians 5:21)?

13. Why should I be confused when God is the author of peace and he gives me knowledge through his Spirit who lives in me (1 Corinthians 14:33; 1 Corinthians 2:12)?

14. Why should I feel like a failure when I am a conqueror in all things through Christ (Romans 8:37)?

15. Why should I let the pressures of life bother me when I can take courage knowing that Jesus has overcome the world and its tribulations (John 16:33)?

SESSION FOUR:
WORLDVIEW

'Do not conform any longer to the pattern of this world, but be transformed by the renewing of your mind. Then you will be able to test and approve what God's will is – his good, pleasing and perfect will.'

Romans 12:2

WORLDVIEW CORE

PREPARATION

This is the first of four sessions in Part B of Freedom In Christ For Young People. Having looked at key truths, we now turn our attention to those things that try to deflect us from truth, our three enemies, the world, the flesh and the devil.

The second book in The Freedom In Christ Discipleship Series, Win The Daily Battle (Monarch 2008), corresponds to Part B of the course. Read pages 11 - 42 in the book for the material that relates to this session.

KEY VERSE
Romans 12: 2 – 'Do not conform any longer to the pattern of this world, but be transformed by the renewing of your mind. Then you will be able to test and approve what God's will is – his good, pleasing and perfect will.'

AIM
To understand that Christians need to make a definite decision to turn away from believing what the world teaches and choose instead to believe what God says is true.

KEY TRUTH
The world we grew up in influenced us to look at life in a particular way and to see that way as 'true.' However, if it doesn't stack up with what God says is true, we need to reject it and bring our beliefs in line with God's truth.

OVERVIEW
Depending on where and when you were brought up, you will have learned to look at the world in a particular way that seems right to you. But is it actually true? You may also have come to believe that there is no such thing as absolute unchangeable truth. But is that right? When we become Christians we need to make a radical decision to stop looking at the world in the way we used to and start seeing it from God's perspective.

Welcome to the second section of the course. The first part looked at some basic truths – this second one is about the things that deflect us from truth. In this session, we're going to look at worldviews; and how we all look at the world in different ways – and they're not always God's ways!

WE ALL HAVE A WORLDVIEW
Have you ever heard someone say that a person is looking at the world 'through rose-tinted glasses'? What that means is that this someone is overly optimistic and a bit unrealistic about what they see. Let me give you an example of optimism:

A kid's Batman costume made by a company called Kenner Products had the following warning on the label: 'Caution: Cape does not enable users to fly'. You'd have to be a huge optimist to buy it thinking that it will help you fly!

The fact is that we all look at the world - at reality if you like - in a particular way, through 'glasses' of some sort. The way that we look at the world is known as our 'worldview'.

YOUR WORLDVIEW IS LIKE A FILTER

Your worldview works like a filter. Everything that you see, everything that happens around you, you put through this filter to work out what it all means.

This course is all about learning to see the world as it really is, to try our best to remove any glasses that are distorting things for us. We want to discover what God's truth is.

HOW DID WE GET OUR WORLDVIEW?

Part of how we look at the world is shaped by our past experiences. So, for example, if you've grown up with a really harsh, overly strict dad, you will probably come to view God as a disciplinarian: someone who's constantly demanding more of you, but is never pleased. But that's not what God is like at all!

We're not going to focus on past experiences today, but on how culture shapes our worldviews. You'll find that you probably wear generally the same kind of glasses as someone who has grown up in the same culture as you, but someone from the South American jungle, or the Chinese countryside, will wear very different glasses. There are many different worldviews. We'll look at three common ones to get the idea. So, let's try on three different types of glasses and see how they fit:

1. A NON-WESTERN WORLDVIEW

This set of glasses is a worldview called 'animism' held by a very large number of people throughout the world. You'll find it in its purest form amongst tribal societies in developing countries, but its influence stretches far beyond that and it's common in many countries of the world across all sections of society.

Most animists believe in some kind of god, but what's really important to them is the idea of a spiritual power found in everything – animal, vegetable, mineral – and lots of spirits going with that. Within this worldview, there are certain people that are experts in the spiritual: 'shamans', 'medicine men' or 'witch doctors'. They are the ones to call on if you have any kind of trouble. Every problem is seen to involve this universal power or a spirit in some way.

Animists often live in fear of evil spirits, or spirits that simply don't like them and want to hurt them. There is also always the worry that an enemy might become spiritually superior, and use this spiritual power against them.

This worldview is found all over the world, and 'new age' and occult practices are increasingly bringing it to the West as well.

2. THE 'MODERN' WORLDVIEW

Most people that have grown up in the West over the last 50 years or so, will have learned to look at the world using the 'modern' worldview, at least to some extent.

This worldview divides everything in to 'the natural' – things that can be scientifically proven and 'the supernatural' – things that can't. The supernatural has no relation to normal, everyday life and is generally not to be taken particularly seriously. God ends up in that category.

This has meant that spiritual things haven't really been included in education (it's just not seen as that important). The modern worldview basically says that if you can't test something and prove it scientifically – it's not true!

Even the Church has been affected by this worldview. Some churches try to get rid of everything supernatural in order to fit in with the world, and some Christian ministers say that they don't believe in miracles, angels and demons or even the Holy Spirit.

3. THE POSTMODERN WORLDVIEW

Lately, the modern worldview has been losing out to something many call the postmodern (meaning 'after modern') worldview. If you have grown up in the West, you have probably been influenced by a mix of modern and post-modern thinking. The younger you are, the more likely it is that you have been influenced by postmodern ways of thinking.

A philosopher named Friedrich Nietzsche summed up the line of thinking that would become postmodernism, when he wrote in 1885:

'There are many kinds of eyes..., and consequently there are many kinds of "truths", and consequently there is no truth.'

No truth! In the modern worldview God may not be seen as truth (as he can't be proved), but truth as a concept remains; in postmodernism, truth does not even exist! Everyone is allowed to make up their own truths – and we are not to challenge what other people believe. Whatever feels right for that person...

This is why, as Christians, we are under real pressure to say that anything anyone does is OK – it's their choice, right? We are under pressure to say that all religions are alright, that all belief systems are equal to ours.

THE BIBLICAL WORLDVIEW

Having tried on these three different looking glasses, which should we choose? Which showed us the best view of the world?

None!

When we become Christians, we need to take off the glasses our culture gave us and learn to look at the world as it really is - how God says it is - and adopt what you might call the Biblical worldview.

Although we can be given a hard time for saying this in our postmodern world, according to the Bible, truth really does exist. In fact, it teaches that God is truth.

What a lot of postmodernists miss is that faith and logic actually work together. Logic shows that truth exists. Just think about that really important question that everyone has a view on: what happens when we die?

- Hinduism teaches that when a soul dies it is reincarnated in another form.

- Christianity teaches that souls spend eternity in either heaven or hell.

- Atheists believe that we have no soul and that when we die our existence simply ends.

- Postmodernism says that you can make up whatever you want to believe as long as you don't upset anyone else.

But surely, all of these can't be true at the same time? Logically, you can't go to heaven and be reincarnated into a fruit fly! Does what we believe before we die influence what happens when we die? Or will everyone – whatever they believe during their time on earth – have the same experience when they die?

Logic tells us that at best only one of these mutually exclusive options can be true, and that what happens to you when you die will be the same for everyone, regardless of what you believe beforehand. If Christians are right, everyone will stand before God and will either go to heaven or hell. If atheists are right, we will all simply return to dust and that will be it. So logic proves the existence of truth.

God is truth, and therefore truth is independent of human thought. It's an absolute, something we can't rid ourselves of, and it's founded on God's unshakable character.

The Biblical worldview has been tested and found reliable by millions of people over thousands of years. It has changed people for the better, and inspired people to do heroic things, like abolishing slavery or helping drug addicts find freedom.

It can be tricky to go against the flow by proclaiming that Jesus is the only way to God, and that there is only one truth. But at the same time, if we know the truth, how can we keep quiet about it?

BEWARE OF MIX 'N' MATCH

It's very important that we realise that our upbringing and experiences have caused us to wear a very specific sort of glasses. If we don't realise this, we simply add a few Christian bits to our already set worldview when we become Christians, and the world looks decidedly odd.

No, we must realise what we're wearing, and take the old glasses off to replace them with a Biblical worldview. Unfortunately, the 'Mix 'n' Match' way of looking at the world is very common.

We will ask the young people (15-18s) to answer some questions to see what type of worldview they have. Although it isn't a terribly serious exercise, it can show us how easy it is for worldviews that are opposite to the Biblical one to slip into our mindsets. Many of us will talk about how Christianity 'feels right' for us, and how we have 'experienced' it. This may be true – which is great – but it cannot be the basis of our faith! Otherwise, what happens on days when we don't feel anything? No, we say this, because we are so influenced by the postmodern worldview.

Os Guinness sums it up like this:

'The Christian faith is not true because it works; it works because it is true....' (Os Guinness, Time for Truth, Baker Books, 2000, pages 79-80).

Christian faith is 'choosing to believe what God says is true' because we have made a decision that the Biblical worldview is how things really are. And, because it is true, we find that when we base our lives on it, it works!

QUESTIONS TO THINK ABOUT AS YOU PREPARE:

If you had been born in a completely different country, how would that change the way you look at the world and what you believe?

1. Which of the three worldviews that we looked at is most like what you have grown up with?

2. How can you decide whether someone's worldview is true?

3. Why do you have the worldview you have in the first place?

4. Can you think of an example where all your friends' worldviews clash with a Biblical worldview?

5. How can we stand up for truth without coming across as arrogant?

6. Can we be friends with people who have beliefs that we disagree with?

WORLDVIEW 11-14

LEADER'S PREPARATION

Pray together:

> ❝ Father of Truth, open our eyes today to see clearly what is the truth in our lives, and what is not. Help us to understand what relates to you and what doesn't and be able to know where our beliefs come from. Amen

YOU MAY NEED

MP3 player with well-known songs

Pair of sunglasses, with black paper over the lenses

Wallace & Gromit, Curse of the Were-Rabbit DVD

Accompanying DVD / DVD player / TV / projector

Dark sunglasses and colour-tinted sunglasses

Bibles

Printed out sheets of Bible verses

Celebrity magazines

Christian stickers (can be simply made by writing 'I love Jesus' on s blank sticker)

Small group questions

Remember – each young person needs a torch (flashlight)!

 ## PRAYER AND DECLARATION

Encourage everyone to join together in saying the following prayer and declaration. You can download the PowerPoint slides with the words for these from the website.

It would be good to suggest that the young people stand up and speak out the declaration clearly and confidently to the heavenly realms. They could shout it out and use appropriate actions!

PRAYER

> ❝ Father, you are the Truth. Open my eyes so that I can see clearly where my life is based on truth and where it is not. Help me to understand where my beliefs come from. Amen.

DECLARATION: IN A CLEAR, CONFIDENT TONE!

 Jesus said that he is the way, the truth and the life. I am going to listen to him.

I confidently command evil lies to leave this place. Anything that comes between me and Jesus is not welcome here. You must go now in Jesus' name.

🔍 STARTING POINT

⚙ INTRODUCTORY ACTIVITIES

THE HUM-ALONG
Preload an MP3-player with some well-known songs, and try to get hold of some headphones to go with it. Pick volunteers to hum along to a song as they listen to it through the headphones. The first person to guess the song gets to go next.

VISUALLY IMPAIRED TAG
Prepare a pair of sunglasses by sticking black paper over the lenses. The person who is 'it' has to wear these glasses as they try to tag as many people as possible, relying only on their peripheral view.

Leader's Note: Trip hazard. Clear the floor of anything the blindfolded players could trip over (e.g. loose carpet, electrical wires, chairs), and remind the players to be careful.

While reviewing the introductory activities ask:

- What music do we like and why?

- How difficult was it when you saw things in a different way to usual?

Give a short summary of the previous session. A good resource for this is the Overview found in the Core of the previous session.

Today we're going to find out that how we see things makes a real difference in our lives.

We have now started the second section of the course.

The first part looked at some basic truths – the second one is about some of the things that get in the way of truth.

Today we're going to consider how we all look at the world in certain ways – not always God's way!

🎞 MOVIE CLIP

DVD clip: Wallace and Gromit, and the Curse of the Were-Rabbit, 2005 (PG)

·Start clip: 00:16:59   End clip: 00:19:58

Wallace has decided to solve the problem of vegetable-eating rabbits, by changing their worldviews – to make them rabbits who detest veg...

↑ WORSHIP ACTIVITY

In advance of the session have these verses printed out on sheets of card. They are available as downloads from the website.

'There is now no condemnation for those who are in Christ Jesus.' (Romans 8:1)

'And we know that in all things God works for the good of those who love him.' (Romans 8:28)

'If God is for us, who can be against us?' (Romans 8:31)

'Jesus said: "Surely I am with you always, to the very end of the age."' (Matthew 28:20

'God has said, "Never will I leave you; never will I forsake you."' (Hebrews 13:5)

'Jesus Christ is the same yesterday and today and forever.' (Hebrews 13:8)

'God is light; in him there is no darkness at all.' (1 John 1:5)

'This is love: not that we loved God, but that he loved us and sent his son as an atoning sacrifice for our sins.' (1 John 4:10)

Spread the Bible verses around the room. Ask the young people to get their torches (flashlights)out, switch them on and turn the lights off. Put on some quiet background music.

Say:

Psalm 119:105 says that the Bible is like a light to us, it guides us and shows us the truth.

We're going to walk around this room [or several rooms if your main meeting room is very small] for a while and every time you find a card, you find a truth from the Bible. Read it out loud – to yourself and to anyone else who happens to be listening. Then place the card down and keep walking until you reach another one.

Do this as worship to God, grateful that he has given us truth to guide us.

◉ DVD CHAPTER 1

Play Session 4, Chapter 1 – 'A Unique View?' – of the accompanying DVD.

Now lead straight into the explanation about worldviews, wearing tinted glasses.

In advance of the session, get a pair of sunglasses that have tinted lenses or get a cheap pair of glasses, and colour the lenses pink (perhaps with a whiteboard pen, or by sticking pink plastic over them). Wear these for the beginning of the talk.

Have you ever heard the saying that someone is looking at the world 'through rose-tinted glasses?'

What that means is that this someone is overly optimistic, a bit unrealistic, about what they see. Let me give you an example of optimism:

A kid's Batman costume made by a company called Kenner Products had the following warning on the label:

'Caution: Cape does not enable users to fly.' You'd have to be a huge optimist to buy it thinking that it will help you fly!

Now, I'm wearing my rose-tinted glasses today – you all look gorgeous, all rosy and healthy! Are you an optimist like me, seeing everything better than it is?

Or maybe you're a pessimist? [change into a pair of dark sunglasses]

Maybe you see the world in its worst possible light – wow, it is dark and gloomy in here! [take glasses off]

The fact is that we have all learned to look at the world - at reality - in a particular way, through 'glasses' of some sort. A particular way of seeing the world is called a 'worldview'.

YOUR WORLDVIEW IS LIKE A FILTER

Your worldview works like a filter. Everything that you see, everything that happens around you, you put through this filter to work out what it all means.

Illustration - food from around the world:

Get some simple party snacks from around the world (a frozen food shop / aisle is probably the best place to look) and let the group try out different ones. If your budget is tight just explain that this is a food-tasting moment and not a full on dinner experience! Try to get your group to try new things. Don't forget to ask around your church as there may be some great cooks who would love to prepare something for you.

Discussion:

• If you could choose to be from another country where would you come from?

• If you were from a different country how might you see the world differently?

This course is all about learning to see the world as it really is - to try our best to remove any glasses that are distorting things for us. We want to discover what God's truth is.

◉ DVD CHAPTER 2

Play Session 4, chapter 2 – 'My View, My Truth?' – of the accompanying DVD.

Now lead straight into the overview.

OVERVIEW

How do we get our worldview?

Part of how we look at the world is shaped by our past experiences.

So, for example, if you've grown up with a really harsh, overly strict parent, you will probably come to view God as a disciplinarian, someone who's constantly demanding more of you, but is never pleased.

But that's not what God is like at all!

If your best friend always puts you down you might think that when Jesus says he's your friend he might do the same – that you always have to do things to impress him.

But that's not what Jesus is like.

If you constantly argue in your family you might think that being part of God's family is a constant argument.

But that's not what it is like.

CULTURE

Something else that has a huge impact on our worldview is culture.

We all tend to look at things in a similar way to other people brought up in the same part of the world as we were. Remind them of the food from around the world.

If you had grown up in the South American jungle or the Chinese countryside you would see things differently.

Discussion:

Divide into groups and hand out two or three celebrity magazines to each group. Assign a leader to each group initially to ask the two questions below, then lead on to talking about the questions relating to God's view further down the page. Try to encourage your group leaders to allow thoughts to be shared without looking for right or wrong answers.

• How do you think that the magazines we read and TV we watch affects our worldview?

• If you believed that science could answer every question, how would this affect your worldview?

The truth is that our culture massively affects our worldview.

The media tell us that to be loved and fit in we have to look a certain way and have the right stuff.

Is this what God says?

We are told that science and being clever can explain and solve everything.

Can you explain God in a science textbook?

Leader's Note: Even though these questions are very important what we want the young people to learn is that they can and should think things through / question / challenge / balance and consider implications. We are trying to allow a safe place for them to encounter God's truth through his Holy Spirit. For a fun twist, hand out tinted and dark sunglasses for the groups to wear as they are reading through the magazines. This can work with each person taking a turn if you only have a couple of pairs.

THE MAIN POINT

Many of the worldviews affecting us from our culture say different things about truth:

- Some say that truth is only that which can be proved by science

- Other worldviews say that there is no such thing as truth

- And others say that whatever you feel is right for you can be your truth

This is not what the Bible says. The Bible says that God is truth, no matter what science says and no matter what you feel like.

BEWARE OF MIX 'N' MATCH

It's very important that we realise that our upbringing and experiences have caused us to wear a very specific sort of glasses, to look at reality in a particular way.

If we don't realise this, we simply add a few Christian bits to our already set worldview when we become Christians, and the world looks decidedly odd [perhaps stick some Christian stickers to your rose-tinted glasses at this point].

◎ DVD CHAPTER 3

Play Session 4, chapter 3 – 'What Is Truth?' – of the accompanying DVD.

'DON'T LET THE WORLD SQUEEZE YOU INTO ITS MOULD'

Christian faith is: 'choosing to believe what God says is true' because we have made a decision that the Bible's worldview is how things really are.

By all means look at the facts, check that Christianity is reasonable. Once you are happy, make a firm decision to believe God's word whether it feels true or not, no matter what those around you may say.

- Have you done that?

- Are you ready to do that?

Now ask a leader to share their story about when they decided to follow Jesus.

- Include points from the above process

- Share a little about what was going on in their life at that time.

- What prompted them?

- Did they look at and weigh up the facts?

- How did they check those facts out?

- How did they come to the decision?

- How has it gone since?

- Do they have three top tips that help sustain this?

RESPONSE

Using a PowerPoint slide read together Psalm 119:105:

'Your word is a lamp to my feet and a light for my path.'

Challenge the young people to write this down on page 20 of the Youth Guide 11-14 and learn it in the next week.

SMALL GROUPS & PRAYER FOCUS

1. What does the world tell us we have to do to fit in and be loved? What does the Bible say?

2. How do people respond when they get hurt? What does the Bible say?

3. What are some of the things that affect the way we see the world?

4. In what ways do you think the Bible can guide us?

5. Can we be friends with people who have beliefs that we disagree with? Why?

Prayer:

Father God, we're sorry for when we're more affected by the world around us than by you. We're sorry when we make decisions based on what's cool, what our horoscope told us or how the media has influenced us. We choose now to follow you properly, and be influenced and guided by your Word. Thank you that the Bible is true and a light to our lives. Amen

⭐ AND THERE'S MORE!

Draw the young people's attention to the activities on page 19 of the Youth Guide 11-14. In particular, focus perhaps on the 'Think' section:

'How much time do I spend reading the Bible compared to magazines or other stuff that affects my worldview? Do I need to balance things out a bit more?'

? CLOSING QUESTION

Ask them to consider this question over the coming week (on page 21 of the Youth Guide 11-14):

If you know you are saint, why do you think that you still often mess up?

Remember to remind the young people about the date for the Steps To Freedom Away Day/ Weekend.

WORLDVIEW 15-18

LEADER'S PREPARATION

Pray together:

> Father of Truth, open our eyes today to see clearly what is the truth in our lives, and what is not. Help us to understand what relates to you and what doesn't and be able to know where our beliefs come from. Amen

YOU MAY NEED
Food from around the world

Accompanying DVD / DVD player / TV / projector

Printed out worldview descriptions

Printed out Bible verses

Torches (flashlights)

Dark sunglasses

Tinted glasses/normal glasses with pink plastic stuck on or whiteboard pen

Bibles

Remember – each young person needs a torch (flashlight)!

PRAYER AND DECLARATION

Encourage everyone to join together in saying the following prayer and declaration. You can download the PowerPoint slides with the words for these from the website.

It would be good to suggest that the young people stand up and speak out the declaration clearly and confidently to the heavenly realms. They could shout it out and use appropriate actions!

PRAYER:

> Father you are truth. Open my eyes so that I can see clearly where my life is based on truth and where it is not. Help me to understand where my beliefs come from. Amen.

DECLARATION:

> Jesus said that he is the way, the truth and the life. I am going to listen to him. I confidently command evil lies to leave this place. Anything that comes between me and Jesus is not welcome here. You must go now in Jesus' name!

🔍 STARTING POINT

FOOD FROM AROUND THE WORLD

As part of your welcome drinks, get some simple party snacks from around the world from a frozen food shop / aisle and let the group try out different ones. If your budget is tight just explain that this is a food-tasting moment and not a full on dinner experience! Try to get your group to try new things. Don't forget to ask around your church as there may be some great cooks who would love to prepare something for you.

Discussion:

- If you could choose to be from another country where would you come from?

- If you were from a different country how might you see the world differently?

Give a short summary of the previous session. A good resource for this is the Overview found in the Core of the previous session.

We have now started the second section of the course. The first part looked at some basic truths – the second one is about some of the things that get in the way of truth.

Today we're going to look at worldviews, and how we all look at the world in certain ways – not always God's ways!

◉ DVD CHAPTER 1

Play Session 4, chapter 1 – 'A Unique View?' – of the accompanying DVD.

Now, wearing tinted glasses, lead straight into the explanation about worldviews.

Leader's Prep: Get a pair of sunglasses that have tinted lenses or get a cheap pair of glasses and colour the lenses pink (perhaps with a whiteboard pen, or by sticking pink plastic over them). Wear these for the beginning of the talk.

Have you ever heard the saying that someone is looking at the world 'through rose-tinted glasses?'

What that means is that someone is overly optimistic and a bit unrealistic, about what they see. Let me give you an example of optimism: a kid's Batman costume made by a company called Kenner Products had the following warning on the label: 'Caution: Cape does not enable users to fly.' You'd have to be a huge optimist to buy it thinking that it will help you fly!

Now, I'm wearing my rose-tinted glasses today – you all look gorgeous, all rosy and healthy! Are you an optimist like me, seeing everything better than it is?

Or maybe you're a pessimist? [change into a pair of dark sunglasses]

Maybe you see the world in its worst possible light – wow, it is dark and gloomy in here! [take glasses off]

The fact is that we all look at the world in a particular way, through 'glasses' of some sort. A particular way of seeing the world is called a 'worldview'.

YOUR WORLDVIEW IS LIKE A FILTER

Your worldview works like a filter. Everything that you see, everything that happens around you, you put through this filter to work out what it all means.

Most Westerners claim to believe in God but in the Western worldview he is often seen as irrelevant to our lives. When push comes to shove, we have been taught to rely on things that we can see, touch and prove scientifically.

If you were brought up in the West and experienced lots of stuff going wrong, your first thought would probably be to find out why by looking for logical scientific reasons.

It's not that logic and science are wrong or bad, it's just that they are not giving you the whole story. They are not taking the whole of reality – specifically the reality of the spiritual world – into account.

Can we really believe that all this (look around you for a second) came about by chance? There's got to be more to the world than what we can see, touch or prove through experiments.

Trouble is we don't realise we were taught a worldview. It happened just like you learned to speak – you simply absorbed it. If you had been brought up in Sweden, you'd have grown up speaking Swedish. In the same way, we just absorb the way we look at the world from those around us: parents, friends, teachers, the TV and so on.

It's quite scary to think that, if you had been brought up somewhere else, you would see the world in a completely different way.

How can you know what to believe?

This course is all about learning to see the world as it really is - to try our best to remove any glasses that are distorting things for us. We want to discover what God's truth is.

◉ DVD CHAPTER 2

Play Session 4, chapter 2 – 'My View, My Truth?' – of the accompanying DVD.

UNDERSTANDING WHAT YOU ARE REALLY SAYING

Print off the first three worldviews (available as downloads), cut them up into their relevant paragraphs and stick them round the room.

Divide your group into three and ask them to go round the room on rotation to read and discuss each of the worldviews.

Keep the Biblical worldview to the end. Review the others and bring it into the discussion at the appropriate time.

1. A Non-Western Worldview

This set of glasses is a worldview called 'animism.' It's found in its purest form amongst tribal societies in developing countries, but is widespread in many countries beyond that across all levels of society.

Most animists believe in some kind of god, but that what's really important is the idea of a spiritual power, found in everything – animal, vegetable, mineral. Within this worldview, there are certain people that are experts of the spiritual: shamans, medicine men or witch doctors. They are the ones to call on if you have any kind of trouble. Every problem is seen to involve a spirit in some way.

Animists often live in fear of evil spirits, or spirits that simply don't like them and want to hurt them.

There is also always the worry that an enemy might become spiritually superior, and use this spiritual power against them.

This worldview is found all over the world, and 'new age' and occult practices have brought some of its beliefs into the West as well.

2. The 'Modern' Worldview

Most people that have grown up in the West over the last 50 years or so will have learned to look at the world using the 'modern' worldview, at least to some extent.

This worldview divides everything in to 'the natural' – things that can be scientifically proven – and 'the supernatural' – things that can't. The supernatural has no relation to normal, everyday life and is generally not to be taken particularly seriously. God ends up in that category.

This has meant that spiritual things haven't really been included in education (it's just not seen as that important). The modern worldview basically says that if you can't test something and prove it scientifically – it's not true!

Even the Church has been affected by this worldview. Some churches try to get rid of everything supernatural in order to fit in with the world, and some Christian ministers say that they don't believe in miracles, angels and demons, or even the Holy Spirit.

3. The Postmodern Worldview

Lately, the modern worldview has been losing out to something many call the postmodern (meaning 'after modern') worldview. If you have grown up in the West, you have probably been influenced by a mix of modern and post-modern thinking.

A philosopher named Friedrich Nietzsche summed up the line of thinking that would become postmodernism, when he wrote in 1885:

'There are many kinds of eyes..., and consequently there are many kinds of "truths", and consequently there is no truth.'

No truth! In the modern worldview God may not be seen as truth (as he can't be proved), but truth as a concept remains; in postmodernism, truth does not even exist! Everyone is allowed to make up their own truths – but we are not to challenge what other people believe. Whatever feels right for that person...

This is why, as Christians, we are under real pressure to say that anything anyone does is OK – it's their choice, right? We are under pressure to say that all religions are alright and even that all belief systems are equal to ours.

4. The Biblical Worldview

Having tried on these three different looking glasses, which should we choose? Which showed us the best view of the world?

None!

We need to change the way we have learned to see reality until it agrees with how the Bible says the world is.

Although we can be given a hard time for saying this in our postmodern world, according to the Bible, truth really does exist. In fact, it teaches that God is truth.

⬆ WORSHIP ACTIVITY

In advance of the session have these verses printed out on sheets of card. They are available as downloads from the website.

'There is now no condemnation for those who are in Christ Jesus.' (Romans 8:1)

'And we know that in all things God works for the good of those who love him.' (Romans 8:28)

'If God is for us, who can be against us?' (Romans 8:31)

'Jesus said: "Surely I am with you always, to the very end of the age."' (Matthew 28:20)

'God has said, "Never will I leave you; never will I forsake you."' (Hebrews 13:5)

'Jesus Christ is the same yesterday and today and forever.' (Hebrews 13:8)

'God is light; in him there is no darkness at all.' (1 John 1:5)

'This is love: not that we loved God, but that he loved us and sent his son as an atoning sacrifice for our sins.' (1 John 4:10)

Spread the Bible verses around the room. Ask the young people to get their torches (flashlights) out, switch them on and turn the lights off. Put on some quiet background music.

Say:

Psalm 119:105 says that the Bible is like a light to us, it guides us and shows us the truth.

We're going to walk around this room [or several rooms if your main meeting room is very small] for a while and every time you find a card, you find a truth from the Bible. Read it out loud – to yourself and to anyone else who happens to be listening. Then place the card down and keep walking until you reach another one.

WHAT'S THE POINT?

Direct the young people's attention to page 18 of the Youth Guide 15-18 where it says:

- We each have a different worldview, or perspective, which can affect the way we see God and ourselves.

- The culture in which we live and our past experiences can affect and distort the way we look at the world.

- We need to choose to look at ourselves and God through a Biblical worldview and not mix and match it with any other perspective that is not as true.

◉ DVD CHAPTER 3

Play Session 4, chapter 3 – 'What Is Truth?' – of the accompanying DVD.

Now lead straight into the following section.

'DON'T LET THE WORLD SQUEEZE YOU INTO ITS MOULD'
Christian faith is 'choosing to believe what God says is true'

By all means look at the facts, check that Christianity is reasonable. But, once you are happy, make a firm decision to believe God's word whether it feels true or not, no matter what those around you may say.

Have you done that?

Are you ready to do that?

Now ask a leader to share their story about when they decided to follow Jesus. Include points from the above process.

- What was going on in their life at that time?

- What prompted them?

- Did they look at and weigh up the facts?

- How did they check those facts out?

- How did they come to the decision?

- How has it gone since?

- Do they have three top tips that help sustain this?

ACTIVITY

Ask the group to take the 'Which Worldview?' test on page 20 of the Youth Guide 15-18. (Make sure it doesn't feel too serious!) Say:

Although this test wasn't very serious, it can show us how easy it is for worldviews that are opposite to the Biblical one to slip into our mindsets. Many of us will talk about how Christianity feels right for us, and how we have experienced it. This may be true – which is great – but it cannot be the basis of our faith! Otherwise, what happens on days when we don't feel anything?

Someone called Os Guinness sums it up like this:

'The Christian faith is not true because it works; it works because it is true....' (Os Guinness, Time for Truth, Baker Books, 2000, pages 79-80).

Christian faith is 'choosing to believe what God says is true' because we have made a decision that the Biblical worldview is how things really are.

RESPONSE

SOAPBOX

Discuss:

1. What does the world tell us we have to do to fit in and be loved? What does the Bible say?

2. How do people respond when they get hurt? What does the Bible say?

3. What are some of the things that affect the way we see the world?

4. In what ways do you think the Bible can guide us?

5. Can we be friends with people who have beliefs that we disagree with? Why?

Prayer

Father God, we're sorry for when we're more affected by the world around us than by you. We're sorry when we make decisions based on what's cool, what our horoscope told us or how the media has influenced us. We choose now to follow you properly, and be influenced and guided by your word. Thank you that the Bible is true and a light to our lives. Amen.

AND THERE'S MORE!

Using a PowerPoint slide read together Psalm 119:105:

'Your word is a lamp to my feet and a light for my path.'

Challenge the young people to write this verse on page 19 of their Youth Guide 11-18 and learn it in the next week.

CLOSING QUESTION

Question for next week - see page 21 of the Youth Guide 15-18:

If we know we are saints, why is it that we still so often mess up?

Remember to remind the young people about the date for the Steps To Freedom Away Day/ Weekend.

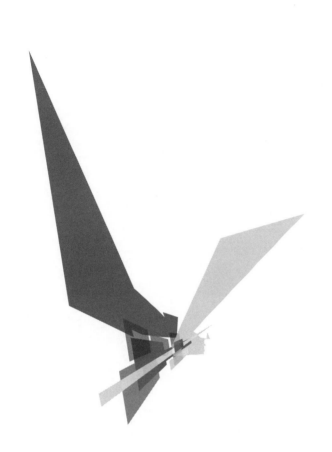

SESSION FIVE:
BIG CHOICES

'You, however, are controlled not by the flesh but by the Spirit, if the Spirit of God lives in you.'

Romans 8:9

BIG CHOICES CORE

INTRODUCTION

In this session, we're going to try to understand what the Bible means by the word 'flesh', and how our flesh can stop us from growing as Christians.

Sometimes we think that becoming a Christian is like flicking a switch – immediately we will automatically do everything right! Pretty soon we realise that this isn't the case. We often don't feel any different at all compared to before we became Christians, we still have some bad habits and sometimes it feels like the temptation to do something wrong is even stronger than before. Why is this?

Think about these two questions:

* What changed when we became Christians?

* What did not change when we became Christians?

WHAT CHANGED?

Whether we feel them or not, some dramatic changes took place when we became Christians:

- We are a new creation (2 Corinthians 5:17) and have a new heart and a new Spirit within us.

- Our new heart wants what God wants; it's not naturally directed to sin. It lets us know quickly if we have sinned – a very good sign that we are saved.

- We have new life 'in Christ' right now together with the significance, security and acceptance we were designed for.

- Before we became Christians, whether we realised it or not, the devil was our boss – we did things he wanted us to do. Now, we have a new boss – God (Colossians 1:13).

- We received forgiveness for stuff we have done wrong.

- We entered into a relationship with God.

- We will now go to heaven when we die.

WHAT DIDN'T CHANGE?

Let's look at three things that didn't happen when we became Christians:

- Our body didn't change

- Although we have changed dramatically on the inside, on the outside we look the same as before.

- Our 'flesh' was not taken away.

We learned in an earlier session that we were designed to be significant, secure and accepted. From our first breath we have instinctively wanted to feel significant, secure and accepted but often don't. We therefore set about looking for ways to get those legitimate feelings. Because we did not know God, we turned to other things: food, shopping, making people like us, etc. Eventually those things become our ways of coping, of feeling better. They become ingrained habits. These are part of what the Bible calls "the flesh".

When we became Christians, unfortunately no one pressed a 'CLEAR ALL' button in our minds to automatically replace our old way of being with new godly ways of thinking and reacting.

Instead, we have to train ourselves to think in a way that is in line with God's truth. The Bible calls this 'renewing our minds'. We do this by replacing old ways of thinking – based on lies – with new ways of thinking – based on truth.

At its most basic, the term "flesh" refers to our physical bodies and by extension to the instincts and urges that it has. You could perhaps sum up the Biblical concept of the flesh by saying it is "the urge to do what comes naturally to a fallen human being".

WHY 'FLESH'?

You may be wondering why in this cool, ultra-modern course (!) we are using an old-fashioned word - 'flesh' - when most modern translations of the Bible don't. 'Flesh' is an unfamiliar word to the modern ear in this context, but it's exactly what the original Bible text says. The Greek word used in the New Testament ('sarx') was the word used to describe, for example, meat you would buy from a butcher or the flesh on your leg. Many modern Bible translations do not translate the word 'flesh' literally but interpret it and use a phrase such as 'sinful nature' or 'old nature' (though you will normally find a footnote explaining what they have done). We understand completely why they do that – using a direct translation without explanation would not make a great deal of sense to modern readers, especially young people.

However, we are concerned that use of the term 'nature' might be unhelpful because, as we saw in the first two sessions, Christians definitely do not any longer have a nature that is sinful but we share God's nature. Deep down inside at the most fundamental level of our nature and identity we are now holy and righteous.

A phrase such as 'sinful tendency' might perhaps be a more helpful interpretation. It accurately conveys the concept that we have something inside us that pulls us towards sin without implying that we ourselves are back in the position of being fundamentally sinful at the level of our very nature. For the sake of clarity, however, we are going to stick with the literal translation 'flesh'. (You may find it interesting to look at a modern translation such as the English Standard Version that does generally translate the word literally as 'flesh'.)

SIN IS NOT DEAD
Something else didn't change: sin didn't die

Now, let's be clear: we can't defeat sin. The good news is that Jesus has already done it!

But sin is still alive and kicking, tempting us every day to take the quick route to significance, security and acceptance.

OUR CHOICES
Even though nothing can take away the fact that God loves us and has saved us, it's down to us to choose to be one of three different types of people (outlined in 1 Corinthians 2:14 - 3:3):

1. Natural Norman ('the man without the Spirit' 1 Corinthians 2:14 & Ephesians 2:1-3)

Norman is like everyone who is not yet a Christian:

* he is physically alive but spiritually dead.

* he is separated from God.

* he is living independently from God.

* his actions and choices are based on the flesh – his human ways of coping.

This doesn't necessarily mean that Norman is unhappy – he has probably learned ways to feel good about himself without involving God. But in the long run, he will struggle to find things to meet his needs, and he will not have a firm spiritual basis to cope with difficulties in life. Ultimately, of course, unless Norman comes to Christ, he will find that he has no right to enter the Kingdom of Heaven.

2. Spiritual Sam (1 Corinthians 2:15)

Sam is living in a way that all Christians can:

- he has been transformed through faith in Christ.

- he has received forgiveness and acceptance into God's family and has realised who he is in Christ.

- he makes choices by listening to God's Spirit rather than the flesh.

- he is getting rid of old ways of thinking and replacing them with truth (ie renewing his mind).

- he experiences joy and peace, instead of stress and turmoil.

- he demonstrates the fruit of the Spirit (Galatians 5:22, 23).

- sometimes he messes up but knows he can shake off temptation and not let it run his life (Romans 6:11-14).

Sam's way of life is what we're all aiming for – but don't dismiss it as an impossible dream! Did you know that God has already given you everything you need for this kind of life? (Don't believe us? Have a look at 2 Peter 1:3 and Ephesians 1:3!).

3. Fleshly Fred (1 Corinthians 3:3)

Fred has had the same life-changing experience as Sam - his is a Christian, a new creation - but, instead of following the impulses of the Spirit, he follows the impulses of the flesh. He has the option – the freedom – to walk according to the Spirit, but chooses not to, either on purpose or perhaps because he doesn't really understand the freedom that he has.

His daily life looks more like Norman's than Sam's:

- he thinks a lot of wrong thoughts and dwells on them.

- he experiences a lot of negative feelings.

- his body shows signs of stress.

He is still a Christian, has a relationship with God and is going to heaven but is not living to his full potential.

Fred also tends to get 'stuck' in certain sins.

We probably all recognise this a bit. Maybe we keep returning time and again to comfort eating, losing our temper, gossiping or sexual sin. In the end we feel completely hopeless and feel (wrongly) that we can never escape.

Fred is still saved, but he is not living his life as well as he could; he's not as happy as he could be, he doesn't achieve the things for God that he could do.

THINGS THAT STOP US FROM GROWING

God has given us everything we need to live like Sam. So we don't need to go to special services to get 'zapped' or pray the 'right' prayer. But we do need to learn to deal with the things that stop us from growing:

- Ignorance

Lots of us live lives like Fred simply because we don't know better. We haven't been told the truth of who we are in Christ. Maybe you're like a lot of Christians who have spent your whole life listening to preachers telling you what to **do**, rather than who you **are**.

- Deception (Colossians 2:8)

It's hard to spot if you're being deceived, because it feels like the truth to you. But if you're not growing as a Christian, deception might be the reason why.

You might also be deceived if you often think thoughts like these:

> 'This might work for others, but my case is different and it won't work for me'

> 'I could never have faith like so-and-so'

> 'God could never use me'

- Unresolved personal and spiritual conflicts

We often think that we have the right to be angry or upset with someone, but it actually stops us from growing. For example, if you have never truly forgiven someone who hurt you, you are leaving a big door open to the devil to confuse your thinking and stop you connecting with truth. If you don't close that door by doing what God tells you to do; forgiving the person that has hurt you, you are unlikely to grow as a Christian.

Later on in the course, you're going to get the chance to spend some quality time listening to the Holy Spirit and letting him point out the doors that are still open in your life (this is part of a process that we call 'The Steps to Freedom in Christ'). You'll get the chance then to close those doors and move on to a life with more freedom. Often, it's only when you have gone through a process like that, that you start really understanding some basic Christians concepts, like how much God loves you!

CHOOSING TO WALK BY THE SPIRIT EVERY DAY

Once we have decided to believe truth no matter how we feel and we have dealt with our unresolved spiritual conflict, we are truly free to make a choice every day – obey the flesh or obey the Holy Spirit.

You might be surprised how many people, whom you might consider amazing, mature Christians, hear from their flesh every day messages such as 'you are useless, hopeless and a waste of space!' The person who is worth your admiration is the one who chooses simply not to listen to their flesh, but knows that their significance, acceptance and security are in Christ.

What does it mean to 'walk by the Spirit'?

Now, it's important to know that walking by the Spirit is **not**:

- Just a good feeling. You might feel happy when you make the right choice, or you might not. It won't change what's true or right.

- An excuse to do whatever we want. When we follow the promptings of the Spirit, rather than the flesh, we will act in line with God's guidelines. In other words, the Spirit won't tell you to do something (e.g. steal something) that goes against God's character.

- Obeying lots of rules and getting obsessed by them. God won't love us any more or any less, because we follow rules. Walking by the Spirit is about having the freedom to choose not to do the wrong thing.

On the other hand, walking by the Spirit is:

- Real freedom: 'Where the Spirit of the Lord is, there is freedom' (2 Corinthians 3:17). The devil can't make you walk in the flesh.

- Being led: not pushed along or forced to go somewhere (John 10:27).

- Walking at God's pace, in the right direction. We walk together with Jesus, not running ahead, nor staying behind (Matthew 11:28-30).

You can tell that you're walking by the Spirit if your life is marked out more and more by love, joy, peace, patience, kindness, goodness, faithfulness, gentleness and self-control. These are the fruit of the Spirit (Galatians 5:22-23), which will grow in your life over time.

Maybe you're thinking that you're more like Fred than Sam – what should you do? We need to submit to God by confessing our sin, then resist the devil by turning our back on it and taking hold of our authority in Christ. Finally we need to keep renewing our minds. We will look at these things as we go through the course.

It boils down to a choice we all have to make, every day to walk by the flesh or by the Spirit. What is amazing is that God has given us everything we need to live all out as a Christian, even if it does not feel like it. 2 Peter 1:3 says: 'His divine power has given us everything we need for life and godliness through our knowledge of him who called us by his own glory and goodness.'

QUESTIONS TO THINK ABOUT AS YOU PREPARE:

1. Remember the closing question from last time. Even though you're a saint, why do you think we often still feel like doing the wrong thing?

2. Are the people you hang out with most like Norman, Sam or Fred? Who are you most like? Why?

3. Does it surprise you that a Christian can live pretty much like a non-Christian? Why? Why not?

4. Why do you think people can feel insecure, useless, guilty and worried if they live by the flesh?

5. Do you believe that it's possible to defeat the flesh?

6. What barriers do you think people face to growing as Christians?

7. How can you tell if someone is living by the Spirit?

BIG CHOICES 11-14

LEADER'S PREPARATION

Pray together:

> ❝ Father God, I choose to be guided by the Holy Spirit. Help me not to make choices guided by my flesh. Amen.

YOU MAY NEED

'Would you rather?' alternatives

Balloons with Bible verses rolled up inside them (these will need preparation by adding verses from downloadable psalm sheet)

Charlie & the Chocolate Factory DVD

Accompanying DVD / DVD player / TV / projector

Large sheets of paper / flipchart and post-it notes

Pens and marker pens

Masking tape, 36 sheets of paper with a footprint on one side and either a mine or arrow on the other

Selection of fruit

Bibles

 ## PRAYER AND DECLARATION

Encourage everyone to join together in saying the following prayer and declaration. You can download the PowerPoint slides with the words for these from the website.

It would be good to suggest that the young people stand up and speak out the declaration clearly and confidently to the heavenly realms. They could shout it out and use appropriate actions!

PRAYER

> ❝ Lord, I choose to be guided by your Holy Spirit. Teach me to make choices that lead to freedom. Amen

DECLARATION: IN A CLEAR, CONFIDENT TONE!

> ❝ I am walking with the Lord Jesus. I am not interested in being influenced by anyone who is his enemy so you must be gone in the name of Jesus. Now!

Start by giving a short summary of the previous session. A good resource for this is the Overview found in the Core of the previous session.

INTRODUCTORY ACTIVITIES

WOULD YOU RATHER?

Explain that this session is all about the choices we make so we are going to play a game that involves choices.

Ask the young people to get up and go to one side of the room or the other depending on their answer.

Ask a couple of young people after each round why they chose that particular one.

Alternatives - there is no sitting on the fence:

- McDonalds or Subway?

- sleep on a big doughnut or in custard?

- have incredibly long fingers or incredibly long toes?

- be able to fly or breathe under water?

- have dinner with Shrek or Homer Simpson?

- go back in time or forward in time?

- eat cheese flavoured trifle or banana flavoured pizza?

- be so small people can't see you or so tall you can see everyone?

WINK, THINK

Have half the group sit on chairs in a circle, with the other half of the group each standing behind one of the chairs.

One player should be left with a vacant chair in front of him. (Add a leader to the game to make up the numbers, if necessary.) The player with the vacant chair in front of him must aim to wink subtly at someone sitting down, who should at that point leave her seat and move to the chair in front of the person who winked at her.

If a player notices the player in front of her beginning to get up, she may reach out and grab him to stop him leaving. However, everyone standing up must keep their hands behind their backs unless the player in front of them moves.

Explain:

In the same way that in this game, we felt drawn away from our partners, sometimes in life we feel a pull away from God. But God is not like the person behind us in this game. He doesn't force us to stay. What we need to learn is that we also have the freedom to choose to stay!

⊚ DVD CHAPTER 1

Play Session 5, chapter 1 – 'Choice' – of the accompanying DVD.

Ask the group

- What choices do you make every day?

- What was the toughest choice you had to make today?

- What was the toughest choice you have ever had to make?

Choices are an integral part of our everyday lives. We just need to realise and acknowledge it!

⬆ WORSHIP ACTIVITY

Print out or photocopy the worship phrases from the Psalms (available in the downloadable material for this session).

Cut out the phrases, roll them up and stick them inside colourful balloons which you then inflate.

Throw the balloons around the group and one by one get the young people to pop them. Every time a balloon is popped get one of the young people to read the Psalm aloud on the piece of paper in praise to God.

Leader's Note: Be aware of anyone in your group who is afraid of balloons or loud bangs. You could always stick the phrases on paper planes and throw around instead.

▦ MOVIE CLIP

Today we're going to try to understand what the Bible means by the word 'flesh', and how our flesh can stop us from growing as Christians.

DVD clip: Charlie and the Chocolate Factory (PG)

Start clip: 00:41:00

End clip: 00:47:35

In this clip the children are given their first glimpse of Willy Wonka's chocolate factory, but Augustus Gloop finds it impossible to cope with the temptation of all that melted chocolate.

Discussion:

Following on from the DVD clip and depending on the size of your group, divide into two or three groups and then ask the leaders to explain about bad habits and lead the discussion below.

- What do you get tempted by?

- How do you avoid this temptation, or do you think there is nothing wrong and do nothing?

Have some young leaders or leaders share some of their temptations to start things off if needed.

Explain:

Sometimes we think that becoming a Christian is like flicking a switch – immediately we will automatically do everything right!

Pretty soon we realise that this isn't the case – we often don't feel any different at all from before we became Christians; we still have some bad habits and sometimes it feels like the temptation to do something wrong is even stronger than before.

Discussion:

- Why is this?

- Is there anything we can do about it?

Well, even though we became new creations when we gave our lives to Jesus, our old ways of reacting to things and our old ways of thinking are still there. We've learned how to think, react and cope with things as we've grown up, and it's not necessarily the way that the Bible says.

These old ways of thinking, reacting and coping are what the Bible calls 'the flesh'.

As our way of thinking, reacting and coping didn't change overnight when we became Christians, we have to train ourselves to think in line with God's truth instead – the Bible calls this 'renewing our mind'.

Come back together.

◎ DVD CHAPTER 2

Play Session 5, chapter 2 – 'Genuine Choice' – of the accompanying DVD.

OUR CHOICES

Even though nothing can take away the fact that God loves us and has saved us, it's down to us to choose to become like one of three different types of people.

Use three large sheets of paper and draw the outline of a person on each. Write / stick labels on the sheets with the characteristics of the three person types.

Alternatively ask for three volunteers to have labels stuck onto them. (use large post-its). Emphasise they are only stand-ins and not being type-cast!

Person Types (explain that the cheesy names are deliberate):

Leader's Note: draw the young people's attention to page 23 of the Youth Guide 11-14 where the young people can write in the pictures the characteristics of each person type.

1. Natural Norman ('the man without the Spirit' 1 Corinthians 2:14 & Ephesians 2:1-3)

Norman is like everyone who is not yet a Christian:

- he doesn't have the spiritual life Jesus came to give

- he is separated from God.

- he doesn't care about or know God.

- his flesh/feelings direct his actions and choices.

This doesn't necessarily mean that Norman is unhappy – he has probably learned ways to feel good about himself without involving God.

But in the long run, he will struggle to find things to meet his needs, and he will not know he is secure, significant and accepted as he is.

Ultimately, of course, unless Norman accepts the life that Jesus came to give him this will never change.

2. Spiritual Sam (1 Corinthians 2:15)

Sam is what all Christians could be like:

- he has been changed through believing in Jesus.

- he has received: forgiveness, acceptance in God's family and has realised how much he is worth in Christ.

- he is guided by God's Spirit rather than the flesh.

- he is getting rid of old ways of thinking and replacing them with truth.

- he experiences joy and peace, instead of stress and worry.

- he is still tempted to mess up and still does sometimes but realises that he doesn't always have to give in. (Romans 6:11-14).

Sam is what we're all aiming for and it is not impossible to become like him! God has already given us everything that we need for this kind of life (2 Peter 1:3).

3. Fleshly Fred (1 Corinthians 3:3)

Fred has had the same life-changing experience as Sam, but instead of following the God's Spirit he follows what we are calling 'the flesh'. He has the option – the freedom – to follow God's Spirit, but chooses not to, either on purpose or perhaps because he doesn't really understand the freedom that he has.

His daily life looks more like Norman's than Sam's:

- he lets wrong thoughts fill his mind and dwells on them

- he lets negative feelings rule his life.

- this could affect his well being

He's just not living to his full potential!

Fred also tends to get 'stuck' in messing up over and over again. There are some particular things he does, which are wrong and which damage him, but which he just can't seem to stop doing.

We might recognise this.

Maybe we keep returning time and again to bad language or losing our temper. In the end we can feel completely hopeless and feel (wrongly) that we can never escape.

Fred still has a relationship with God and is going to heaven but he is not living life to the max, he's not as happy as he could be, and he could be changing the world around him instead of going round and round in circles.

 ## THE MAIN POINT

THINGS THAT STOP US FROM GROWING

The incredible thing is that God has already given us everything we need to live like Sam. Living like he does is not a matter of going to the 'right' special events or festivals, or getting prayed for by the right person or praying the 'right' prayer.

All these are good things but we need to realise that our growth in the Lord is down to us. We can do it already with God's help.

The starting point is to learn to deal with the things that stop us from growing.

 ## DVD CHAPTER 3

Play Session 5, chapter 3 – 'Choosing Freedom' – of the accompanying DVD.

Explain:

We have EVERYTHING we need to grow as Christians. 2 Peter 1:3 is an amazing verse that says:

'His divine power has given us everything we need for life and godliness through our knowledge of him who called us by his own glory and goodness.'

GAME – WALKING IN GOD'S FOOTPRINTS

Mark a grid on the floor – 6 x 6 squares

Put a piece of paper on each square with a footprint on.

On the other side of each piece of paper put a picture of an arrow or a mine.

There must be at least one arrow on each row.

Ask the young people to take it in turns to try and cross the grid, turning the paper over as they go. Each time they step on a mine they are out. When they have finished their turn, they must make sure that all arrows and mines are face down. The trick is for the next player to try and remember the safe route.

The first person to cross the grid is the winner.

CHOOSING TO WALK BY THE SPIRIT

We can choose every day whether to obey our flesh, our old way of doing things, or the Holy Spirit.

We can choose to think, react and cope with life in God's way, or in the ways we were used to before we became Christians.

Walking by the Spirit means real freedom, being led by God rather than pushed along; it means walking through life together with God.

You can tell that you're walking by the Spirit if your life is marked out by

- love
- joy
- peace
- patience
- kindness
- goodness
- faithfulness
- gentleness
- self-control

These are the fruit of the Spirit (Galatians 5:22-23), which will grow in your life over time.

Maybe you've realised in this session that you're more like Fred than Sam. If so, what should you do?

Start by confessing your sin to God – admitting that you've been living 'in the flesh' – and then choose to walking in the Spirit.

It's a choice we all have to make. Every day.

RESPONSE

Buy a load of fruit (the more variety, the better), cut it up and put it on a tray in the middle of the group.

Hand out napkins.

Explain:

This activity is a sign you can use to say to God that you are making a choice to live by his Spirit and have the fruit that will eventually come with that.

Ask the young people to commit to making the choice every day to live by God's Spirit and not the flesh that we have learned about today. As a symbol of this, encourage the group to eat the fruit laid out.

To live God's way and not be held back by following ourselves.

SMALL GROUPS & PRAYER FOCUS

1. Remember the question from last time. Since we're all saints, why do you think we still often feel like doing the wrong thing?

2. Are your friends most like Norman, Sam or Fred? Who are you most like?

3. Does it surprise you that a Christian can live pretty much like a non-Christian? What should make a difference?

4. Do you believe that it's possible to defeat the flesh? Why? Why not?

5. What things do you think hold back people and stop them growing as a Christians?

6. How can you tell if you are living being guided by God's Spirit?

⭐ AND THERE'S MORE!

Point out the two sections on page 23 of the Youth Guide 11-14 to do at home this week:

- Challenge: Spend some time alone with God every day this week. Write down anything that he says or puts into your mind, and think about renewing your mind with God's truth.

- Think: If you are living by the Spirit, your life will be full of the characteristics of God – love, joy, peace, etc. What barriers do you think there are in your life to growing as a Christian? What can you do about them?

You could use the opportunity to remind them that The Steps To Freedom In Christ will help them deal with some of the barriers.

❓ CLOSING QUESTION

Refer the young people to the question to consider during the coming week, on page 24 of the Youth Guide 11-14:

Are there sins that you keep falling back to, sins that you can't seem to stop committing? Why do you think that is?

BIG CHOICES 15-18

PRAYER AND DECLARATION

Encourage everyone to join together in saying the following prayer and declaration. You can download the PowerPoint slides with the words for these from the website.

It would be good to suggest that the young people stand up and speak out the declaration clearly and confidently to the heavenly realms. They could shout it out and use appropriate actions!

PRAYER:

❝ Lord, I choose to be guided by your Holy Spirit. Teach me to make choices that lead to freedom. Amen

DECLARATION:

❝ I am walking with the Lord Jesus. I am not interested in being influenced by anyone who is his enemy so you must be gone in the name of Jesus. Now!

🔍 STARTING POINT

As part of the welcome drinks, and once everyone has arrived, walk round with a bag of sweets with distinctive types (such as Haribo Starmix). Pass the bag from person to person quickly so that they have to choose under pressure. Some will just reach in and grab a couple, but others will try to look in and select specific sweets.

Afterwards point out to the group that even when we are given things we still like to make choices.

Start by giving a short summary of the previous session. A good resource for this is the Overview found in the Core of the previous session.

◉ DVD CHAPTER 1

Play Session 5, chapter 1 – 'Choice' – of the accompanying DVD.

Ask the group:

- What choices do you make every day?

- What was the toughest choice you had to make today?

- What was the toughest choice you have ever had to make?

Choice is an integral part of our everyday lives. We just need to realise and acknowledge it!

△ SOAPBOX

- Are you someone who likes to make a definite choice when you are being given something like the sweets a moment ago?

- Why do you think that is?

- What about the people who were not bothered which sweet they received. Why didn't you care which one ended up in your mouth?

- How much do you think about the choices that you make?

Some of us are more impulsive than others. Some of us are more reflective. Some of us are not even really aware that there is a choice involved. The fact is that, however we respond, we are all given the opportunity to choose how we are going to live.

Sometimes the biggest challenge is to choose to do something that we just do not feel like doing. We might choose to worship God even when everything in us feels like doing the opposite. The thing that we forget is that if we choose God's way, it can change the way we are feeling. Topsy turvy but true.

◎ DVD CHAPTER 2

Play Session 5, chapter 2 – 'Genuine Choice' – of the accompanying DVD.

⬆ WORSHIP ACTIVITY

Print out the worship phrases from the Psalms from the downloadable resources for this session.

Cut out the phrases, roll them up and stick them inside colourful balloons which you then inflate.

Throw the balloons round the group and one by one get the young people to pop them. Every time a balloon is popped, get one of the young people to read the Psalm aloud on the piece of paper in praise to God.

Leader's Note: Be aware of anyone in your group who is afraid of balloons or loud bangs. You could always stick the phrases on paper aeroplanes and throw around instead.

Read out the What's The Point? section on page 22 of the Youth Guide 15-18 which says:

- As Christians, our old sinful nature is gone but we still have our old ways of thinking, reacting and coping, characteristics known as 'the flesh', and we have to choose to change. We have to unlearn our 'fleshly' way of thinking and learn how to think in line with God's truth – the Bible calls this 'renewing our mind'. It's all about choice – we will still be tempted to sin but we can choose to walk by the Spirit and not give in to temptation.

- As Christians, our old sinful nature is gone but we still have our old ways of thinking, reacting and coping, characteristics known as 'the flesh', and we have to choose to change.

- We have to unlearn our 'fleshly' way of thinking and learn how to think in line with God's truth – the Bible calls this 'renewing our mind'.

It's all about choice – we will still be tempted to sin but we can choose to walk by the Spirit and not give in to temptation.

WALKING BY THE SPIRIT OR THE FLESH?

Even though nothing can take away the fact that God loves us and has saved us, it's down to us to choose to be like one of three different types of people...

Divide the young people into three groups, giving each group the paragraphs for a 'person', then explain that they have 10 minutes to read and prepare a 1 minute drama / presentation displaying their person's characteristics.

Alternatively use three large sheets of paper and draw the outline of a person on each, use the sheets to write/ stick labels of the characteristics of the three person types.

Person Types (explain that the cheesy names are deliberate!):

Natural Norman ('the man without the Spirit' 1 Corinthians 2:14 & Ephesians 2:1-3)

Norman is like everyone who is not yet a Christian:

- he doesn't have the spiritual life Jesus came to give

- he is separated from God

- he doesn't care about or know God

- his flesh/feelings direct his actions and choices

This doesn't necessarily mean that Norman is unhappy – he has probably learned ways to feel good about himself without involving God.

But in the long run, he will struggle to find things to meet his needs, and he will not know how secure, significant and accepted he is.

Ultimately, of course, unless Norman accepts the life that Jesus came to give him, this outlook will never change.

Spiritual Sam (1 Corinthians 2:15)

Sam is what all Christians could be like:

- he has been changed through believing in Jesus.

- he has received forgiveness, acceptance in God's family and has realised how much he is worth in Christ.

- he is guided by God's Spirit rather than the flesh.

- he is getting rid of old ways of thinking and replacing them with truth.

- he experiences joy and peace, instead of stress and upset.

- he is still tempted to mess up and still does sometimes but realises that he doesn't always have to give in. (Romans 6:11-14).

Sam is what we're all aiming for and it really is possible for us to live like him!

God has already given us everything that we need for this kind of life (2 Peter 1:3).

Fleshly Fred (1 Corinthians 3:3)

Fred has had the same life-changing experience as Sam, but instead of following God's Spirit he follows what we are calling 'the flesh'. He has the option – the freedom – to follow God's Spirit, but chooses not to, either on purpose or perhaps because he doesn't really understand the freedom that he has.

His daily life looks more like Norman's than Sam's:

- he lets wrong thoughts fill his mind and dwells on them

- he lets negative feelings rule his life.

- this probably affects his sense of well-being

He's just not living to his full potential!

Fred also tends to get 'stuck' in messing up over and over again. There are some particular things he does, which are wrong and which damage him, but which he just can't seem to stop doing.

We might recognise this.

Maybe we keep returning time and again to bad language or losing our temper. In the end we can feel completely hopeless and feel (wrongly) that we can never escape.

Fred still has a relationship with God and is going to heaven but he is not living life to the max, he's not as happy as he could be. He could be changing the world around him instead of going round and round in circles.

After each group has presented, give out the 'persons' write up and encourage discussion. If possible steer the conversation onto the following points:

- Things that stop us from growing

- The incredible thing is that God has given us everything we need to live like Sam. So we don't need to go to special events or festivals, or get prayed for or pray the 'right' prayer.

- All these things are good but we can do it already with God's help.

- We need to learn to deal with the things that stop us from growing.

-

⦿ DVD CHAPTER 3

Play Session 5, chapter 3 – 'Choosing Freedom' – of the accompanying DVD.

Explain:

We have EVERYTHING we need to grow as Christians. 2 Peter 1:3 is an amazing verse that says:

'His divine power has given us everything we need for life and godliness through our knowledge of him who called us by his own glory and goodness.'

We can choose every day whether to obey our flesh, our old way of doing things, or the Holy Spirit.

We can choose to think, react and cope with life in God's way, or in the ways we were used to before we became Christians.

Walking by the Spirit means real freedom, being led by God rather than pushed along; it means walking through life together with God.

You can tell that you're walking by the Spirit if your life is marked more and more by:

- love
- joy
- peace
- patience
- kindness

- goodness
- faithfulness
- gentleness
- self-control

These are the fruit of the Spirit (Galatians 5:22-23), which will grow in your life over time.

Maybe you've realised in this session that you're more like Fred than Sam. If so, what should you do?

Start by confessing your sin to God – admitting that you've been living 'in the flesh' – and then choose to walk in the Spirit.

It's a choice we all have to make. Every day.

Discussion:

- Remember the question from last time: Since we're all saints, why do you think we still often feel like doing the wrong thing?

- Are your friends most like Norman, Sam or Fred? Who are you most like?

- Does it surprise you that a Christian can live pretty much like a non-Christian? What should make a difference?

- Do you believe that it's possible to defeat the flesh? Why? Why not?

- What things do you think hold back people and stop them growing as a Christians?

- How can you tell if you are living being guided by God's Spirit?

RESPONSE

Buy a load of fruit (the more variety, the better), cut it up and put it on a tray in the middle of the group.

Hand out napkins.

Explain:

This activity is a sign you can use to say to God that you are making a choice today to live by God's Spirit and have the fruit that comes with that.

Ask the young people to commit to making the choice every day to live by God's Spirit and not the flesh that we have learned about today. As a symbol of this encourage the group to eat the fruit laid out.

AND THERE'S MORE!

Run through with the young people the material on pages 24 - 25 of the Youth Guide 11-18.

Encourage them particularly to do the 'Challenge' section at home:

Take five minutes to be quiet with God. Ask him to show you areas of your life where you have not been renewing your mind and are still thinking in ways that are not in line with God's truth. Write these down and make the choice to change.

And also the 'Think' section:

As a Christian, does it sometimes seem like you are tempted more than ever to do the stuff you shouldn't? Remember that the Bible tells us the power of sin is broken in our lives (Romans 6:5-18) and we are free now to turn our backs on it and choose freedom.

CLOSING QUESTION

Ask them to consider this question before next time (page 25 of the Youth Guide 11-18):

Are there sins that keep happening over and over, that you keep going back to, sins that you can't seem to stop committing? Why do you think that is?

SESSION SIX:
DEMOLISHING STRONGHOLDS

'We demolish arguments and every pretension
that sets itself up against the knowledge of
God, and we take captive every thought to
make it obedient to Christ.'

2 Corinthians 10:5

DEMOLISHING STRONGHOLDS
CORE

PREPARATION

This is the third of four sessions in Part B of Freedom In Christ For Young People in which we are considering our enemies. In this session we continue to look at 'the flesh' and consider a particular aspect of it: strongholds.

The second book in The Freedom In Christ Discipleship Series, Win The Daily Battle (Monarch 2008), corresponds to Part B of the course. Read pages 84-111 in the book for the material that relates to the flesh.

KEY VERSE

2 Corinthians 10:5 – 'We demolish arguments and every pretension that sets itself up against the knowledge of God, and we take captive every thought to make it obedient to Christ.'

AIM

To understand what 'strongholds' are and where they come from.

KEY TRUTH

All of us have mental strongholds, ways of thinking that are not in line with God's truth, but we can choose to tear them down by replacing the lies with truth.

OVERVIEW

The environment in which we grew up, traumatic experiences in the past and giving in to temptations have led to the development of 'strongholds' in our minds, which prevent us living according to the truth. Becoming a Christian does not instantly change the way we have learned to think, but we can demolish strongholds by choosing actively to renew our minds with the truth of God's Word.

INTRODUCTION

In this session we're going to think about an aspect of the flesh that is particularly stubborn and can really stop us growing as Christians: 'strongholds'. We will see that we can truly be free from these strongholds.

WHAT IS A STRONGHOLD?

Sometimes a little thought is planted in our mind by something that happens to us – maybe we're bullied, or worse – or someone says something negative about us ('you're useless', 'you're a failure', 'you're ugly').

Perhaps we've believed it for so long it becomes part of our lives and we can't imagine ever getting over it.

2 Corinthians 10:3-5 says this:

'For though we live in the world, we do not wage war as the world does. The weapons we fight with are not the weapons of the world. On the contrary, they have divine power to demolish strongholds. We demolish arguments and every pretension that sets itself up against the knowledge of God, and we take captive every thought to make it obedient to Christ.'

We need God and his Word to come and check over the thoughts and attitudes of our hearts and demolish those that aren't true.

Galatians 5:1 says: 'It is for freedom that Christ has set us free.' Very many Christians aren't experiencing this kind of freedom: they believe the truth at some level, but they struggle to let that truth make a difference in their everyday lives.

If you're one of the many who struggle to really connect with this truth, it's probably because of mental 'strongholds'.

Strongholds are connected to the flesh, which we looked at in the last session. As we said, our life (our families, circumstances, friends etc.) has 'programmed' us to believe certain things. When we became Christians, although we became brand new creations in Christ, no one pressed a 'clear all' button in our mind. We still have things we believe that aren't true; things that predispose us to act in a certain way (strongholds). They are ways that we have learned to think and behave (just like learning to write). If you had to learn to write with the hand you don't normally write with then after a time of trying you should be able to. If we are continually told that we are useless or ugly or we keep giving in to a certain temptation we will start to believe lies about ourselves or feel that we can't say no when we are being tempted.

A stronghold is another word for a fortress, a castle, that's been carefully built to be able to withstand attack. Our set thoughts and attitudes are just like that sometimes; various events slowly and carefully build something in our minds that get harder and harder to attack and break down.

Strongholds make us feel hopeless, and we start to believe that, even though we are a new creation, things won't ever change. However, God promises us life in all its fullness.

If you struggle to do something that you know God wants you to do, or if you find it impossible to stop doing something you know God doesn't want you to do, it's likely to be a stronghold that's getting in the way. It's not that God is asking the impossible of us. He would never ask us to do something we couldn't do, that's just not his style!

If we've never found out how to tear down strongholds, we might continue to use excuses to explain them away: 'that's just the way I am – I can't change'. If we get really angry; 'well, that's just me, I've always had a short temper'.

If we feel insecure, inferior to others or paranoid, there's probably a mental stronghold behind it.

HOW STRONGHOLDS COME TO BE

Our environment

Ever since we were born, we've picked up lots of ways of thinking from the environment that we happened to be born into. Our families, communities, schools and friends have all had an impact. It's like how we learned to speak English because we were born into an English-speaking family; we just picked it up. If we had been brought up in a French home, we would naturally speak French. In the same way as we pick up our mother tongue, we also pick up values and ways to behave from our environment. Perhaps you grew up hearing that you were useless, ugly or lazy. If you believed those things, you will probably have a stronghold of believing that you're inferior to everyone else.

Traumatic Experiences

Traumatic experiences can also set up strongholds because they are so hurtful; eg. a death in the home, a divorce or abuse.

We'll talk more later on in the course about how we can be set free from past experiences like these. For now, we need to understand that it's not the traumatic experiences themselves that cause the stronghold, but the lies that we believe as a result of it.

For example, if in the past you were bullied, you may well have come to see yourself as a helpless victim. It might have been true at one time, but it's not true any more.

Or if your parents have gone through a divorce, you might wrongly have believed it had something to do with you. You carry guilt with you, and it affects every decision you make.

These strongholds can be torn down with truth. You can go back to the past experiences and look at them in the light of who you are now – a child of God. You will see that you don't need to be a helpless victim, because you are a new creation in Christ. And you will discover that you don't need to carry guilt around with you, because Jesus has taken all your guilt on himself.

One problem with strongholds is that if you **believe** something that's not true, you will also **feel** something that isn't true. You may feel rejected when you're not rejected. You may feel helpless to change when actually you're not.

Temptation

Another time for strongholds to form or to become stronger is when we keep giving in to temptation. In fact Satan tempts us in order to build strongholds in our lives, causing us to go around in circles feeling helpless and hopeless.

As we saw in Session 1, we were all made with the need to be significant, secure and accepted. All temptation is an attempt to get you to fulfil those needs anywhere apart from God. Satan has observed your behaviour over the years and he knows exactly where you're vulnerable, and that's where he'll attack.

For example, at some traumatic point in your life (a fight at home, someone abusing you, pressure at school or anything else), Satan might plant a thought in your mind, tempting you to let off some steam, and show that you're in control of some part of your life, by drinking too much. This might over time become your way of coping, and Satan knows that you are vulnerable – he doesn't need to convince you, just plant a thought. After a while, a strong destructive stronghold will have formed in your mind, and you will think that you're unable to stop drinking too much if you want to have a good time or let off some steam.

The truth is, we really don't have to give into that temptation. 1 Corinthians 10:13 says: '...when you are tempted God will also provide a way out so that you can stand up under it.'

Often when we are tempted, it doesn't feel like there's a way out – so where is that way of escape? The answer is to use what we call 'threshold thinking'. God has provided a way of escape from all temptation – where is it? Right at the threshold. Right at the beginning, when the tempting thought first comes into your mind. This is our opportunity to 'take captive every thought to make it obedient to Christ' (2 Corinthians 10:5).

Suppose you are trying to give up smoking. When the meeting is over you remember that you were asked to get some milk on the way home, or the whole family would eat dry cereal in the morning. There are two places you could go: one sells milk only but the other sells milk and cigarettes. Which one are you going to go to? Your chance to make the right choice comes when you first think about it. As soon as you decide to go towards the place where they sell cigarettes, you can rationalise as much as you like ('well, the milk is cheaper') but whether you admit it to yourself or not, you know very well that you are being drawn to the cigarettes. After this, your chances of turning around are shrinking by the minute. In your mind, you're already there – Satan is working on your mind before you have even got to the cigarettes behind the counter. As soon as you buy them and smoke one, the tempter becomes the accuser and you feel guilty and stupid. The answer? To reject the tempting thought to go to the place where cigarettes are sold as soon as it appears.

There's a saying that goes: 'you can't stop a bird from flying over your head, but you can stop it from building a nest in your hair.' A lot of thoughts pass through your mind every day, and your job is to decide which thoughts you allow to stay. Once you allow a thought to land, before you know it, it has built a nest and made itself at home! This is what 'taking every thought captive' (2 Corinthians 10:5) means. Your mind is your own and you are in charge of it. Not every thought that comes into your mind is your own but you are the one who decides which can land and which you simply dismiss.

Tempting thoughts that you don't reject straight away lead to action. Repeating the action will result in a habit. Leave the habit undisturbed for a while, and you'll have a stronghold.

WHAT STRONGHOLDS DO TO US

Wrong View Of Reality

When we talked about worldviews a couple of weeks ago, we said that worldviews can act like a pair of glasses, in effect distorting our view of reality. Strongholds do the same thing and can distort our view of reality in a big way.

For example, if we have had a dad that was never around, we might have a stronghold of rejection. When we look at life through those lenses we start to believe that we are rejected and unloved by God the Father as well. We hear people laughing and assume they are laughing at us. We get left out of a conversation and immediately conclude it's because we're worthless and that nobody cares about us.

It's in these situations that we must allow the Word of God to speak into our lives and break down this stronghold. We must decide to believe God's truth, and that he knows better than us.

Bad Choices

Strongholds push us towards making bad choices because we are basing our decisions on something that actually isn't true - not a great basis for our lives! Every day we have to make the choice whether to do things God's way or to trust our own feelings and instincts more. Unfortunately, some of those feelings and instincts are strongholds that blur our vision to the warning signs that God has put up for us.

Every time we decide to choose God's way – whether we feel like it or not – we will change a little bit, until gradually it gets easier to make the right choices.

Demolishing Strongholds

The good news is that we don't have to put up with strongholds!

Just like a well-functioning computer regularly checks for viruses, so should we. First, we need to get rid of the enemy's influence and we'll have the opportunity to do this when we go through The Steps To Freedom In Christ. Once you've done that, a stronghold is just a habit to shake. You can choose to believe the truth instead of the lie and change the habit.

You may have already become aware of some strongholds in your life. When you go through The Steps To Freedom In Christ, you will no doubt find out more. Then in session 10 we will show you a structured way to dismantle those strongholds that we call 'stronghold-busting'. It's not a simple walk in the park, but it can revolutionise your life!

QUESTIONS TO THINK ABOUT AS YOU PREPARE

1. Can you now explain why we get stuck with certain sins sometimes?

2. One definition of a stronghold is 'anything you know is right that you can't do, or anything that you know is wrong that you can't stop doing.' If you find yourself doing something that you know is wrong, can you stop?

3. How can you prepare yourself for future temptation?

4. What advice would you give to a friend who struggles with temptation?

5. Can you think of a time where you have decided to believe what God has said is true, even when you haven't felt like it?

DEMOLISHING STRONGHOLDS
11-14

LEADER'S PREPARATION

Pray together:

❝ Father God, thank you that you give us real freedom. May today be one step on the way for us all to experience full freedom in Christ. Amen.

YOU MAY NEED

Ice blocks / empty plastic bottle

Two or three ice blocks with T-shirt frozen inside

Hammer / safety gloves and goggles or swimming goggles / towel / mop / buckets

Newspapers / sticky tape / measuring tape

Prizes

Fondue set with melted chocolate / bowl of melted chocolate

Tray of cut up food for the fondue

Accompanying DVD / DVD player / TV / projector

Building Blocks

'Jenga' sets

Plastic building blocks (like 'Duplo')

Downloadable PowerPoint material

Bibles

Small group questions

Leaders prepared to share a personal story about freedom from a stronghold

PRAYER AND DECLARATION

Encourage everyone to join together in saying the following prayer and declaration. You can download the PowerPoint slides with the words for these from the website.

It would be good to suggest that the young people stand up and speak out the declaration clearly and confidently to the heavenly realms. They could shout it out and use appropriate actions!

PRAYER

❝ Heavenly Father, I thank you that I can have true freedom in my life because of Jesus. Would you come now by your Holy Spirit and show me how to live more in that freedom today. In Jesus' name, Amen.

DECLARATION: IN A CLEAR, CONFIDENT TONE!

❝ Jesus lives in me, so evil has no rights in my life. I am going to listen to the advice of the Holy Spirit; therefore there will be peace and quiet in this place. The enemy must leave right now – go!

🔍 STARTING POINT

Start by giving a short summary of the previous session. A good resource for this is the Overview found in the Core of the previous session.

INTRODUCTORY ACTIVITIES

THE LITERAL ICEBREAKER

Prepare this activity a few days earlier: fill two or more ice cream tubs with water and stick in the freezer.

Divide your group into as many teams as you have frozen water tubs.

Give each group a lump of ice on a strong tray, a hammer and/or any other (relatively safe) implement you can think of, and a large soft drinks bottle.

Whichever team manages to get all their ice into their bottle first is the winner. Or give the groups a set length of time, and see which team can get the most ice into their bottle in this time.

ICED T-SHIRT

Instead of just water in the ice cream tubs, immerse a t-shirt in the water and freeze the tub with the t-shirt in it.

Again give each group a strong tray, a hammer and/or any other (relatively safe) implement you can think of and the winner is the first team to have a member put the t-shirt on.

Leader's Note: Risk assess these activities on both your group and your venue - you might not want to play this game on your best carpet or antique coffee table! We would advise using safety gloves and goggles or swimming goggles. If you only have two or three pairs, corner off the area and give each person in the group a set amount of time for their turn and then they must swap with another team member. It would also be wise to have towels, mops and buckets to clear up at the end.

NEWSPAPER TOWERS

Divide the group into two or three teams.

Give each group a number of newspapers and a roll of sticky tape.

The aim of the game is to make the best castle possible in 3 minutes.

Marks awarded for style, height, innovation etc.

Ask one of the leaders to be the judge and award prizes.

DVD CHAPTER 1

Play Session 6, chapter 1 – 'Finding Truth' – of the accompanying DVD.

Ask the group:

- Have you ever believed anything that wasn't true?

- How did it feel?

It does have an effect on us!

WORSHIP ACTIVITY

Try to get your hands on a fondue set – if that is difficult melt some chocolate in the microwave. Then have various treats cut up on a plate ready to be dipped in the chocolate and devoured. E.g. marshmallows, apple, strawberry, banana, bread sticks.

Invite the young people to sit with you in a circle and say:

We come to worship God now, because he is the only one worth our worship and because he is so good to us.

Ephesians 1:7-8 says that God lavished his grace on us. (This means that he loads us, time and time again, with kindness, forgiveness and love.)

1 John 3:1 says:

'How great is the love that the Father has lavished on us, that we should be called children of God!'

To represent the 'lavishness' of God's love, we have this yummy chocolate and lots of treats to dip in and share together.

I encourage you, as you dip your first chosen item into the chocolate, to tell God just one reason why you worship him.

As you taste it, remember how good God is to provide food and everything we need, and how amazing he is that he created all these goodies in the first place.

Leader's note: Remember to cover the chocolate if you are putting it into the microwave, so that it doesn't burn. Assess the risks of whether you should melt the chocolate prior to the session.

STRONGHOLDS

Remember last week we talked about the 'flesh', those wrong ways of thinking we picked up? Today we're going to think about some particularly stubborn wrong ways of thinking that are called 'strongholds'. They really stop us from growing as Christians but we can be free from them.

Get hold of a box of children's wooden building blocks and build a tower as you're speaking (make it as solid as you can to avoid it falling over before you want it to!).

Illustration – build the tower as you talk

Sometimes a little thought is planted in our mind by something that happens to us – maybe we're bullied, or someone says something negative about us ('you're useless', 'you're a failure', 'you're ugly'). Perhaps we've believed it for so long it becomes part of our lives and we can't imagine ever getting over it.

2 Corinthians 10:3-5 says this: [As you finish this reading demolish the tower you have just built]

"For though we live in the world, we do not wage war as the world does. The weapons we fight with are not the weapons of the world. On the contrary, they have divine power to demolish strongholds. We demolish arguments and every pretension that sets itself up against the knowledge of God, and we take captive every thought to make it obedient to Christ."

We need God and his Word to come and check over the thoughts and attitudes of our hearts and demolish those that aren't true.

REAL LIFE STORIES
Have one or more of the leaders give a testimony of how they have experienced freedom from a stronghold in their lives. (Remember to prompt them beforehand).

◎ DVD CHAPTER 2

Play Session 6, chapter 2 – 'False Truth' – of the accompanying DVD.

The challenge is this:

• Are you going to believe what your past experiences have taught you?

• Are you going to believe what God says about you in His Word?

• Do you believe it's true that it is your choice?

Galatians 5:1 says: 'It is for freedom that Christ has set us free.'

Now, a lot of Christians aren't experiencing this kind of freedom. They sort of believe the truth, but they struggle to let that truth make a difference in their everyday lives.

If you struggle to really connect with this truth, it's probably because of these 'strongholds' in your mind.

WHAT IS A STRONGHOLD?
Divide the group into two or three groups; give each group a set of the game 'Jenga'.

Give them 5 minutes to build a strong tower.

Ask the groups to sit around their towers. Explain to the group that strongholds are connected to the 'flesh' (which we talked about last time). As we said, our life - our families, circumstances, friends and so on – has 'programmed' us to believe certain things.

And when we became Christians, although we became brand new creations in Christ, no one pressed a 'clear all' button in our mind. We still have things we believe that aren't true; things that make us act in a certain way.

Ask the groups to look at the strong towers they have made.

These things are called 'strongholds' and are like towers we build in our minds, which come from believing wrong things about ourselves, and these 'towers' kind of start to really affect the way we think and act.

The reason they are called strongholds is that they are difficult to get rid of – like invading a well defended castle. A good way to recognise some strongholds is:

- something that we know is right but we can't do

- something that we know is wrong but we can't stop doing

Strongholds make us feel hopeless, and we start to believe that God can't change things in our lives.

This is the opposite of what God says to us. He is the God of hope. He can do anything.

THE MAIN POINT

Now ask each leader in the groups to lead/share the truth of the next section within their groups.

HOW STRONGHOLDS COME TO BE

There are a few ways that strongholds can be built in us:

Our Environment

Ways of thinking that we've picked up from family, friends, school and so on, can become strongholds. For example, if you've always heard from your family that you're useless, you might finally start believing it. But we need to choose to believe the truth about us – what God says. God wants us to be free from these.

Traumatic Experiences.

Some things that happen to us really hurt us, and they can set the foundation for a stronghold. For example, if you experience a death of someone close to you or a divorce, you can start believing things about yourself that aren't true, like perhaps that it was your fault. God wants us to be free from that.

Temptation

If we keep giving in to temptation, eventually a stronghold will be built. The good news is that we are free not to give in to temptations. 1 Corinthians 10:13 says: '...when you are tempted God will also provide a way out so that you can stand up under it.' God has given us a way of escape every time we are tempted.

Bring the group back together.

POWERPOINT - ILLUSTRATION

We're going to watch a cartoon sequence of someone undergoing temptation. [Download this from the website in advance of the session].

See if you can spot the frame that contains the way of escape that God has provided and tell me at the end.

Show the slides one at a time and read them out.

Ask the young people to suggest where in the clip there was a way out of the temptation.

It was a trick question!

The way of escape was **before** the first frame! Why was she even thinking about driving past the supermarket? If there were a way of checking, you'd probably find that she was already salivating. The thought of what she was going to do was already there, even if she didn't spot it.

We need to learn to reject temptations as soon as the very first thought enters our mind. Imagine that temptations are birds flying around your head. There's a saying that goes: 'you can't stop a bird from flying over your head, but you can stop it from building a nest in your hair.'

Your mind is your own and you are in charge of it. Not every thought that comes into your mind is your own but you are in control of which ones you allow to land. A tempting thought needs to be turned away as soon as you become aware of it.

◎ DVD CHAPTER 3

Play Session 6, chapter 3 – 'Real Truth' – of the accompanying DVD.

Underline what was said in the clip with the group:

*   No matter what has happened to you, if you are a Christian you are not dirty. The Bible says you have been washed absolutely clean.

*   No matter what people have said about you, you are not useless. You can become everything God wants you to be.

*   You are forgiven. You are made new. You don't have to hide any more.

*   It's taken time for these strongholds to develop.

*   And it will take some time – but not nearly as long – for you to get rid of them. But get rid of them you can.

*   Keep making a choice to choose what is true. Despite your feelings. Despite your past experiences.

Want to make a start?

Then put your foot down and decide here and now that you are not going to believe things that aren't true.

HOW TO GET RID OF STRONGHOLDS

Strongholds basically lie to us: for me they make me think that eating will make me happy. [Share one of your own vulnerabilities perhaps.] They also sometimes stop us from choosing to do things God's way. When we need to make decisions, we sometimes trust our feelings more than we trust what God says. Unfortunately, if those feelings come from a stronghold, we are likely to make a bad decision.

That's why we need to know God's truth!

The good news is that we don't have to put up with strongholds!

God's truth is the way to deal with them. It is like the most powerful battering ram and no castle can withstand it!

Allow the groups to destroy the tower they built earlier by throwing large plastic blocks (like 'Duplo') at them – it can take time but with God's promises it will happen.

You are going to get the opportunity to start to deal with any strongholds in your life when we go through The Steps To Freedom In Christ. It is not a magic formula, it is just quality time with God and can change your life!

 RESPONSE

Play a game of Jenga or similar. As you are playing reiterate today's teaching:

[As the tower is being built] When we have hurtful experiences, give in to temptation or believe lies, this can build a stronghold. Maybe we feel useless or that no one loves us. Maybe we feel we can't stop doing something we know is wrong. Maybe we believe that God is not for us.

[When the tower falls] God's truth demolishes any stronghold that we might have in our lives.

Prayer:

Father God, we pray for ourselves and anyone we know who struggles with the strongholds that we've mentioned before you. Help us to break down the barriers that stop us from growing in you. Amen.

SMALL GROUPS & PRAYER FOCUS

1. Can you now explain why we keep messing up?

2. Someone has said that a stronghold is 'anything you know is right that you can't do, or anything that you know is wrong that you can't stop doing.' If you find yourself doing something that you know is wrong, how can you stop?

3. How can you prepare yourself for future temptation?

4. What advice would you give to a friend who struggles with temptation?

5. Can you think of a time when you decided to believe what God has said is true, even when you didn't feel like it?

AND THERE'S MORE!

Draw the young people's attention to page 27 of the Youth Guide 11-14 and specifically to the Challenge and Think sections:

Challenge: You can unlearn a stronghold but you have to want to. Think of something in your life that may be a stronghold and next time you find yourself wanting to think or do that same thing, confront it with some of God's truth from the Bible and ask God for help. If you keep doing that, eventually the lie will be replaced by truth.

Think: Strongholds are 'strong' and you may feel like you will never get rid of them, believing that you can't change... BUT YOU CAN! A stronghold is a lie that has grown from past experiences and Jesus enables you to be free from these! It will take some time and some determination but every Christian can renew their mind.

? CLOSING QUESTION

Ask the young people to consider these questions (on page 27 of the Youth Guide 11-14) during the coming week:

What sort of lies do you think the devil tells us?

Do you think the devil has ever lied to you?

DEMOLISHING STRONGHOLDS
15-18

 PRAYER AND DECLARATION

Encourage everyone to join together in saying the following prayer and declaration. You can download the PowerPoint slides with the words for these from the website.

It would be good to suggest that the young people stand up and speak out the declaration clearly and confidently to the heavenly realms. They could shout it out and use appropriate actions!

PRAYER:
" Heavenly Father, I thank you that I can have true freedom in my life because of Jesus. Would you come now by your Holy Spirit and show me how to live more in that freedom today. In Jesus' name, Amen.

DECLARATION:
" Jesus lives in me, so evil has no rights in my life. I am going to listen to the advice of the Holy Spirit; therefore there will be peace and quiet in this place. The enemy must leave right now – go!

🔍 STARTING POINT

Start by giving a short summary of the previous session. A good resource for this is the Overview found in the Core of the previous session.

◉ DVD CHAPTER 1

Play Session 6, chapter 1 – 'Finding truth' – of the accompanying DVD.

Ask the group:

• Have you ever believed anything that wasn't true?

• How did it feel?

It does have an effect on us!

⌃ SOAPBOX

REAL LIFE STORIES
Have one or more of the leaders give a testimony of how they have experienced freedom from a stronghold in their lives. (Remember to prompt them beforehand).

◉ DVD CHAPTER 2

Play Session 6, chapter 2 – 'False Truth' – of the accompanying DVD.

The challenge is this:

• Are you going to believe what your past experiences have taught you?

• Are you going to believe what God says about you in his word?

• Do you believe it's true that it is your choice?

Galatians 5:1 says: 'It is for freedom that Christ has set us free.'

Now, a lot of Christians aren't experiencing this kind of freedom. They sort of believe the truth, but they struggle to let that truth make a difference in their everyday lives.

If you struggle to really connect with this truth, it's probably because of 'strongholds' in your mind. Lies that we have continued to believe over time can really take hold of us and become 'strongholds'. They are a particularly stubborn part of the flesh.

Our thinking and behaviour become automatic. If you believe people when they say you are ugly and disgusting, you will understandably feel worthless, when actually you are worth so much. And you will act in a way that reflects how you are feeling about yourself.

These strongholds seem unmovable and unchangeable. We can feel as if we can never break free – that we are stuck in a rut doing the same thing over and over again, knowing that it is sin, but somehow unable to stop.

You say sorry to God. But do it again. Say sorry. Then do it again. Say sorry. Then do it again. And it can feel like there is no way out. Do you identify with that?

Shame takes a hold of our life. Being honest with God about our struggles and our 'unholy' thoughts is the first step to breaking them.

We're in church week in, week out, but you would probably never dream of speaking about those things in church.

God doesn't want us to hide these things under a blanket and pretend everything is ok if it isn't.

2 Corinthians 10:5 says:

'We demolish arguments and every pretension that sets itself up against the knowledge of God, and we take captive every thought to make it obedient to Christ.'

To get rid of those lies we need to identify them as lies and then keep a close eye on our thinking. Take every thought captive.

How? Hold every thought up against God's word, the truth. Jesus said "You will know the truth. And the truth will set you free". Don't go with a thought just because it's in your head, or just because it feels true.

Our thoughts are a bit like planes circling around an airport control tower. Just as the tower decides which planes can land, we decide which thoughts we dwell on and continue to think about.

To take a thought captive is like saying, 'I am not going to let this thought take over. I am going to put it in a prison cell and not let it out.

CHALLENGE

You don't have to think it! If it doesn't stack up with God's word, just throw it out. For example, let's say your past experiences have left you feeling dirty or useless. Is that true? Well it certainly feels true to you. The challenge is this. Are you going to believe what past experiences have taught you? Or are you going to believe what God says about you in his Word?

At the end of the day it comes down to your choice.

⬆ WORSHIP ACTIVITY

Try to get your hands on a fondue set – if that is difficult melt some chocolate in the microwave. Then have various treats cut up on a plate ready to be dipped in the chocolate and devoured. Eg marshmallows, apple, strawberry, banana, bread sticks.

Invite the young people to sit with you in a circle.

We come to worship God now, because he is the only one worthy of our worship and because he is so good to us.

Ephesians 1:7-8 says that God lavished his grace on us. (This means that He loads us, time and time again, with kindness, forgiveness and love.)

1 John 3:1 says:

'How great is the love that the Father has lavished on us, that we should be called children of God!'

To represent the 'lavishness' of God's love, we have this yummy chocolate and lots of treats to dip in and share together.

I encourage you, as you dip your first chosen item into the chocolate, to tell God just one reason why you worship him.

As you taste it, remember how good God is to provide food and everything we need, and how amazing he is that he created all these goodies in the first place.

Leader's note: remember to cover the chocolate if you are putting it into the microwave, so that it doesn't burn. Assess the risks of whether you should melt the chocolate prior to the session.

Direct the young people's attention to the 'What's the point?' section on page 26 of the Youth Guide 11-18 which says:

- Strongholds are deeply ingrained attitudes and actions that do not match the truth of God's Word, the Bible.

- We can renew our minds using the Word of God to get rid of thoughts and attitudes in our heart that aren't true.

- When we choose to believe the truth in God's Word, we will grow and make better choices.

⊙ DVD CHAPTER 3

Play Session 6, chapter 3 – 'Real Truth' – of the accompanying DVD.

Underline what was said in the clip with the group:

- No matter what has happened to you, if you are a Christian you are not dirty. The Bible says you have been washed absolutely clean.

- No matter what people have said about you, you are not useless. You can become everything God wants you to be.

- You are forgiven. You are made new. You don't have to hide any more.

- It's taken time for these strongholds to develop.

- And it will take some time – but not nearly as long – for you to get rid of them. But get rid of them you can.

- Keep making a choice to choose what is true. Despite your feelings. Despite your past experiences.

Want to make a start?

Then put your foot down and decide here and now that you are not going to believe things that aren't true.

HOW TO GET RID OF STRONGHOLDS

Strongholds basically lie to us: perhaps they make me think that eating will make me happy. [If you feel able, share a personal example of a stronghold from your own life]. They also sometimes stop us from choosing to do things God's way. When we need to make decisions, we sometimes trust our feelings more than we trust what God says. Unfortunately, those feelings can come from a stronghold.

The good news is that we don't have to put up with strongholds.

God's truth is the way to deal with them.

It is like the most powerful battering ram and no castle can withstand it!

You are going to get the opportunity to deal with any strongholds in your life when we go through The Steps To Freedom In Christ. It is not a magic formula, it is just quality time with God and can change your life.

RESPONSE

Discussion:

- Can you now explain why we keep messing up?

- Someone has said that a stronghold is 'anything you know is right that you can't do, or anything that you know is wrong that you can't stop doing.' If you find yourself doing something that you know is wrong, can you stop?

- How can you prepare yourself for future temptation?

- What advice would you give to a friend who struggles with temptation?

- Can you think of a time when you decided to believe what God has said is true, even when you didn't feel like it?

Play a game of Jenga or similar. As you are playing reiterate today's teaching:

[As the tower is being built] When we have hurtful experiences, give in to temptation or believe lies, this can build a stronghold. Maybe we feel useless or that no one loves us. Maybe we feel we can't stop doing something we know is wrong. Maybe we believe that God is not for us.

[When the tower falls] God's truth demolishes any stronghold that we might have in our lives.

Prayer:

Father God, we pray for ourselves and anyone we know who struggles with the strongholds that we've mentioned before you. Help us to break down the barriers that stop us from growing in you. Amen.

AND THERE'S MORE!

Draw the young people's attention to the questions on page 28 and the Challenge, Think and Pray sections on page 29 of the Youth Guide 15-18.

? CLOSING QUESTION

Question to consider during the next week (page 29 of the Youth Guide 15-18):

What kind of lies does the devil tell us? Do you think you've ever been deceived by the devil?

SESSION SEVEN:
SPIRITUAL REALITY

'Put on the full armour of God so that you can take your stand against the devil's schemes.'

Ephesians 6:11

SPIRITUAL REALITY CORE

PREPARATION

This is the final session of four in Part B of Freedom In Christ For Young People in which we are considering our enemies. Having looked at the world and the flesh, in this session we turn our attention to the devil.

The second book in The Freedom In Christ Discipleship Series, Win The Daily Battle (Monarch 2008), corresponds to Part B of the course. Read pages 43 - 110 in the book for the material that relates to this session.

KEY VERSE

Ephesians 6:11 – 'Put on the full armour of God so that you can take your stand against the devil's schemes.'

AIM

To understand that, although our enemy (the devil) is constantly attempting to get us to believe lies, we don't have to believe every thought that comes into our head. Instead we can hold each one up against truth and choose to accept or reject it.

KEY TRUTH

The battle takes place in our minds. If we are aware of how Satan works, we will not fall for his schemes.

OVERVIEW

It's important to understand that we are in a spiritual battle, which makes dismantling strongholds less straightforward than if it were simply a question of learning to think differently. Every day we face a battle for our minds. However, understanding how Satan works and realising our amazing position in Christ will equip us to win.

INTRODUCTION

In this session we're going to find out the facts about Satan and how best to defend ourselves against him.

Germs are everywhere. They drift in the air all around us. They land on surfaces where food is prepared. If you thought hard enough about them, you might be so concerned that you would do nothing except try to kill them. But are they really a problem? Well, only if you don't take sensible precautions. That's not to say that they can't be dangerous, it's just that they're really easy to beat if you defend yourself properly.

So far we've talked about a couple of things that cause problems in our walk with God; we've mentioned the world and we've talked about the flesh. Well, today we're on to another one - the devil and his demons. Just like germs, we can't see them but they are all around us and can do us real damage.

Living in the West and having a Western worldview, which focuses only on what we can see, touch and prove scientifically, makes us more likely to ignore Satan and demons, even if we acknowledge them theologically. At one time, doctors didn't know about germs. They performed basic operations without washing their hands. People died. If we just ignore the existence of Satan, that would be like acting as if germs don't exist. If we stop washing our hands, germs will eventually get to us and make us ill. We probably don't like the idea of the existence of spiritual evil but ignoring it is not an option. It just means that we become easier targets!

But neither is there any need to get fixated on Satan either! It would be like spending your life searching for germs, obsessing about rooting them out, when they're not really worth obsessing about. Just like it's relatively easy to avoid being infected by germs, avoiding Satan's traps isn't hard once you know all the facts.

THE FACTS

The Bible doesn't give us lots of detailed information about Satan and demons, because – frankly – they're not worth it. But we do need to make sure that we know the facts that are presented to us.

- Satan is not like God

  We tend to think that because we can't see God or Satan and because they're both 'supernatural', they must surely be similar in some ways as if they are equal (or nearly equal) but opposite powers. This is very far from the truth. Whereas God is the Creator, Satan is, like us, simply a created being. Satan would really like us to think that he is equal in power to God, but actually – as someone has said – comparing Satan to God is like comparing an ant to an atomic bomb.

- Satan can be in only one place at one time

  Because Satan is created like you and me, he's got many of the same limitations as we do. He can only be in one place at one time for example. He carries out his work worldwide through an army of demons (also known as 'evil spirits', 'fallen angels' or 'powers and authorities'). In fact, when we use the word 'Satan', we generally use it to refer not just to the one who is the chief of the demons but to all the demons in general. It's important to know, however, that only God is everywhere at once.

- Satan does not know everything

  Satan can't read your mind, nor can he tell the future. Have you ever wondered why we never see the headline 'Psychic wins lottery'? It's interesting to see in the Bible that all interaction between angels and people, or demons and people, are done out loud – have a look for yourself when you get home! Only God knows what's in people's minds.

If you're interested in digging into this a little further, consider Daniel 2. King Nebuchadnezzar demands that his sorcerers reveal the content of his dreams in order to validate their divine origin. The sorcerers, whose normal source of power and information was demons, couldn't read the king's mind. In other words, Satan could not find out what was in the king's mind.

SATAN PUTS THOUGHTS INTO OUR MINDS

Although he can't read our minds, Satan certainly can put things into your mind - and, of course, if he puts a thought in and you run with it, at that point he does know what you are thinking. The spiritual battle takes place in your mind and Satan often wants you to think that the thought he puts into your mind is your own. He may put a disgusting thought into your mind and then condemn you for thinking it - if you believed that the thought was your own, you'd probably also believe his conclusion that you must be sick for having it! A key learning point for the young people in this session will be that not every thought that pops into their mind is actually their own - and they don't have to 'think' it.

Let's consider three Biblical examples in which Satan puts a thought into someone's mind but makes them think that it is their own thought.

"Satan rose up against Israel and incited David to take a census of Israel" (1 Chronicles 21:1). Taking a census is not inherently wrong but in this case it was a clear attempt by the enemy to get David to take his confidence for winning battles off God and rely on his own strength. David is described as a man "after God's own heart". If Satan had come along undisguised and said in an evil voice, "David, why don't you sacrifice some babies to me?" David would have dismissed it out of hand. He would never have wanted to further Satan's agenda. In this case too, if he had realised the source of the idea, he would not have done it. The idea of listening to Satan and obeying him would have been repulsive to him. But he did it because he believed it was his own idea – even though the Bible makes clear that it was not – and that it was a good idea. Even good people who have a heart for God can be deceived.

The second example is found in John 13:2: "The evening meal was being served, and the devil had already prompted Judas Iscariot, son of Simon, to betray Jesus." Satan thought that getting Jesus killed would end the threat he posed. Little did he know! Many have debated Judas' motivation for betraying Jesus. He may have thought that it would help move matters on by forcing Jesus to reveal himself as the conquering Messiah. He may simply have been tempted by what he could do with the money he received. Whatever he was thinking, he probably had no idea that the thought to do it came from Satan – but it did. And when Judas realised the implications of what he had done, he was overcome by remorse and went out and hanged himself.

The third example of Satan putting thoughts into someone's mind is found in Acts 5:3: "Then Peter said, 'Ananias, how is it that Satan has so filled your heart that you have lied to the Holy Spirit and have kept for yourself some of the money you received for the land?'" Here we have another example of Satan getting someone to believe a false idea. Ananias fell for the lie that it was outward show that mattered. What had he done? He had sold some land and given most of the money to the church. That's a great thing to do – in most churches he would have been sincerely thanked and honoured. However, he made out that he had given all the money he received for the land when in fact he kept some back. The result was that he was struck dead.

So here we have people who suffered real damage because they fell for lies fed to them by demons. Satan aims to steal, kill and destroy (John 10:10) and, if he is allowed to, that is exactly what he will do.

How does Satan introduce false ideas to our minds? It is safe to assume that he does not introduce them in a shrieking demonic voice with loads of cackling laughter like in horror films. It must be a lot more subtle than that. In fact, if his aim is to get us to believe that his ideas are our own, it would have to be in a voice that sounds like our thoughts. If he is trying to get you to fall for the lie that you are useless, it's likely that the thought will not be "You are completely useless aren't you?" but is much more likely to sound exactly like your other thoughts and be along the lines of, "I think I must be completely useless".

One of the most important lessons we can learn in this battle for truth that rages in our minds is not to assume that every thought in our head is our own and, therefore, worth thinking. Instead we need to hold our thoughts up against the truth in God's Word. You might find young people asking, "How do I know whether a thought is from the enemy or my own?" They may be missing the point. The real issue is not where the thought came from but whether or not it is true. And that is something we can ascertain only by comparing it carefully to the truth in the Bible. There is no need to get obsessed with demons. We simply need to be aware of them and how they work but make sure that our focus is on Jesus who is the Truth. Whether the source is the TV, a teacher or a demon is not the issue. The real issue is whether or not the thought is true.

SATAN'S TACTICS

Satan is much weaker in his fight against us than you might imagine. Imagine that your Christian life is like a race. Satan doesn't have the power actually to get on the running track to block your path or stop you getting to where God's wants you to go. But he can send his demons to call out from the sidelines.

There are just three tactics they can use: temptation, accusation and deception. He can try and tempt you away (Hey! Come and look what's over there! It will make you feel better – no one needs to know. You know you want to!), or he can shout accusations at you, especially if you have just fallen for a temptation (You're a failure – you're always going to be a failure! You might as well sit down and give up!) or he can tell you blatant lies (Hey, you! You're going the wrong way. The finishing line is back that way!).

Some Christians feel so defeated by what the devil says that they just give up and sit down at this point. Others will stop and argue. Neither of these groups get anywhere closer to the finishing line. To be victorious, pay no attention to the abuse from the side-lines, but just keep running towards Jesus.

SATAN WANTS TO GET A FOOTHOLD IN OUR LIVES

Satan does all the tempting, accusing and deceiving in order that we might open the door of our lives to him. We open the door by sinning which gives him a 'foothold', a point of influence (see Ephesians 4:26-27). Once the door opens, Satan wedges his foot in the opening, and he now has an entrance point to influence your thinking.

If you are tempted, you know it. If you are accused, you know it. But if you are deceived... how would you know? Satan's most effective strategy is deception.

It's very important to stress at this point that we're not talking about Christians being "possessed", ie completely taken over or taken back by demons. At the core of your being, your spirit is connected to God's spirit and Satan can't have you back. You have been bought by the blood of Jesus (1 Peter 1:18-19). Christians can never be owned by Satan but we can unwittingly allow him to have different levels of influence (or footholds) in our minds.

THIS IS OUR DEFENCE

- Understand who you are in Christ

    Ephesians 1:19-22 tells us that Jesus is seated at God's right hand, 'far above all rule and authority, power and dominion.' And do you know what our position is? This is what it says in Ephesians 2:6: 'And God raised us up with Christ and seated us with him in the heavenly realms in Christ Jesus.'

    James 4:7 says 'Submit to God. Resist the devil and he will flee from you.' You are seated with Christ above Satan, and as long as you are submitting yourself to God, Satan has no choice but to flee from you.

    One of the reasons we have included a 'declaration' at the start of every session is to help the young people understand that, in the spiritual world, we - not Satan - are the ones with the real power and authority in Christ.

- Don't be scared.

    Satan would like us to be scared of him, because that gives him some power over us. The reality is that demons have much more cause to be scared of Christians than we have to be scared of them! It's like the obsession with germs we mentioned earlier. If I go around scared of germs, looking for them everywhere, they're going to rule my life! But if I just simply do the small things to neutralise them – like wash my hands – I don't need to waste time thinking about them.

    We simply need to keep submitting to God and keep our eyes fixed on Jesus – then we are safe.

- Guard your mind

    We need to keep our brains switched on at all times so that we can spot when Satan tries to tempt, accuse or deceive us. God works through our intelligence; so don't leave it behind in your faith!

- Know the truth

    If you know God, if you've read the Bible, you will start to know the truth. The better you know the truth, the real thing, the easier it is to spot fakes. If, for example, you've memorised the verse from Ephesians 2:6, saying that you're seated with Christ, when Satan tells you that you're worthless you'll spot the lie at once!

- Get back on track when you fall off

    One of the things Jesus told us to do time and time again is 'Repent'. When we mess up, repentance is not just about saying sorry and carrying on, doing our best to not sin again, but totally turning away from that stuff and closing the doors that we have opened to the devil. It's like you're a train going the wrong way down the tracks. Repentance is picking the train up to face the opposite direction and going God's way.

It's important that we know about Satan and demons and how they work so that we can take sensible precautions. But we don't need to get too worked up about them. So now let's finish this section by focusing on Jesus instead!

SPIRITUAL AUTHORITY

What position do the Father and Son have now?

In Ephesians 1:19-22 we are told that Jesus is seated at God's right hand, the highest seat of power and authority. God has placed everything under his feet and we are told that he is now "head over everything"

Ephesians 1:21: "God has put Christ over all rulers, authorities, powers, and kings, not only in this world but also in the next."

So God is far above Satan. You probably knew that already! The big question is, what is our position in all this? Do we have more or less power than Satan?

Ephesians 2:6 says, "and he raised us up with Christ and gave us a seat with him in the heavens. He did this for those in Christ Jesus."

In Christ, we too are seated at God's right hand, far above (not just slightly above!) Satan and all demonic powers. Because Christ finished the job he came to do, the Church is now given the power and the authority to carry on his work.

QUESTIONS TO THINK ABOUT AS YOU PREPARE

1. What do you think it means in practice to 'put on' the armour of God?

2. If you woke up in the night with the feeling that there was a scary presence in your room, based on James 4:7 and what you've learned, what do you think would be a good way to deal with it?

3. What is your defence against Satan?

4. If you think you're under attack from Satan, what should you do?

5. Looking back at the question we left the young people with at the end of last week's session, do you think you've ever been deceived by Satan? How would you know if you are being deceived right now?

SPIRITUAL REALITY 11-14

LEADER'S PREPARATION

Pray together:

❝ Father God, thank you that you are greater than he who is in the world and for the fact that I do not have to be frightened of evil. I trust in you for protection of everyone in our group today, especially for protection of our minds. Thank you for your victory over evil. Amen.

YOU MAY NEED

Bin bags / large plastic bags filled with scrunched-up balls of newspaper

Masking tape

Two trays

Party poppers

Safety goggles / dust mask / overalls / anti-bacteria spray

Accompanying DVD / DVD player / TV / projector

Monopoly money

Bibles

Print-out of Ephesians 6:10-17, The Armour of God (downloadable from website)

Two newspapers

PRAYER AND DECLARATION

Encourage everyone to join together in saying the following prayer and declaration. You can download the PowerPoint slides with the words for these from the website.

It would be good to suggest that the young people stand up and speak out the declaration clearly and confidently to the heavenly realms. They could shout it out and use appropriate actions!

PRAYER

❝ Father, thank you that Jesus is the victor! I thank you that he is greater than he who is in the world. I want to learn to overcome in the battle for my thoughts. Please show me how to do that. In Jesus' name, Amen.

DECLARATION: IN A CLEAR, CONFIDENT TONE!

> **Sometimes the enemy tries to distract and confuse my thoughts but I will not let him. My mind belongs to me and I tell him to leave me alone now in Jesus' name.**

STARTING POINT

Start by giving a short summary of the previous session. A good resource for this is the Overview found in the Core of the previous session.

INTRODUCTORY ACTIVITIES

BATTLE GAME 1 – NEWSPAPER WAR

Fill several bin bags / large plastic bags with scrunched-up balls of newspaper.

Divide the group into two teams and give them each one side of the room.

Mark the division line with a piece of furniture or strip of masking tape.

Give each team equal amounts of newspaper.

When a signal is given, each team must try to get rid of the newspaper from their side of the room.

Anyone who steps on the opponents' side of the room is disqualified.

After a certain amount of time (you decide, dependent on the stamina of your group!), count down from 10 to 0.

When the game ends, the team with the least newspaper on their side wins.

BATTLE GAME 2 – TRAY WARS

Get two trays and two rolled up newspapers secured with sticky tape.

The game is played in pairs.

Each player holds a tray on the palm of their hand and the newspaper in the other.

As players defend their tray, they must knock their opponent's tray out of their hands.

The first player to drop their tray loses.

Explain:

We've played a couple of battle games. Today we're going to find out about a real life battle that is going on right now – and the battle ground is your mind!

DVD CHAPTER 1

Play Session 7, chapter 1 – 'In A Battle?' of the accompanying DVD.

Ask the group:

Have you ever thought that there is a battle going on around us?

God is in the white corner and Satan is in the black corner

Where do you stand in all this?

Good news! Because you are in Christ, he shares his authority with you, so you can use it to do what he told you to do – to go and make disciples.

WORSHIP ACTIVITY

When people in Britain found out that the Second World War had been won, they went crazy celebrating!

Everyone who had lived through the war had had a rough ride with food shortages, the constant threat of air raids and the fear of invasion. Victory wasn't just a technical term for what the Allied troops had achieved; it was experienced by everyone as feelings of peace, joy, excitement and relief.

When Jesus died on the cross, he won the ultimate victory – he crushed evil forever. Colossians 2:15 says:

'…having disarmed the powers and authorities [of evil], he made a public spectacle of them, triumphing over them by the cross.'

Just like people celebrated and threw parties on VE Day, shouldn't we celebrate the victory that Jesus has won?

Hand out lots of party poppers and get the young people to shout out statements of praise or thanks to God and then fire their party popper.

THE MAIN POINT

Have another leader introduce this session.

Today we're going to find out the facts about Satan and how best to defend ourselves against him.

Then enter the room dressed in goggles and a dust mask (you might be able to get these from different people in your church, e.g. farmers, car mechanics or science teachers), waving an anti-bacterial household cleaning spray in one hand.

Explain:

I've heard a rumour that in this room there are some things called 'germs'. As I grew up I wasn't aware that there was such a thing. I just lived my life happily, not knowing that the danger is everywhere!

Someone told me about them the other day, so now I've given my life to destroying them. There shall be no more germs! I'm going to go around and find every germ there is and spray them to death.

Take off your mask and goggles explaining that...

It would just be ridiculous if I spent all my time looking for germs! I'd get nothing else done in my life. And anyway, I know that if I just wash my hands properly and keep my immune system healthy, germs aren't a big issue. That's not to say that they can't be dangerous, it's just that most of the time they don't stand a chance if we protect ourselves properly.

So far in this course we have talked about a couple of things that sometimes cause problems in our walk with God; we've mentioned the world and we've talked about the flesh.

Well, today we're on to another one - the devil and his demons.

Just like germs, we can't see the devil and demons, they are all around us and they can do us harm - if we let them.

We could just ignore him, but that would be like acting as if germs don't exist. If we stop washing our hands and eating well, germs will eventually get to us and make us ill. In the same way, dismissing the idea of a spiritual reality of evil, only means that we're easier targets.

Invite a leader up to the front.

If Bob [use real name!] buries his head in the sand [make him bend over, away from your listeners, as if putting his head down into sand] – what happens?

He leaves a great big target exposed! [Point at his backside].

So, we mustn't ignore Satan. But we shouldn't get fixated on him either!

It would be like spending your life searching out germs, obsessing about rooting them out, even though they're not really worth obsessing about.

Just like it's relatively easy to avoid being infected by germs, avoiding Satan's traps isn't nearly so hard as you might think it is once you know all the facts.

THE FACTS
Who is who?

Get the group on their feet.

Read out the following list of characteristics – get young people to move to a corresponding side of the room for God or the devil or stay in the middle for both:

Holy	Loving
Wise	Truthful
Cunning	Knows everything
Powerful	Jealous
A liar	Deceitful

The Bible doesn't give us lots of detailed information about Satan and demons, because – frankly – they're not worth it. But we do need to make sure that we know the facts that are presented to us.

One major fact is that Satan is nothing like God.

He's like us in that he can only be in one place at a time. He can't read people's minds either.

Comparing Satan with God is like comparing an ant to an atomic bomb.

Although Satan can't read our minds, he can try to put thoughts into our minds; so because of that and because he's had so much practice observing people over many years – he can often make a pretty good guess at what we're thinking.

Read – or get a young person to read - John 13:2 out loud.

Do you think Judas knew that his idea was from Satan? No, probably not. He probably thought it was his own good idea.

But when he realised what he had done he killed himself. It's important that we realise that not every bad idea or destructive thought that pops into our mind is our own.

Discussion

Divide the group into smaller groups of 4-5 and discuss the following:

- Have the things you've learned so far about Satan surprised you? Scared you?

- Does he seem more or less powerful than you expected?

- Can you think of a time when you've had a bad thought that you now realise probably didn't come from yourself?

Bring the groups back together and present your findings.

 ## THE MAIN POINT

 ## DVD CHAPTER 2

Play Session 7, chapter 2 – 'Fighting Dirty' – of the accompanying DVD.

Explain:

Satan's strategy to get us off course is to tempt, accuse and trick us. For example, a thought pops into our mind saying that we're useless.

If at that point we believe that lie and give up, Satan has managed to neutralise a Christian who is full of potential.

It's not much better if we start arguing with the thought. That will stop us in our tracks as well.

You see he wants us to have negative thoughts like "I'm no good", or "I'll never be able to".

He wants to trick us into not depending on God with thoughts like "I can sort this out on my own" or "I'll decide such and such".

The best thing to do is to pay no attention to lies like these. You can do that if you know that they are lies, if you know the truth from God's Word. It's difficult if you don't.

Satan does all the tempting, accusing and tricking in order that we might open the door to our lives to him. We open the door by sinning.

Once the door opens, Satan wedges his foot in the opening, and he now has an entrance point to influence you even more.

But remember that no Christian can be possessed by Satan, only influenced, because we are already 'owned' by God.

◉ DVD CHAPTER 3

Play Session 7, chapter 3 – 'Our Defence' – of the accompanying DVD.

Explain that we are now going to look at some ways to defend ourselves.

ILLUSTRATION – OUR DEFENCE
We defend ourselves best by:

- Firstly, not being scared. Satan has got more reason to fear you that you have to fear him.

- Secondly, we need to remember that we are children of God and as such have power and authority in the spiritual world.

- Thirdly, we need to keep our brains switched on at all times to spot when we're being tricked.

- Finally, we need to know the truth.

Show some Monopoly or toy money to the group.

What do you think I could get for this if I went shopping?

Why nothing?

How do you know that it's not real?

You know, because you've seen real money.

If you know God, if you've read the Bible, you will start to know the truth.

The better you know the truth, the real thing, the easier it is to spot fake thoughts and kick them out.

RESIST THE DEVIL

James 4:7 says, 'Submit to God. Resist the devil and he will flee from you.'

That means as long as you are giving yourself totally to God, as a child of God you have authority over Satan, and he has no choice but to go away when you tell him to.

We don't want to get obsessed with Satan and demons - like we don't want to get obsessed with germs - just take simple precautions.

But when doctors didn't know that there were germs, they didn't sterilise their instruments or scrub their hands and people died.

Christians who don't know that there is a battle going on for their minds don't see any need to put on the armour of God and 'take every thought captive to make it obedient to Christ' (2 Corinthians 10:5). That makes them vulnerable to attack.

RESPONSE

Give everyone a print-out of Ephesians 6:10-17 (The Armour of God).

Explain that the armour of God provides all the protection they will ever need.

Ask the young people to remain seated as you read through the passage slowly, and encourage them to think about the different parts of the armour, and whether they have put them on.

Next, ask everyone to stand up.

With the group work out an action for each part of the armour (e.g. hold one flat hand out as the shield).

When you have actions for each part, read through the passage out loud together, doing the actions as you read.

You might like to explain that:

- The belt of truth stands against the devil's tricks.

- The breastplate of righteousness stands against Satan's accusations.

- The shield of faith stands against Satan's attack on our minds, which is where the main battle takes place.

- The armour of God needs to be on all the time.

Draw their attention to the picture on page 31 of the Youth Guide 11-14. Encourage them to write in the names of the different pieces of armour.

Finish by praying something like this:

Father God, I thank you that you have provided all we need for protection against evil. Help us know what is true and recognise thoughts that aren't. Would you encourage us to kick those thoughts and lies out. We thank you that you have saved us once and for all. Amen.

SMALL GROUPS & PRAYER FOCUS

1. What do you think it means in practice to 'put on' the armour of God?

2. If you woke up in the night with the feeling that there was a scary presence in your room, based on James 4:7 and what you've learned, what do you think would be a good way to deal with it?

3. What is your defence against Satan?

4. If you think you're under attack from Satan, what should you do?

5. Looking back at the question from last week, do you think you've ever been deceived or tricked by Satan?

⭐ AND THERE'S MORE!

Page 31 of the Youth Guide is designed to get the young people into the habit of taking hold of their authority over the enemy. The Challenge section says:

'Read Ephesians 6:10-18 every morning this week and as you do, pretend that you are putting on an actual suit of armour. As you put on each piece pray that God would help you wear that item today.'

Draw their attention also to the Think section:

'Jesus named Satan "the father of lies" (John 8:44). If we believe his lies, he can influence our lives. Truth always beats a lie; just like turning on a light in a dark room gets rid of the darkness. The better we know God's truth, the more we can spot a lie and kick it out.'

❓ CLOSING QUESTION

The question for next week (on page 33 of the Youth Guide 11-14) is:

'If we can't always trust what we feel, then why has God given us feelings and how should we react to them?'

In addition to that, ask them to pay particular attention to all the different feelings they will experience over the coming week and write a list down that they can bring back to the next session.

Leader's Note: Send a text message to the group to remind them about these questions a couple of days before the next session.

SPIRITUAL REALITY 15-18

 ## PRAYER AND DECLARATION

Encourage everyone to join together in saying the following prayer and declaration. You can download the PowerPoint slides with the words for these from the website.

It would be good to suggest that the young people stand up and speak out the declaration clearly and confidently to the heavenly realms. They could shout it out and use appropriate actions!

PRAYER

❝ Father, thank you that Jesus is the victor! I thank you that he is greater than he who is in the world. I want to learn to overcome in the battle for my thoughts. Please show me how to do that. In Jesus' name, Amen.

DECLARATION: IN A CLEAR, CONFIDENT TONE!

❝ Sometimes the enemy tries to distract and confuse my thoughts but I will not let him. My mind belongs to me and I tell him to leave me alone now in Jesus' name.

🔍 STARTING POINT

Go straight into the session explaining that you will have the refreshments later on in the session.

Start by giving a short summary of the previous session. A good resource for this is the Overview found in the Core of the previous session.

◎ DVD CHAPTER 1

Play Session 7, chapter 1 – 'In A Battle?' – of the accompanying DVD.

Ask the group: have you ever thought that there is a battle going on around us? Is that a scary thought?

⌂ SOAPBOX

Divide the young people into groups of three.

Ask a leader to paraphrase what was said in the DVD (encourage them not simply to repeat it but instead give it a personal angle) and give their opinion to the group.

Ask the groups to discuss if they agree with what was said in the DVD. Have they ever considered this concept before?

Hand out the script print-out from the DVD (in the downloadable material for this session).

'In the white corner, the side of light and life is God! In the black corner, the side of darkness and evil, is the devil, Satan.

Satan would love you to believe that his power and God's power are the same and that there's a kind of tug-of-war with helpless old you in the middle and there's God on one side and the devil on the other. But nothing could be further from the truth.

In fact in Colossians 2 we find out that, at the cross, Jesus overcame evil once and for all and after that was raised to the position of the right hand of God, the position of ultimate power and authority in the entire universe.'

Challenge your young people to answer these questions:

Jesus is at the right hand of God but what about you? Where do you stand in all this?

Then explain the good news:

Because you are in Christ, he shares his power and authority with you. You too are seated at the right hand of the Father.

INTRODUCING THE SESSION
So far we've talked about a couple of things that cause problems in our walk with God; we've mentioned the world and we've talked about the flesh.

Well, today we're on to another one - the devil and his demons.

Just like germs, we can't see the devil and demons, they are all around us and they can do us harm - if we let them.

We could just ignore him, but that would be like acting as if germs don't exist. If we stop washing our hands, germs will eventually get to us and make us ill. In the same way, dismissing the idea of a spiritual reality of evil, only means that we're easier targets.

⊙ DVD CHAPTER 2

Play Session 7, chapter 2 – 'Fighting Dirty' – of the accompanying DVD.

Explain:

Satan's strategy to get us off course is to tempt, accuse and trick us. So, we mustn't ignore Satan. But we shouldn't get fixated on him either!

It would be like spending your life searching out germs, obsessing about rooting them out, whilst they're not really worth obsessing about.

Just like it's relatively easy to avoid being infected by germs, avoiding Satan's traps isn't hard once you know all the facts.

THE FACTS
On a large / flipchart paper draw a line down the middle. On one side of the line write 'God' and on the other write 'Satan'. Ask the group to shout out what they know about each - write down what they say. Consider using someone else to write down what they say.

Reflect on what has been said and make sure you cover the following:

• Satan is not like God

We tend to think that because we can't see God or Satan and because they're both 'supernatural', they must surely be similar in some ways as if they are equal (or nearly equal) but opposite powers. This is very far from the truth. God is the Creator but Satan is, like us, simply a created being. Satan would really like us to think that he is equal in power to God, but actually – as someone has said – comparing Satan to God is like comparing an ant to an atomic bomb.

• Satan can be in only one place at one time

Because Satan is created like you and me, he's got many of the same limitations as we do. He can only be in one place at one time for example. He carries out his work worldwide through an army of demons (also known as 'evil spirits', 'fallen angels' or 'powers and authorities'). In fact, when we use the word 'Satan', we generally use it to refer not just to the one who is the chief of the demons but to all the demons in general. It's important to know, however, that only God is everywhere at once.

• Satan does not know everything

Satan can't read your mind, nor can he tell the future. Have you ever wondered why we never see the headline 'Psychic wins lottery'? It's interesting to see in the Bible that all interaction between angels and people, or demons and people, are done out loud – have a look for yourself when you get home! Only God knows what's in people's minds.

Leader's Note: For Biblical evidence for this last point see the part in the Core section on Daniel and

Nebuchadnezzar on page 161.

SATAN PUTS THOUGHTS INTO OUR MINDS

Although he can't read our minds, Satan can put things **into** your mind – the Bible clearly teaches that he can. Because of this and due to how much practice he has had observing people over many years, he can often make a pretty good guess at what we're thinking.

He may put a disgusting thought into your mind and then condemn you for thinking it. If you believed that the thought was your own, you'd probably also believe his conclusion that you must be sick for having it!

Let's look at an example in which Satan put a thought into someone's mind but made them think that it was their own thought:

"Satan rose up against Israel and incited David to take a census of Israel" (1 Chronicles 21:1).

Getting David to take a census was a clear attempt by the enemy to get David to take his confidence for winning battles off God and rely on his own strength.

David is described as a man "after God's own heart". If Satan had come along undisguised and given David the thought in an evil voice with an evil laugh like in a horror movie, David would have realised it was Satan and wouldn't have taken the census. No way would he want to listen to the devil.

But he did it because he believed it was his own idea – even though the Bible makes clear that it was not – and that it was a good idea. Even good people who have a heart for God can be deceived.

So if Satan doesn't use an evil voice when he speaks his thoughts to us, what do they sound like? If his aim is to get us to believe that his ideas are our own, it would have to be in a voice that sounds like our thoughts.

If he is trying to get you to fall for the lie that you are useless, the thought will not be "You are completely useless aren't you?" but is much more likely to sound exactly like your other thoughts and be along the lines of, "I think I must be completely useless".

How do we know whether a thought is from the enemy or is our own? Well, in a sense we don't need to work that out. The main question is not where the thought comes from but whether it is true.

And that is something we can work out only by comparing it carefully to the truth in the Bible. Whether the thought comes from the TV, a teacher or a demon is not the main issue. The real issue is whether or not the thought is true. If it's not, just throw it out - don't think it. Your mind is your own and you are in charge of it.

So let's not focus on demons. Let's focus on Jesus who is the Truth!

Ask:

• Have the things you've learned so far about Satan surprised you? Scared you?

• Does he seem more or less powerful than you expected?

• Can you think of a time when you've had a bad thought that you now realise probably didn't come from yourself?

SATAN TRIES TO TEMPT, ACCUSE AND DECEIVE US.

There are three main ways Satan attacks: he can tempt us, accuse us and deceive us.

We can all think of a time that we have been tempted. The tempter isn't the opposite sex or a chocolate bar. These are just objects that Satan or his underlings use.

We all know what it feels like to be accused. How many of us have struggled with thoughts like 'I'm stupid', 'I'm no good' or 'I'll never change', 'God doesn't love me?' Every one of us.

But what about when we are deceived? How would you know? That's difficult to recognise, and that's Satan's prime strategy.

↑ WORSHIP ACTIVITY

When people in Britain found out that the Second World War had been won, they went crazy celebrating!

Everyone who had lived through the war had had a rough ride with food shortages, the constant threat of air raids and the fear of invasion. Victory wasn't just a technical term for what the Allied troops had achieved; it was experienced by everyone as feelings of peace, joy, excitement and relief.

When Jesus died on the cross, he won the ultimate victory – he crushed evil forever. Colossians 2:15 says:

'...having disarmed the powers and authorities [of evil], he made a public spectacle of them, triumphing over them by the cross.'

Just like people celebrated and threw parties on VE Day, shouldn't we celebrate the victory that Jesus has won?!

Hand out lots of party poppers and get the young people to shout out statements of praise or thanks to God and then fire their party popper.

Review with the young people the material on page 30 of the Youth Guide 15-18 under 'What's The Point?' which says:

- Christians are the bull's eye target for the enemy who will try to bring us down by tempting, accusing and deceiving us.

- Comparing Satan's power to God's power is like comparing an ant to an atomic bomb!

- Jesus is far above Satan and demonic powers and because Christians belong to Christ, we have authority over the kingdom of darkness. That is amazing.

DVD CHAPTER 3

Play Session 7, chapter 3 – 'Our Defence' – of the accompanying DVD.

Satan wants to stop us being effective for Jesus. He wants to get a foothold in our lives.

Explain that we are now going to look at some ways to defend ourselves.

SMALL GROUPS & PRAYER FOCUS

Leader's Note: Now hand over to small groups, make sure that you have asked one young person from each group prior to the session to prepare for this section. Also serve the refreshments during this group time.

The next section is designed to be led by a young person in small groups using the downloadable sheet.

OUR DEFENCE

• Understand who you are in Christ.

Ephesians 1:19-22 tells us that Jesus is seated at God's right hand, 'far above all rule and authority, power and dominion.'

And do you know what our position is? This is what it says in Ephesians 2:6: 'And God raised us up with Christ and seated us with him in the heavenly realms in Christ Jesus.'

In Christ, we too are seated at God's right hand, far above (not just slightly above!) Satan and all demonic powers. Because Christ finished the job he came to do, the Church is now given the power and the authority to carry on his work.

James 4:7 says 'Submit to God. Resist the devil and he will flee from you.' You are seated with Christ above Satan, and as long as you are submitting yourself to God, Satan has no choice but to flee from you. That is why we can command him to go away.

• Don't be scared.

Satan would like us to be scared of him, because that gives him some power over us. The reality is that demons have much more cause to be scared of Christians than we have to be scared of them! It's like being obsessed with germs. If I go around scared of germs, looking for them everywhere, they're going to rule my life! But if I just simply do the small things to neutralise them – like wash my hands – I don't really need spend any time thinking about them.

We simply need to keep submitting to God and keep our eyes fixed on Jesus.

• Guard your minds.

We need to keep our brains switched on at all times so that we can spot when Satan tries to tempt, accuse or deceive us. God works through our minds; so don't leave it behind in your faith!

• Know the truth.

If you know God, if you've read the Bible, you will start to know the truth. The better you know the truth, the real thing, the easier it is to spot fakes. If you've memorised the verse from Ephesians 2:6, saying that you're seated with Christ, when Satan tells you that you're worthless you'll spot the lie at once!

• Get back on track when you fall off.

One of the things Jesus told us to do time and time again was 'Repent.' When we mess up, repentance is not just about saying sorry and carrying on, doing our best to not sin again, but totally turning away from that stuff and closing the doors that we have opened to the devil. It's like you're on a train going the wrong way down the tracks. Repentance is picking the train up to face the opposite direction and going God's way.

So there's no need to get obsessed with Satan and demons. Let's now focus on Jesus instead!

RESPONSE

Coming back together, discuss any points that arise from the groups and then consider these questions:

- What do you think it means in practice to 'put on' the armour of God?

- If you woke up in the night with the feeling that there was a scary presence in your room, based on James 4:7 and what you've learned, what do you think would be a good way to deal with it?

- What is your defence against Satan?

- If you think you're under attack from Satan, what should you do?

- Looking back at the question from last week; do you think you've ever been deceived or tricked by Satan?

-

⭐ AND THERE'S MORE!

Draw the young people's attention to page 32 of the Youth Guide 15-18 and ask them to consider the questions there during the week:

- Why are we easier targets for Satan if we ignore the fact that a spiritual battle is going on?

- How do we know that Satan is so much less powerful than God?

- As Christians, why do we have authority over the devil?

- What are the things that we can do to defend ourselves against the devil's temptations, accusations and lies?

Also refer them to the sections on page 33:

Challenge: Can you think of a time when you have felt tempted, accused or deceived? The belt of truth is what we need to expose the lies of the evil one. This week your challenge is to read the book of Ephesians and every day write down one verse that contains a truth that stands out to you.

Think: Do you know who you are in Jesus? The Bible tells us that God has seated us in the heavenly realms with Jesus and we have his power and authority over the kingdom of darkness. If we stay close to God and don't give in to Satan, he has to get lost when we resist him (James 4:7)!

Finish by praying something like this:

Father God, I thank you that you have provided all we need for protection against evil. Help us know what is true and recognise thoughts that aren't. Would you encourage us to kick those thoughts and lies out? We thank you that you have saved us once and for all. Amen.

And / Or

Lord God, sometimes it can be really difficult to be aware of lies but I know that you have given me all that I need to grow as a Christian. Help me to take hold of my freedom by knowing how to resist the devil. Amen

? CLOSING QUESTION

Question to consider for next week (page 33 Youth Guide 15-18):

If we can't always trust what we feel, then why has God given us feelings and how should we react to them?

In addition to that, ask them to pay particular attention to all the different feelings they will experience over the coming week and write a list down that they can bring back to the next session.

Leader's Note: Send a text message to the group to remind them about these questions a couple of days before the next session.

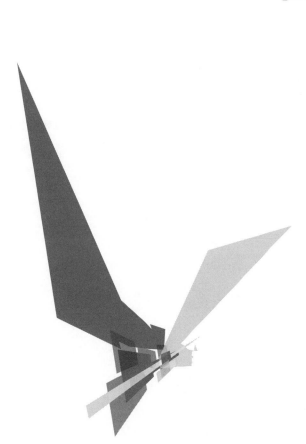

SESSION EIGHT:
HANDLING OUR EMOTIONS

'Cast all your anxiety on him because he cares for you. Be self-controlled and alert. Your enemy the devil prowls around like a roaring lion looking for someone to devour.'

1 Peter 5:7-8

HANDLING OUR EMOTIONS CORE

PREPARATION

This is the first session of two plus the Steps To Freedom in Part C of Freedom In Christ For Young People in which we turn our attention to resolving the negative effects of the past.

The third book in The Freedom In Christ Discipleship Series, Break Free, Stay Free (Monarch 2008), corresponds to Part C of the course. Read pages 12 - 55 in the book for some key principles and the material that relates to this session.

KEY VERSE

1 Peter 5:7-8 – 'Cast all your anxiety on him because he cares for you. Be self-controlled and alert. Your enemy the devil prowls around like a roaring lion looking for someone to devour.'

AIM

To understand our emotional nature and how it is related to what we believe.

KEY TRUTH

Our emotions are essentially a product of our thoughts and a barometer of our spiritual health.

OVERVIEW

We can't control our emotions directly but they are, in a general sense, the result of what we choose to believe. If we don't have a proper understanding of God and his Word, and who we are in Christ, it will be signalled to us through our emotions. Failure to handle emotions well may make us vulnerable to spiritual attack. The more we commit ourselves to the truth and choose to believe that what God says is true, the more we are able to handle our feelings.

INTRODUCTION

We are now starting the third section of the course in which we will look at resolving the negative effects of the past.

We're going to start by considering our emotions. Everyone has emotions – we know that from experience! Some are pleasant and some are not so nice. We're going to think in this session about how we deal with them. We have focused a lot so far on believing what is true rather than in placing our trust on what we feel. That is an important Biblical principle that we must always remember. But perhaps we have given you the impression that our emotions are a bad thing. In reality, they were, of course, given to us by God and are a good thing. It's just a question of understanding why God gave them to us and what they show us.

The good news is that God doesn't expect us to just change our feelings at the snap of a finger. But we can learn how to be emotionally honest and healthy over time. We do this by changing what we believe and how we behave.

WHAT ARE MY EMOTIONS?

Your emotions are to your soul, what your ability to feel pleasure and pain are to your body.

Let's look at pain for a moment. Imagine that someone offered to take away all your physical pain for life. Would you accept the offer?

It might sound great to begin with, especially if you have a sore back, regular head aches or something like that. But, it would be dangerous!

You wouldn't feel any pain if you stepped on a nail, or sat too close to a fire. Without pain, you'd be a hopeless mass of scars within a matter of weeks. God gave us pain for our own protection – it's a gift.

Our emotions are the same. They tell us what is going on inside. For example if you are feeling down it might be because you believe that you really aren't worth much which is, of course, a lie.

FEELINGS ARE A RESULT OF WHAT WE CHOOSE TO BELIEVE

What we believe, or choose to think, can make us feel the way we do. The problem is that, if what we believe doesn't reflect what is true, then what we feel will not reflect what is actually happening.

Imagine – girls – that you have a boyfriend. He's been acted weirdly over the weekend. You start to worry that something is wrong. Then, on Monday morning, you get a text message from him asking you to meet him at a certain coffee shop on Friday afternoon. You think, 'oh no, he's going to break up with me!' First you get angry at his insensitivity, just sending you a text like that. By Thursday you're depressed, because you have convinced yourself that your relationship is going to end. By Friday afternoon you are an emotional mess – all because of what you were thinking, and none of it based on reality! At your meeting, your boyfriend surprises you with flowers and a gift; it was an anniversary you had forgotten about. Now, how would you feel? You spent all week feeling bad because you didn't know the truth. Those feelings were not based on reality.

If you always depend on your interpretation of reality, your feelings will be all over the place. If you depend on believing God's Word, your feelings will reflect reality and the truth about who you are.

A key message for the young people to take from this session is: **if what you believe does not reflect the truth, then what you feel will not reflect reality**. The more we choose to believe that what God says is true, the more we will have feelings that reflect reality.

If you decide to follow your feelings, rather than what God says is true, Satan will have an easy job fooling you. You'll probably agree with him when he tells you that you're a 'worthless excuse for a Christian', even though God clearly says in the Bible that you are a forgiven and accepted child of God.

If we don't spot that some emotions are based on lies, we can allow the enemy to get a foothold in our lives; an entrance point for him to influence us.

For example, 1 Peter 5:7-8 shows that anxiety (which is an emotion) can cause problems if we do not handle it well. It starts with a well-known sentence that you may well have on a bookmark in your Bible or on a poster on your wall: "Cast all your anxiety on him because he cares for you." The passage continues with another couple of sentences that are just as well-known: "Be self-controlled and alert. Your enemy the devil prowls around like a roaring lion looking for someone to devour." Even though it's likely that you knew both of those passages well, you probably did not realise that they follow one another directly. They are both part of the same idea. Peter is telling us that if we let anxiety get a grip of us, we are making ourselves much more vulnerable to the enemy's schemes against us.

Satan is actively prowling around looking to take advantage of our emotions to get a foothold in our lives.

You can't instantly change what you feel. But you can decide what to do so that your emotions don't lead you into sin. The Bible says: 'In your anger do not sin … and don't give the devil a foothold.' (Ephesians 4:26-27). If you're overcome by anger – make a wise decision what to do with it! Make sure that it doesn't develop into bitterness or unforgiveness towards other people, or you might as well put up a welcome banner for the enemy.

LEARNING TO HANDLE EMOTIONS WELL

Your emotions are like when your computer or iPod tells you there is a problem. They are there to let you know that there's a potentially serious problem inside the metal casing. If you don't stop to fix the problem, sooner or later you can expect some big trouble.

There are three ways that you can react when the error message appears:

1. You could take a piece of tape and put it over the message and think, 'no problem, the message has gone!'

2. You could explode in anger, take a hammer and smash the screen– at least it fixes the pressing issue of the message being there.

3. You could admit that there is a problem and try and fix it.

You can deal with your emotions in much the same way:

COVER IT UP

Sometimes we cover up our emotions, and choose not to deal with them. Doing this is both unhealthy and dishonest.

Listen to how King David felt when he lived in denial:

'When I kept silent, my bones wasted away through my groaning all day long...' (Psalm 32:3).

If we bottle up our feelings for too long, they will take over our lives and can even affect our bodies by making us ill.

EXPLODE

Another way of handling our emotions is to just let them out immediately without thinking about who gets hit by our emotional outburst. This is not healthy for the people around us. It might feel good for us to get stuff off our chests, but it could really hurt our friends, our families or whoever else happened to be standing in the way.

James 1:19-20 says this:

'Everyone should be quick to listen, slow to speak and slow to become angry, because our anger does not produce the righteousness that God desires.' (TNIV)

BE HONEST

So what should we do when the error message appears indicating a problem? When we feel angry, anxious or depressed? The healthy way to handle our emotions is to be honest and admit how we feel.

It starts by admitting our feelings to God. God already knows your thoughts and emotions, so you might as well tell him how you feel! He's big enough to deal with an outburst or a tantrum from us now and then. He is your closest friend.

Jesus was honest with his emotions; he admitted his grief at the death of Lazarus, and he talked about his sorrow in Gethsemane. If the Lord of the universe needs to be expressive and honest like that, what about you and me?

HANDLING PAST TRAUMAS

We've been talking about day-to-day emotions, but what about major traumas from the past?

Some of us carry around emotional baggage, traumatic experiences that have scarred us emotionally. It could be some form of abuse, a frightening experience or the death of someone we loved. It keeps affecting us negatively for a long time afterwards, by making us angry or scared or depressed. God doesn't want emotional pain from our past to affect us today. Forgiving people is really important here and we're looking at that next week.

Often, traumatic experiences make you believe lies about God and yourself. If you are bullied and told that you are rubbish, perhaps you start believing it. If you thought that God wasn't there for you, then maybe you start to question his love for you.

This becomes a mental stronghold (remember we talked about those a couple of weeks ago?) that distorts your understanding of who you are and who God is. But since you are a child of God, who you are is not decided by your past, but by Christ's work on the cross and his resurrection. Nobody can fix our past, but we can be free from its negative control over us by knowing the truth of who we are in Christ.

CHANGING HOW WE FEEL

If we feel overwhelmed by negative emotions, what can we do about it?

Well, let's look at a situation in the Bible which seemed overwhelming at the start: Israel v the Philistines (1 Samuel 17). The Philistines were trying to save themselves from a bloodbath by sending a giant – Goliath – to challenge Israel. The Israelite army got freaked out – because they didn't have any giants!

Then David comes along, pulls out his slingshot, says: 'How dare you challenge the armies of the living God?' and kills Goliath.

Both David and the Israelite army faced the same giant. The army compared the giant to themselves, and were scared. David compared the giant to God, and knew he couldn't lose.

You are not affected so much by what's around you, as by how you see or interpret what's around you.

Faith in God can really make that big a difference in our life. Faith, if you remember, is just believing what's true and behaving accordingly. When we do that, understanding what's really true from God's Word rather than what experiences and people have made us believe, we're 'renewing our mind', as the Bible calls it. We're deciding to believe what's true, even when we don't feel like it.

Again, if what we believe does not reflect the truth, then what we feel does not reflect reality.

- Do you agree that it's not the stuff around you that affects how you feel, but the way you see or interpret that stuff?

- If you sometimes feel overwhelmed by negative emotions, how can you start to look at your situation in a way that reflects what's actually true?

QUESTIONS TO THINK ABOUT AS YOU PREPARE

1. When you experience a strong negative emotion, do you tend to cover it up, explode or be honest about it?

2. Read Psalm 109:6-15. Does it surprise you that something like that is in the Bible? Have you ever felt like David? Have you ever prayed like that? Would it be right to pray that way?

3. Is there anything that you feel that you can't say to God that he doesn't already know? How does God feel about your emotions? How does he feel about honesty?

HANDLING OUR EMOTIONS 11-14

 ## PRAYER AND DECLARATION

Encourage everyone to join together in saying the following prayer and declaration. You can download the PowerPoint slides with the words for these from the website.

It would be good to suggest that the young people stand up and speak out the declaration clearly and confidently to the heavenly realms. They could shout it out and use appropriate actions!

PRAYER

❝❝ Father, thank you for giving me emotions, both good ones to enjoy and bad ones to show when there's a problem. Help me to understand how they can help me in my day-to-day experiences. Please help all of us to hear from your Holy Spirit today and act on his advice. In Jesus' name. Amen.

DECLARATION: IN A CLEAR, CONFIDENT TONE!

❝❝ I am Jesus' friend. Enemies of the Lord Jesus are not welcome here. It doesn't matter whether I shout it out or just whisper it; I can banish any enemy of God's. I have authority as a child of Jesus. So leave now, in Jesus' name.

STARTING POINT

Start by giving a short summary of the previous session. A good resource for this is the Overview found in the Core of the previous session.

INTRODUCTORY ACTIVITIES

EMOTIONAL CHARADES

Divide your group into two teams.

Line them up in two lines with a leader at the front, who is slightly separate from each line. Give each of the leaders a copy of the list of emotions below.

The person in the front of the line must go to the leader who whispers an emotion off the list to the player.

This person must then try to act out this emotion without using any sounds or writing.

When the team has guessed correctly, the player runs to the end of the line and it's the next person's turn.

The winner is the team that goes through all their team members (if you have a small group), or the team that has gone through the most players in e.g. 5 minutes.

List of emotions:

Happy	Confused
Sad	Depressed
Angry	Anxious
Excited	Relieved
Disappointed	Disgusted

THE ANGRY GAME

Either in small groups, just for fun, or with a few volunteers up front, play the angry game.

The idea is for two people to stare at each other looking angry until one person laughs.

The person that manages not to laugh is the winner.

DVD CHAPTER 1

Play Session 8, chapter 1 – 'Feelings' – of the accompanying DVD.

Ask the group:

How do you handle your feelings?

Actually the Bible teaches that everything about us was created by God.

- Our physical appearance

- Our heart

- Our ability to dream

All God-given.

That means that our emotions were created by God too.

God understands that there will be days where we are laughing and days where we are crying.

That's life.

WORSHIP ACTIVITY

Gather together lots of different strips of fabric, make them about 5 cm by 80-100 cm (2 inches wide by 3 to 4 feet long). Make sure you have lots of different colours, and enough for each young person to be able to choose a couple. You could use tissue paper (and sticky tape) instead of fabric, if that's easier to get hold of.

Say something like:

As we're coming to worship God, I'd like you to think about how you're feeling right now.

Look at the strips of fabric.

Can you see any colours that represent how you feel?

Pick out a couple of strips of fabric that represent how you feel.

We are going to bring our emotions – whether good or bad – into our worship today.

Have the young people explain why they've chosen the colours they've chosen.

Then pray a simple prayer committing the whole group to God, however they're feeling.

Encourage the young people to hold their strips of fabric in open hands while they pray.

Play a CD of (or sing) one or two of your group's favourite worship songs.

THE MAIN POINT

We are now starting the third section of the course!

Everyone has emotions – you will all know that from experience! At this point you could ask who kept a list of their feelings over the last week and see who had the most different types.

Some are pleasant and some are not so nice. We're going to think today about how we deal with all those emotions.

Ask them to turn to page 35 of their Youth Guide 11-14 and do the Just For Fun exercise and show their responses to their neighbour.

'SIMON SAYS'

Begin by explaining the rules that whatever follows the command "Simon Says", must be obeyed. If someone does not do what is commanded when the words "Simon says" are spoken by the leader, that player is "out". Likewise, a player is "out" if he obeys the command of a leader to do something that is NOT preceded by the words "Simon Says."

Suggested actions:

Nod your head	Jump on one leg
Wiggle your fingers	Shake your head
Jump up	Digest your food
Shake your left leg	Make your heart beat
Shake your right leg	Be happy
Stick your tongue out	Be sad
Stand on one leg	

Thank your volunteer and ask him/her to sit down.

Explain:

We just saw Bob [insert name of volunteer] use his brain and his body all at the same time – well done Bob!

Let's think a bit about how that worked;

I gave a command to Bob, which went in through his ears and reached his brain, where he made a decision to follow my command.

His brain then sent an impulse to the body part in question and he jumped, shook his head or whatever. So his brain was controlling his body and made it work.

What happened when I asked him to digest his food?

Probably not very much; we can't make our body digest food or our hearts beat, it happens automatically.

And what happened when I told him to be happy, or to be sad?

Well, he might have made a face, looking like he was sad or happy – but was he really?

We can't switch our emotions on and off just like that. We have no control over them. They just happen, a bit like digesting or breathing.

⊙ DVD CHAPTER 2

Play Session 8, chapter 2 – 'Focus On God's Truth' – of the accompanying DVD.

Now go straight into the overview.

OVERVIEW
Just as the clips says; the good news is that God doesn't expect us to just change how we react to things at the snap of a finger. We do what God wants by changing what we can control: what we believe and how we behave.

1. WHAT ARE MY EMOTIONS?

Ask the group:

• What makes you mad?

• What makes you happy?

• What makes you cry?

Your emotions are like signals, announcing when things are right and good and also warning us when something is wrong.

They tell you when something needs dealing with in your life. You might think it would be great if you never felt depressed, or anxious or angry. No it wouldn't.

These emotions tell us if something is wrong. People with leprosy cannot feel pain – again you might think 'great' – but actually what happens is that sufferers really damage their bodies because they cannot feel that something bad is happening to them. If they were sitting too close to a fire, they wouldn't feel it.

2. LEARNING TO HANDLE EMOTIONS WELL

Ask:

• What do you do when you get mad?

• What do you do when you get a laughing fit at the wrong time?

• What do you do when someone says something hurtful to you?

There are basically three ways that you can respond when you feel a negative emotion:

• you could try to forget about it or cover it up

• you could let it all out at once in a big explosion

• you could admit that there's something wrong and be honest about your feelings

The first option, to cover it up, will only hurt yourself. In fact, some people even get physically ill when they do this.

The second one, letting it all out in a big explosion is not healthy for the people around you.

The best way is the third way - to be honest about them, first of all to God. He's your closest friend and big enough to be able to deal with your emotions! He already knows how you're feeling anyway. God wants to hear how we are doing and he will with any way that we are feeling.

3. OUR FEELINGS DON'T HAVE TO CONTROL US

Ask:

• Do we have a choice in how we react?

• How else could we react?

We have a choice how we react in situations. Sometimes we can think we don't have a choice.

For example, if anyone says something hurtful and we feel angry, we don't have to retaliate. We have control over what we believe and how we behave and actually what we believe and how we behave will then affect our feelings.

4. FOLLOWING FEELINGS MAKES US VULNERABLE TO ATTACK
Ask:

• What happens if we let our feelings control our actions?

If you decide to follow your feelings, rather than what God says is true, Satan will have an easy job fooling you.

You'll probably agree with him when he tells you that you're a 'worthless excuse for a Christian' even though God clearly says in the Bible that you are a forgiven and accepted child of God.

If we don't spot that some emotions are based on lies, we can allow the enemy to get a foothold in our lives; an entrance point for him to influence us.

5. CHANGING HOW WE FEEL
If we feel overwhelmed by negative emotions, what can we do about it?

Well, let's look at a situation in the Bible which seemed overwhelming at the start: Israel v the Philistines (1 Samuel 17).

The Philistines were trying to save themselves from a bloodbath by sending a giant – Goliath – to challenge Israel. The Israelite army freaked out – because they didn't have any giants!

Then David came along, pulled out his slingshot, said:

'How dare you challenge the armies of the living God?' and killed Goliath.

Both David and the Israelite army faced the same giant.

The army compared the giant to themselves, and were scared.

David compared the giant to God, and knew he couldn't lose.

Can faith in God make that kind of difference in our lives?

Absolutely!

And it's not blind faith - it's recognising what is actually true.

Often we have learned from past events to feel helpless and hopeless.

As a Christian that is not true.

It is a bit like the software on a computer.

Instead of letting past events program you to feel negative in a situation, you can change the software.

The Bible calls this renewing your mind; understanding what is really true about God; committing yourself to believe that what God says is true, even if it doesn't feel true.

◉ DVD CHAPTER 3

Play Session 8, chapter 3 – 'Be Real' – of the accompanying DVD.

You are not affected so much by what's around you, as by how you see or interpret what's around you.

Discussion

- Do you agree that it's not the stuff around you that affects how you feel, but the way you see or interpret that stuff?

- If you sometimes feel overwhelmed by negative emotions, how can you begin to try and look at your situation in a way that reflects what's actually true?

Bring all the groups back together.

RESPONSE

Give out postcards or blank cards.

Read Psalm 109:6-15 – David pouring his heart out to God about how he feels about someone.

Explain:

One of the biggest lessons we have learned today is about being honest with God about how we feel.

So as a response we are going to write a postcard to God about how we feel about a particular situation or just how life is going at the moment.

Finish by praying something like this:

Father God, we thank you that you want us to have joy instead of sadness, love instead of anger and peace instead of anxiety. Thank you that as your children we can know the truth of who we are and handle our emotions well. Amen.

SMALL GROUPS & PRAYER FOCUS

When you experience a strong negative emotion, do you tend to cover it up, explode or be honest about it?

Read Psalm 109:6-15 again. Does it surprise you that something like that is in the Bible? Have you ever felt like David? Have you ever prayed like that? Would it be right to pray that way?

Is there anything that you feel you can't say to God that he doesn't already know? How does God feel about your emotions? How does he feel about honesty?

AND THERE'S MORE!

Draw your group's attention to the key verses (1 Peter 5:7-8) printed on page 34 of their Youth Guide 11-14 and then to the Challenge section on page 35 which says:

'This week be really truthful with God. After all he already knows what you are thinking. Tell him exactly how you are feeling and thinking, even if it seems bad but ask him to help you handle your emotions the way he wants.'

Encourage them to do that in order to stop the enemy using their emotions to take advantage of them.

? CLOSING QUESTION

Look at the question for next week (on page 37 of the Youth Guide 11-14):

'Think of the worst thing anyone ever did to you. Why should you forgive that person? Can you think of any good reasons why you shouldn't forgive someone?'

Assure them that they won't be asked next week to tell anyone what the 'worst thing' is but that we will be looking at how God wants to set them free from it.

HANDLING OUR EMOTIONS 15-18

LEADER'S PREPARATION

Pray together:

❝ Father God, I thank you for giving us emotions, both good ones to enjoy and bad ones to show us there's a problem. Help everyone in the group hear from you today. Amen.

YOU MAY NEED
Accompanying DVD / DVD player / TV / projector

Coloured strips of fabric/tissue paper

Postcards or pieces of plain card

Pens

CD player and worship CD/worship leader

Bibles

PRAYER AND DECLARATION

Encourage everyone to join together in saying the following prayer and declaration. You can download the PowerPoint slides with the words for these from the website.

It would be good to suggest that the young people stand up and speak out the declaration clearly and confidently to the heavenly realms. They could shout it out and use appropriate actions!

PRAYER:

❝ Father, thank you for giving me emotions, both good ones to enjoy and bad ones to show when there's a problem. Help me to understand how they can help me in my day-to-day experiences. Please help all of us to hear from your Holy Spirit today and act on his advice. In Jesus' name, Amen.

DECLARATION:

❝ I am Jesus' friend. Enemies of the Lord Jesus are not welcome here. It doesn't matter whether I shout it out or just whisper it; I can banish any enemy of God's. I have authority as a child of Jesus. So leave now, in Jesus' name.

🔍 STARTING POINT

During the welcome drinks, find out how everyone's week has gone. Ask them how they are feeling and what has caused them to feel that way. Try to get some balance of emotions. Ask them if they kept a list of the different emotions they experienced - see whose list has the most different emotions on it.

Give a short summary of the previous session. A good resource for this is the Overview found in the Core of the previous session.

◎ DVD CHAPTER 1

Play Session 8, chapter 1 – 'Feelings' – of the accompanying DVD.

Ask the group:

How do you handle your feelings?

Actually the Bible teaches that everything about us was created by God.

- Our physical appearance

- Our heart

- Our ability to dream

All God-given.

That means that our emotions were created by God too.

God understands that there will be days where we are laughing and days when we are crying. Ecclesiastes 3:1a, 4, says; 'There is a time for everything...a time to weep and a time to laugh, a time to mourn and a time to dance...'

That's life.

⌂ SOAPBOX

If suitable share a personal story, it can make us vulnerable when we share about our own emotions so only share what you feel comfortable with and willing for others to know.

WHAT ARE MY EMOTIONS?
Your emotions are to your soul, what your ability to feel pain is to your body.

Imagine that someone offered to take away all your physical pain for life. Would you accept the offer?

It might sound great to begin with, especially if you have a sore back, regular head aches or something like that. But, it would be dangerous!

You wouldn't feel any pain if you stepped on a nail, or sat too close to a fire. Without pain, you'd be a hopeless mass of scars within a matter of weeks. God gave us pain for our own protection – it's a gift.

Our emotions are the same. They tell us what is going on inside. For example if you are feeling down it might be because you are convinced that you really aren't worth much and you might begin to behave accordingly.

⊚ DVD CHAPTER 2

Play Session 8, chapter 2 – 'Focus On God's Truth' – of the accompanying DVD.

Ask another leader to start talking about Jeremiah in Lamentations 3 and what he went through. Encourage them not just to repeat what the DVD said but to draw out the points it made about how Jeremiah was feeling and what he was going through.

If you are 'feeling' down about yourself, the way to change those feelings is to look at what you are believing. Is it actually right (based on what is really true) or is it driven just by your circumstances?

Ask the group to close their eyes and be quiet. Allow some time for the group to settle then ask them to answer these questions:

• Do you think God has abandoned you or that his promises apply to everyone else but somehow don't apply to you?

• Do you think that you are hopeless, that you will never amount to anything?

Ask them to open their eyes and then say:

'Please believe that it is not true - I encourage you to change that belief! God has not abandoned you. All his promises apply to you. You are not hopeless and you are already very important. I know that because the Bible says it very clearly and it is the truth.' (Try to make eye contact with every young person in the room as you say this. If necessary say it a few times).

Or

Write out that response ('Please believe that it is not true...') and in pairs get them to read it out to each other giving as much eye contact as possible.

Leaders note: This is a sensitive subject and might make emotion rise to the surface in some members of the group. You might need to conclude with a prayer or allow a minute before moving on.

Realising those truths is great but sometimes you may be facing some terrible circumstances. We're not saying "Just snap out of it".

What we are saying is, don't let those circumstances rob you of the great truths that have not changed. You are a child of God. He is for you. He has a great plan for you that is much bigger than those circumstances. He has got stuff for you to do. Despite everything, you can become the person he wants you to be. You can be a disciple of Jesus. No matter what the current situation, ultimately it will not be able to hold you back from those things.

The main thing is to concentrate on making sure you are believing what is true. It's not about making stuff up, it's about reminding yourself what is true anyway and choosing – maybe through gritted teeth at first – to believe it.

You start with what God says in his Word.

Your feelings won't change instantly. You can't just switch them on and off. However, you can control what you choose to believe. And your feelings will change over time as you commit yourself to what is true.

But if you start with your feelings, they will lead you all over the place.

 WORSHIP ACTIVITY

Gather together lots of different strips of fabric, make them about 5 cm by 80-100 cm (2 inches wide by 3 to 4 feet long). Make sure you have lots of different colours, and enough for each young person to be able to choose a couple. You could potentially use tissue paper (and sticky tape) instead of fabric, if that's easier to get hold of.

Say something like:

As we're coming to worship God, I'd like you to think about how you're feeling right now.

Look at the strips of fabric.

Can you see any colours that represent how you feel?

Pick out a couple of strips of fabrics that represent how you feel.

We are going to bring our emotions – whether good or bad – into our worship today.

Have the young people explain why they've chosen the colours they've chosen.

Then pray a simple prayer committing the whole group to God, however they're feeling.

Encourage the young people to hold their strips of fabric in open hands while they pray.

Play a CD of, or sing one or two of your group's favourite worship songs.

LEARNING TO HANDLE EMOTIONS WELL
Refer the young people to page 34 of the Youth Guide 15-18 and read through the What's The Point section which has the following three bulletpoints:

- Our emotions were created by God and show the deep parts of our character and whether our thoughts line up with the truth in God's Word.

- Be honest with God. He is your closest friend. He can handle any of your emotions and loves you as his child.

- Don't act on how you feel but act on what God says is true.

Your emotions are like when your computer or iPod tells you there is a problem. The error message that comes up is there to let you know that there's a potentially serious problem inside the metal casing. If you don't stop to fix the problem, sooner or later you can expect some big trouble.

There are three ways that you can react when the error message appears:

- You could take a piece of tape and put it over the message and think, 'no problem, the message has gone!'

- You could explode in anger, take a hammer and smash the screen– at least it fixes the pressing issue of the message being there.

- You could admit that there is a problem and try and fix it.

You can deal with your emotions in much the same way.

Divide your young people into groups and hand out the Handling Our Emotions sheet (in the downloadable material for this session). If suitable ask the groups to illustrate creatively the three responses to emotions when they come back together to share their thoughts. Here are the topics covered:

Responses we can make to our emotions

- Cover it up

- Explode

- Be honest

Handling past traumas

Changing how we feel

DISCUSSION

Bring the groups back together and discuss their findings. Use these questions to help:

- When you experience a strong negative emotion, do you tend to cover it up, explode or be honest about it?

- Read Psalm 109:6-15. Does it surprise you that something like that is in the Bible? Have you ever felt like David? Have you ever prayed like that? Would it be right to pray that way?

- Is there anything that you feel that you can't say to God that he doesn't already know? How does God feel about your emotions? How does he feel about honesty?

⊚ DVD CHAPTER 3

Play Session 8, chapter 3 – 'Be Real' – of the accompanying DVD.

Explain: you are not affected so much by what's around you, as by how you see or interpret what's around you.

Faith in God can really make a difference in our lives – it means recognising what's true. When we do that – when we understand what's really true rather than believe what our experiences and other people have made us believe – we are 'renewing our mind', as the Bible calls it. You're deciding to believe what's true, even when you don't feel like it.

Again, if what we believe does not reflect the truth, then what we feel does not reflect reality.

- What do you think?

- Do you agree that it's not the stuff around you that affects how you feel, but the way you see or interpret that stuff?

- If you sometimes feel overwhelmed by negative emotions, how can you start to look at your situation in a way that reflects what's actually true?

↗ RESPONSE

Give out postcards or pieces of card.

Read Psalm 109:6-15 – David pouring his heart out to God about how he feels about someone.

Explain:

One of the biggest lessons we have learned today is about being honest with God about how we feel. So, as a response, we are going to write a postcard to God about how we feel about a particular situation or just how life is going at the moment.

Finish by praying something like this:

Father God, we thank you that you want us to have joy instead of sadness, love instead of anger and peace instead of anxiety. Thank you that as your children we can know the truth of who we are and handle our emotions well. Amen.

⭐ AND THERE'S MORE!

Draw the group's attention to page 36 of the Youth Guide 15-18 and encourage them to consider the questions at home:

- Our emotions are reactions to the way we see the world around us but what if the way we perceive things is wrong?

- Sometimes emotions feel like they control us but how can we change our emotions over time?

- If we always follow our feelings, will our lives show the freedom Jesus gives us? Why? Why not?

- Although useful, we can't trust emotions to be right. What can we trust as truth to base our lives on?

-

❓ CLOSING QUESTION

Ask the group to consider the question on page 37 of the Youth Guide 15-18 before next week:

'Think of the worst thing anyone ever did to you. Why should you forgive that person? Can you think of any good reasons why you shouldn't forgive someone?'

Assure them that they won't be asked next week to tell anyone what the 'worst thing' is but that we will be looking at how God wants to set them free from it.

HANDLING OUR EMOTIONS
GROUP DISCUSSION SHEET

This sheet can be downloaded from the website so you can easily print it off.

RESPONSES WE CAN MAKE TO OUR EMOTIONS

Cover it up

- How might we cover up our emotions?

Listen to how King David felt when he lived in denial:

'When I kept silent, my bones wasted away through my groaning all day long...' (Psalm 32:3).

If we bottle up our feelings for too long, they will take over our lives and can even affect our bodies by making us ill.

Explode

- What makes you mad?

- Do you have immediate responses to things?

- Is this healthy, for us or for those around us?

James 1:19 and 20 says this:

'Everyone should be quick to listen, slow to speak and slow to become angry, because our anger does not produce the righteousness that God desires.' (TNIV)

Be honest

- So what should we do when the 'error message' comes up, when we feel angry, anxious or depressed?

The healthy way to handle our emotions is to be honest and admit how we feel.

It starts by admitting our feelings to God. God already knows your thoughts and emotions, so you might as well tell him how you feel! He's big enough to deal with an outburst or a tantrum from us now and then. He is our closest friend.

Jesus was honest with his emotions; he admitted his grief at the death of Lazarus (John 11:33-35), and he talked about his sorrow in Gethsemane (Mark 26:36-39).

- If the Lord of the universe needs to be expressive and honest like that, what about you and me?

HANDLING PAST TRAUMAS
We've been talking about how to handle day-to-day emotions, but what about major traumas from the past?

Some of us carry around emotional baggage, traumatic experiences that have scarred us emotionally.

It could be some form of abuse, a frightening experience or the death of someone we loved. It keeps affecting us negatively a long time afterwards, by making us angry or scared or depressed.

God doesn't want emotional pain from our past to affect us today. Forgiving people is really important here and we're looking at that next week.

Often, traumatic experiences make you believe lies about God and yourself. If you are bullied and told that you are rubbish, perhaps you start believing it. If you thought that God wasn't there for you, then maybe you start to question his love for you.

This becomes a stronghold in your mind (remember we talked about those a couple of weeks ago?) that distorts your understanding of who you are and who God is.

But since you are a child of God, who you are is not decided by your past but by Christ's past - by his work on the cross and his resurrection. Nobody can change our past, but we can be free from its negative control over us by knowing the truth of who we are in Christ.

CHANGING HOW WE FEEL

- If we feel overwhelmed by negative emotions, what can we do about it?

Let's look at a situation in the Bible which seemed overwhelming: Israel v the Philistines (you can read the whole story in 1 Samuel 17).

The Philistines were trying to save themselves from a bloodbath by sending a giant – Goliath – to challenge Israel. The Israelite army freaked out – because they didn't have any giants and didn't see how they could possibly beat him!

Then David, probably a young teenager, came along, pulled out his slingshot, said: 'How dare you challenge the armies of the living God?' and killed Goliath.

Both David and the Israelite army faced the same giant. The army compared the giant to themselves, and were scared. David compared the giant to God, and knew he couldn't lose.

- Which of them, David or the Israelite army, looked at the situation as it really was?

- Can seeing a situation differently really make that much difference?

SESSION NINE:
FORGIVENESS

'In anger his master turned him over to the jailers to be tortured, until he should pay back all he owed. This is how my heavenly Father will treat each of you unless you forgive your brother from your heart.'

Matthew 18:34-35

FORGIVENESS CORE

INTRODUCTION

Do you know what it is that gives Satan the greatest opportunity to defeat Christians? Cults, sex, drugs? No, in our experience it's all about forgiveness.

One of the main reasons why some Christians don't grow very much is because they don't understand why forgiving others is crucial to their own freedom. They only have a hazy idea of what forgiveness really is. Sometimes they believe wrongly that what has been done to them is so bad that they can't forgive the person who did it.

The truth is that nothing will stop you moving on more than not forgiving someone who has hurt you. An easy way for Satan to stop you from growing is to make you believe that you shouldn't forgive.

Helping your young people understand the truths in this session will benefit them hugely for the rest of their lives.

WHY FORGIVE?

Think of the worst thing anyone has ever done to you. Why should you forgive them for that? That's a very good question! Let's look at the reasons:

- It's required by God

In Matthew 6:9-15, Jesus gave us what we refer to as 'The Lord's Prayer'. In it is this little phrase: "Forgive us our debts, as we also have forgiven our debtors". When you pray that, if you have not forgiven those who owe you something, you might not be asking God for very much!

He then makes it even more explicit and says (verses 14-15), "For if you forgive men when they sin against you, your heavenly Father will also forgive you. But if you do not forgive men their sins, your Father will not forgive your sins."

Your relationship with God is inextricably bound up with your relationship with other people. You really can't have a righteous relationship with God in isolation from your relationships with other people.

We need to be careful not to apply this wrongly. Because you are in Christ, your sins are forgiven and you are going to heaven. What is at stake, however, is your daily relationship with God. If there are people that you have not forgiven, God won't let you be comfortable and you won't have freedom until you do!

We think that forgiveness is an issue between us and the person who hurt us. Here, however, Jesus makes it an issue between him and us.

- It's essential for our freedom

The clearest teaching on forgiveness that Jesus gave is in Matthew 18:21-35. It's the story of a servant who owed his master an unimaginably large amount of money (millions in today's terms). There was no way he could ever pay it back. His kind master simply let him off the debt. However, the servant himself was owed some money - about 3 months' wages - by someone else. Rather than following his master's example and forgiving the debt, he insisted on being repaid, even to the point of having the other person thrown into prison. When the master caught up with what had happened, he was understandably furious with the servant and "turned him over to the jailers to be tortured, until he should pay back all he owed" (verse 34).

Elsewhere in the New Testament, the word used here for 'torture' refers to spiritual torment.

Jesus finishes the story by saying (verse 35), "This is how my heavenly Father will treat each of you unless you forgive your brother from your heart."

Jesus warns that, if you do not forgive from your heart, you will suffer some kind of spiritual torment. In other words, you are opening a door to the enemy's influence in your life.

We see the same principle in 2 Corinthians 2:10-11 where Paul says that we forgive "in order that Satan might not outwit us".

Not to forgive someone is to leave a door open to Satan. All that anger and bitterness gives him plenty of space to make a foothold, a place for himself in our lives.

- Because we now understand justice, mercy and grace

Let's think about how God relates to us. He is just and cannot be unjust or unrighteous. Justice means simply giving people what they deserve. If he exercised justice and gave us what we deserve, we would all go to hell.

But God is also merciful and he found a way to forgive and accept us - through Christ's death. Mercy is not giving people what they deserve. We are told to be merciful to others as God has been merciful to us (Luke 6:36). In other words, we are not to give people what they deserve.

But God has gone much further than that. He has given us abundant life, his Spirit, hope and a future, every spiritual blessing.... and much more! He has given us what we don't deserve - and that is what grace is. We too are to go even further in our relationships, to love one another and give people what they don't deserve.

To sum up:

> Justice = giving people what they deserve
>
> Mercy = not giving people what they deserve
>
> Grace = giving people what they don't deserve

It all begins with the relationship that God has established with us: freely you have received, freely give (Matthew 10:8). We are to relate to other people in exactly the same way that God relates to us.

- To stop the pain

Imagine that you walk past a fisherman and you accidentally get snagged by a fish hook in your cheek. What do you do? Well, it wasn't your fault. Should you get so angry with the fisherman that you refuse to take the hook out? That would be ridiculous! You're stuck to another person and it hurts. Why wouldn't you want to take it out?

This is how we act sometimes though. We think that if we forgive someone, we let **them** off the hook, but in fact; by not forgiving them **we** stay hooked to the pain and the past. We're the ones with the hook in us!

WHAT IS FORGIVENESS?
It's really important that we understand what forgiveness is - and what it is not.

- It's from the heart

Forgiving from the heart isn't a simple 'I forgive so and so' mumbled under our breath. You need to put all the pain on the table before God, remember every hurt, in order to truly forgive. It's simply being honest with God. We suggest the following prayer:

'Lord, I choose to forgive _____ (name the person) for _____ (specifically what they did or failed to do), which made me feel _____ (tell the Lord every hurt and pain he brings to mind).'

- It's not forgetting

God doesn't forget our sins – how could he if he is all-knowing? – but he chooses not to not bring them up and use them against us.

If someone says to you, "I've forgiven you... but two years ago you did this", do you know what they have actually said? "I haven't forgiven you. I am still taking the past and using it against you." So part of the choice we make when we forgive is to say, "I am going to let that go. I am not going to bring up the past and use it against you ever again."

You can't get rid of a hurt simply by trying to forget it.

- Not putting up with sin

God forgives, but he doesn't put up with sin. If someone is beating you up, although it's hard, you should forgive him. But this doesn't mean that you shouldn't call the police, since what he's doing is wrong and illegal.

And forgiving certainly doesn't mean that you let the person do it again. You can forgive but at the same time put a stop to abuse by removing yourself from the situation or calling in the appropriate authority.

- Not seeking revenge

When we have been wronged, we want revenge. That's understandable. But what does God say?

"Don't insist on getting even; that's not for you to do. 'I'll do the judging,' says God. 'I'll take care of it.'" (Romans 12:19).

One day, the person who did that awful thing to you will come face to face with God. He is called "the righteous judge" and he will demand payment for the wrong that was done. He will do the getting even. They will have some explaining to do.

You see, when you forgive, although you are letting the person off your hook, you are not letting them off God's hook. When you choose to forgive, you are not saying 'It didn't matter' but you are choosing to hand it over to God and let him deal with it in his perfect wisdom.

CONCLUSION

Forgiveness is to set a prisoner free and then realise that you were the prisoner! It's primarily an issue between you and God. God loves you and wants you to be free from the past, that's why he commands you to forgive. It's got very little to do with the person that hurt you.

Forgiveness is for our own benefit. It is not about who was right or wrong but about clearing the rubbish out of our lives and leaving it there.

QUESTIONS TO THINK ABOUT AS YOU PREPARE

1. Would you say that you have been forgiven a little or a lot by God?

2. Do you ever think that your sins aren't as 'bad' as others' sins?

3. Do you think it's necessary to remember hurts from the past in order to truly forgive?

4. Who continues to suffer when there's no forgiveness?

5. Has what you have seen so far changed what you think about forgiveness?

6. Next time someone offends or hurts you, will you be quicker to forgive? Why / why not?

FORGIVENESS 11-14

LEADER'S PREPARATION

Pray together:

❝ Father, I thank you that you have forgiven me and adopted me as your child. Help all of us in the group to forgive other people and therefore find true freedom. Amen.

YOU MAY NEED

Large mixing bowls with flour

Two bags of Maltesers

List of treasure hunt items to collect

Bible verses for worship activity

Accompanying DVD / DVD player / TV / projector

Medium-sized stones/marbles

Bibles

Small group questions

 PRAYER AND DECLARATION

Encourage everyone to join together in saying the following prayer and declaration. You can download the PowerPoint slides with the words for these from the website.

It would be good to suggest that the young people stand up and speak out the declaration clearly and confidently to the heavenly realms. They could shout it out and use appropriate actions!

PRAYER

❝ Thank you Father that you have forgiven me and that I am now adopted as your child. Please help me and others here understand what it is to forgive and find true freedom. Amen.

DECLARATION: IN A CLEAR, CONFIDENT TONE!

❝ Jesus has forgiven all my sins, I am not guilty. I don't have to listen to the enemy's lies and distractions. I have authority in Christ and am able to instruct any evil to go from this place in his name, so leave now!

STARTING POINT

Start by giving a short summary of the previous session. A good resource for this is the Overview found in the Core of the previous session.

INTRODUCTORY ACTIVITIES

MALTESER FISHING
Get two large mixing bowls and put an equal amount of Maltesers in a layer of flour at the bottom of each.

Split the group into two teams and get the players one at a time to come up and 'fish' for a Malteser from the flour using only their mouths.

The winning team is the first to fish all the Maltesers out of their bowl.

PAIRS TREASURE HUNT
Organise a simple treasure hunt.

Give the young people a list of about 10 items that they need to collect (eg. a pen, a scarf, a spoon etc, adapt for your venue).

Divide the group into pairs, providing string for them to tie their arms and legs together (so that they are joined together side by side).

They must hunt as a pair and not separate at any point.

The winner is the pair who have found all the things on the list.

DVD CHAPTER 1

Play Session 9, chapter 1 – 'Forgive?' – of the accompanying DVD.

Explain:

Sometimes it's a bit tricky to get to where we want to go when we're stuck to another person. It's like that if we don't forgive someone. We remain stuck to them.

WORSHIP ACTIVITY

Worship God for his forgiveness, using the Bible verses below.

Print them out several times on slips of paper (there is a downloadable sheet for you to use) and put them in a bowl in the middle of the room.

Give each young person three drawing pins.

Ask the young people to drop a drawing pin into the bowl as a sign that they are letting go of the stuff that hurts them in their lives and take a verse in its place.

Once everyone has three pieces of paper get them to read out the verses one at a time as praise to God.

Verses:

'There is now no condemnation for those who are in Christ Jesus' (Romans 8:1)

'O my soul, bless God, don't forget a single blessing! He forgives your sins—every one. He heals your diseases—every one.' (Psalm 103:3-5 The Message)

'Blessed are those whose transgressions are forgiven, whose sins are covered. Blessed are those whose sin the Lord does not count against them...' (Psalm 32:1-2a)

'The Lord is compassionate and gracious, slow to anger, abounding in love.' (Psalm 103:8)

'In Jesus we have redemption through his blood, the forgiveness of sins, in accordance with the riches of God's grace.' (Ephesians 1:7)

'As far as sunrise is from sunset, he has separated us from our sins.' (Psalm 103:12 The Message)

'If we confess our sins, he is faithful and just and will forgive us our sins and purify us from all unrighteousness' (1 John 1:9)

'For he has rescued us from the dominion of darkness and brought us into the kingdom of the Son he loves, in whom we have redemption, the forgiveness of sins.' (Colossians 1:13-14)

INTRODUCTION

One of the main reasons why some Christians don't grow very much is because they don't forgive someone who has hurt them.

We'll talk today about why we should forgive and what forgiveness really is.

Before you start speaking, hand out slips of paper with the following Bible verses on. Give them to people who are confident readers, and ask them to find the place in the Bible now and put their slip of paper there to mark the place.

- Matthew 6:14-15

- Matthew 18:32-35

- Luke 6:36

- 2 Corinthians 2:10-11

- Romans 12:19

Do you know what it is that gives Satan the greatest opportunity to defeat Christians? Cults, sex, drugs?

No, it's all about forgiveness.

There's nothing that stops you from moving on more than not forgiving someone who has hurt you. Satan's best way to stop you from growing is to make you believe that you shouldn't forgive.

⊙ DVD CHAPTER 2

Play Session 9, chapter 2 – 'Christ Forgave' – of the accompanying DVD.

Ask the group:

Why do they believe you should forgive?

WHY FORGIVE?

Remember the question you took away from last week's session; think of the worst thing anyone has ever done to you – but don't say it out loud! [Pause]

Why should you forgive that? Let's look at the reasons:

• It's required by God

Get the person with Matthew 6:14-15 to stand up and read the passage.

This doesn't mean that you're going to hell just because you don't forgive someone, but it means that you won't be comfortable and you won't have freedom until you do!

• It's essential for our freedom

In Matthew 18:21-35 Jesus told the story of a servant who owed his master an unimaginably large amount of money (millions in today's terms). There was no way he could ever pay it back. His kind master simply let him off the debt. However, the servant himself was owed some money - about 3 months' wages - by someone else. Rather than following his master's example and forgiving the debt, he insisted on being repaid, even to the point of having the other person thrown into prison. When the master caught up with what had happened, he was furious! This is what happened next.

Get the person with Matthew 18:32-35 to stand up and read the passage.

Jesus warns that, if you do not forgive from your heart, it's as if you have been turned over to the torturers. You will suffer some kind of spiritual torment. In other words, you are opening a door to the enemy's influence in your life.

• Because of our own debt

It would be clear to anyone listening to that story that the first servant ought to have forgiven the second one. It seems absurd to be forgiven so much and then go around nit-picking at others.

It's exactly the same for us. We are called to extend the mercy that we have found in God to the people around us.

Get the person with Luke 6:36 to stand up and read the passage.

Mercy is not giving people what they deserve. That's the least asked of us. What God shows us is grace; giving people what they don't deserve.

• Not to give Satan an opportunity

Get the person with 2 Corinthians 2:10-11 to stand up and read the passage.

Not to forgive someone is to leave a door open to Satan. All that anger and bitterness gives him plenty of space to make a place for himself in our lives.

- To stop the pain

Imagine that you walk past a fisherman and you accidentally get snagged by a fishhook in your cheek. What do you do? Well, it wasn't your fault. Should you get so angry with the fisherman that you refuse to take the hook out?! That would be ridiculous! You're stuck to another person and it hurts, why wouldn't you want to take it out?

This is how we act sometimes though. We can think that if we forgive someone we let them off the hook, but in fact by not forgiving them we stay hooked to the pain and the past. We're the ones with the hook in us!

◎ DVD CHAPTER 3

Play Session 9, chapter 3 – 'Forgiving To Be Free' – of the accompanying DVD.

Now go straight into the overview.

OVERVIEW – WHAT IS FORGIVENESS?

Start with a brief activity: 'Not Really Sorry '

Sit the young people in a circle.

Have each player in turn roll one die.

When someone rolls a six, he should take a piece of charcoal or a lipstick and make a mark on the face of a player of his choice.

After he has done this, he should say 'sorry', but he doesn't have to sound like he means it!

If a player does not roll a six, he should simply pass the die to the player on his left.

Have wet wipes to help players remove the marks from their faces at the end of the game.

Forgiveness isn't always easy, particularly if you're not sure the other person is really sorry!

IT'S FROM THE HEART
Forgiving from the heart isn't a simple 'I forgive so and so' mumbled under our breath. You need to put all the pain on the table before God, remember every hurt, in order to truly forgive.

We suggest the following prayer and this is what you will be invited to use when we go through The Steps To Freedom In Christ:

'Dear God, I choose to forgive .... (name the person) for .... (what they said or did that hurt you), which made me feel .... (tell God every hurt and pain he brings to mind).'

IT'S NOT FORGETTING
God doesn't forget our sins – how could he if he knows everything? – but he chooses not to remember them, not to bring them up and use them against us. You can't get rid of a hurt by simply trying to forget it.

IT'S NOT PUTTING UP WITH SIN

God forgives, but he doesn't put up with sin. If your friend is beating you up, although it's hard you should try to forgive him. This doesn't mean that you shouldn't call the police, since what he's doing is wrong and illegal.

Sometimes you might need to tell someone that you think they're doing the wrong thing, or you might need to remove yourself from the situation. This doesn't mean that you don't forgive them.

IT'S NOT SEEKING REVENGE
Get the person with Romans 12:19 to stand up and read the passage.

When you forgive, although you are letting the person off your hook, you are not letting them off God's hook. The situation doesn't necessarily change but you are free.

Forgiveness is to set a prisoner free and then realise that you were the prisoner. It's primarily an issue between you and God. God loves you and wants you to be free from the past. That's why he commands us to forgive. It's got very little to do with the person that hurt you.

Forgiveness is for our own benefit. It is not about who was right or wrong but about clearing the rubbish out of our lives and leaving it there.

 # RESPONSE

Leader's Note: The best place for the young people to do the actual forgiving is during the Steps To Freedom In Christ Away Day/Weekend which should be the next session of the course. However, we don't want to rob them of the opportunity of making a response to what God has said to them in this session if they want to. Select whichever of these alternatives seems appropriate:

Either:

Get together as many bricks or rocks as you have people in your group and hand them out. Ask everyone to stand, holding the brick in their hands

Many of us will have unforgiveness in our hearts, burdening us and stopping us from growing.

We're going to have a moment of silence now. Ask the Holy Spirit to remind you of anyone you need to forgive [leave pause].

If you are ready to make a choice now to forgive those people that God has brought to mind, you can do that now quietly in your own heart using the prayer on page 71 of the Youth Guide 11-14.

Great feeling of freedom, isn't it!

Or:

We're going to have a moment of silence now. Ask the Holy Spirit to remind you of anyone you need to forgive [leave pause].

If you are ready to make a choice to forgive those people when we go through The Steps To Freedom next time, tell God now.

As a symbol of letting go of these people that we have been connected to through unforgiveness, you can now put your brick down on the floor. (Or drop it in a bucket of water.)

Leader's note: you may need a bit of extra time on this bit as there could be all sorts of thoughts and emotions welling up in different members of the group. Allow space for tears and make sure there are enough leaders around if anyone needs added support or care.

Closing prayer:

Lord, thank you that you have heard the cries of our hearts today and that you have enabled us to make a choice to forgive people for what they have done to us. As we drop these bricks down we thank you that this is the end of these issues and we can know true forgiveness in You, Amen.

SMALL GROUPS & PRAYER FOCUS

1. Would you say that you have been forgiven a little or a lot by God?

2. Do you ever think that your sins aren't as 'bad' as other people's?

3. Do you think it's necessary to remember hurts from the past in order to truly forgive?

4. Who continues to suffer when there's no forgiveness; the person who has hurt someone or the person who has been hurt?

5. Has this session changed what you think about forgiveness or not?

6. Next time someone offends or hurts you, will you be quicker to forgive? Why / why not?

AND THERE'S MORE!

Refer the young people to the questions in their Youth Guide 11-14 on page 40:

*   Why does God say we should forgive people?

*   Why is forgiveness so important for our own freedom?

*   Who will unforgiveness damage more; the person who caused the pain or the person who feels the pain? Why?

*   If God forgave you everything, should there be anything you cannot forgive someone else?

Suggest that they take some time in the next day or two to fill in their answers.

? CLOSING QUESTION

There is a question to think about before next week on page 41 of the Youth Guide 11-14:

'Have you grown as a Christian as quickly as you wanted? If not, what do you think is in the way?'

FORGIVENESS 15-18

LEADER'S PREPARATION

Pray together:

> Father, I thank you that you have forgiven me and adopted me as your child. Help all of us in the group to forgive other people and therefore find true freedom. Amen.

YOU MAY NEED
Accompanying DVD / DVD player / TV / projector

Bricks/rocks

Bucket of water

Bowl

Bible verses printed out on strips of paper

Drawing pins

Bibles

PRAYER AND DECLARATION

Encourage everyone to join together in saying the following prayer and declaration. You can download the PowerPoint slides with the words for these from the website.

It would be good to suggest that the young people stand up and speak out the declaration clearly and confidently to the heavenly realms. They could shout it out and use appropriate actions!

PRAYER

> Thank you Father that you have forgiven me and that I am now adopted as your child. Please help me and others here understand what it is to forgive and find true freedom. Amen.

DECLARATION: IN A CLEAR, CONFIDENT TONE!

> Jesus has forgiven all my sins, I am not guilty. I don't have to listen to the enemy's lies and distractions. I have authority in Christ and am able to instruct any evil to go from this place in his name, so leave now!

STARTING POINT

Start by giving a short summary of the previous session. A good resource for this is the Overview found in the Core of the previous session.

Before you start speaking, hand out slips of paper with the following Bible verses on. Give them to people who are confident readers, and ask them to find the place in the Bible now and put their slip of paper there to mark the place.

- Matthew 6:14-15

- Matthew 18:32-35

- Luke 6:36

- 2 Corinthians 2:10-11

- Romans 12:19

⊙ DVD CHAPTER 1

Play Session 9, chapter 1 – 'Forgive?' – of the accompanying DVD.

Explain:

Imagine being tied to someone else all the time or being a Siamese twin. It's a bit tricky to get to where we want to go when we're stuck to another person. That's exactly what it's like when we don't forgive someone. We remain stuck to them and we find it hard to get to where we want to go.

⊙ DVD CHAPTER 2

Play Session 9, chapter 2 – 'Christ Forgave' – of the accompanying DVD.

⌂ SOAPBOX

Share a personal story similar to the one in the DVD where you have been hurt.

Ask the group:

- What is your reaction when you get hurt?

- What do we look for from those who hurt us?

- What does Jesus suggest?

- Does he do more than suggest?

- What example does he set?

Ask then what they think of this statement:

'All he's asking you to do is forgive as you have been forgiven. To put your relationship with that other person on the same basis he has put his relationship with you.'

GETTING REAL

'That's all very well' we say, 'but I can't just shrug off what they did and say it didn't matter.'

No, you can't. It did matter. It was nasty. It was wrong. And it's as well to be honest and say that. God doesn't ask us to do mind over matter stuff, to pretend it was OK when it wasn't.

Forgiveness isn't about forgetting what has happened. It is actually about being honest with God about what happened, who did it and how it made you feel.

Ask the group: have you ever wanted want revenge?

Here's the key point of forgiveness that very many people miss. Read Romans 12:19:

"Don't insist on getting even; that's not for you to do. 'I'll do the judging,' says God. 'I'll take care of it.'"

One day, the person who did that awful thing to you will come face to face with God. He is called "the righteous judge" and he will demand payment for the wrong that was done. He will do the getting even. They will have some explaining to do.

All God is saying to you is "Look, I have a perfectly clear view of what happened. The rights and wrongs. Will you trust me with it, knowing that I will take care of it, that I will make everything right in the end?"

WHY FORGIVE?

Leader's Note: try asking some young people to lead this next part of the session, invite them out for a coffee or round for dinner and help them decide how best to share this part with the group.

WHY FORGIVE?

Remember the question you took away from last week's session; think of the worst thing anyone has ever done to you – but don't say it out loud! [Pause]

Why should you forgive that? Let's look at the reasons:

• It's required by God

Get the person with Matthew 6:14-15 to stand up and read the passage.

This doesn't mean that you're going to hell just because you don't forgive someone, but it means that you won't be comfortable and you won't have freedom until you do!

• It's essential for our freedom

In Matthew 18:21-35 Jesus told the story of a servant who owed his master an unimaginably large amount of money (millions in today's terms). There was no way he could ever pay it back. His kind master simply let him off the debt. However, the servant himself was owed some money - about 3 months' wages - by someone else. Rather than following his master's example and forgiving the debt, he insisted on being repaid, even to the point of having the other person thrown into prison. When the master caught up with what had happened, he was furious! This is what happened next.

Get the person with Matthew 18:32-35 to stand up and read the passage.

Jesus warns that, if you do not forgive from your heart, it's as if you have been turned over to the torturers. You will suffer some kind of spiritual torment. In other words, you are opening a door to the enemy's influence in your life.

• Because of our own debt

It would be clear to anyone listening to that story that the first servant ought to have forgiven the second one. It seems absurd to be forgiven so much and then go around nit-picking at others.

It's exactly the same for us. We are called to extend the mercy that we have found in God to the people around us.

Get the person with Luke 6:36 to stand up and read the passage.

Mercy is not giving people what they deserve. That's the least asked of us. What God shows us is grace; giving people what they don't deserve.

- Not to give Satan an opportunity

Get the person with 2 Corinthians 2:10-11 to stand up and read the passage.

Not to forgive someone is to leave a door open to Satan. All that anger and bitterness gives him plenty of space to make a place for himself in our lives.

- To stop the pain

Imagine that you walk past a fisherman and you accidentally get snagged by a fishhook in your cheek. What do you do? Well, it wasn't your fault. Should you get so angry with the fisherman that you refuse to take the hook out?! That would be ridiculous! You're stuck to another person and it hurts, why wouldn't you want to take it out?

This is how we act sometimes though. We can think that if we forgive someone we let them off the hook, but in fact by not forgiving them we stay hooked to the pain and the past. We're the ones with the hook in us!

⬆ WORSHIP ACTIVITY

Worship God for his forgiveness, using the Bible verses below.

Print them out several times on slips of paper (there is a downloadable sheet for you to use) and put them in a bowl in the middle of the room.

Give each young person three drawing pins.

Ask the young people to drop a drawing pin into the bowl as a sign that they are letting go of the stuff that hurts them in their lives and take a verse in its place.

Once everyone has three pieces of paper, get them to read out the verses one at a time as praise to God.

Verses:

'There is now no condemnation for those who are in Christ Jesus' (Romans 8:1)

'O my soul, bless God, don't forget a single blessing! He forgives your sins—every one. He heals your diseases—every one.' (Psalm 103:3-5 The Message)

'Blessed are those whose transgressions are forgiven, whose sins are covered. Blessed are those whose sin the Lord does not count against them...' (Psalm 32:1-2a)

'The Lord is compassionate and gracious, slow to anger, abounding in love.' (Psalm 103:8)

'In Jesus we have redemption through his blood, the forgiveness of sins, in accordance with the riches of God's grace.' (Ephesians 1:7)

'As far as sunrise is from sunset, he has separated us from our sins.' (Psalm 103:12 The Message)

'If we confess our sins, he is faithful and just and will forgive us our sins and purify us from all unrighteousness' (1 John 1:9)

'For he has rescued us from the dominion of darkness and brought us into the kingdom of the Son he loves, in whom we have redemption, the forgiveness of sins.' (Colossians 1:13-14)

WHAT DIFFERENCE DOES IT MAKE?

Ask the young people to turn to page 38 of their Youth Guide 15-18 and read through the bullet points in the 'What's the point?' section which say:

- Forgiveness is about freedom. We forgive so that we can be free from our past.

- When we forgive others we are simply following God's example. He has forgiven us for everything that we have ever done wrong.

- Unforgiveness is one of the biggest ways that the devil has of holding us back in our relationship with God.

◉ DVD CHAPTER 3

Play Session 9, chapter 3 – 'Forgiving To Be Free' – of the accompanying DVD.

Explain:

Maybe you are thinking, "But this is all so big I just can't do it. I can't forgive."

That's a lie from the enemy. Forgiveness is not a feeling that suddenly comes over you, it's a choice.

What does God's Word say? 'I can do everything through him who gives me strength.' (Philippians 4:13). That is true whether it feels true or not. This is one of those times where we have to act according to what God's Word says rather than what we may be feeling.

You can make a choice to forgive. I wish I could do it for you but no one else can do it for you. It is totally up to you.

Forgiveness brings freedom and true forgiveness from your heart will eventually take away the pain.

IT'S FROM THE HEART

Jesus told us to forgive from the heart if we want to be free. Forgiving from the heart isn't a simple 'I forgive so and so' mumbled under our breath. You need to put all the pain on the table before God, remember every hurt, in order to truly forgive.

We suggest a prayer that you can use to do this. It's on page 41 of the Youth Guide 15-18. This is what you will be invited to use when we go through The Steps To Freedom In Christ:

'Dear God, I choose to forgive .... (name of person) for .... (specifically what they did or failed to do), which made me feel .... (verbally tell God every hurt and pain he brings to your mind).'

WHAT IS FORGIVENESS?

- It's not forgetting

God doesn't forget our sins – how could he if he knows everything? – but he chooses not to bring them up and use them against us. You can't get rid of a hurt by simply trying to forget it. But when we truly forgive, we are making a choice not to use what was done against the person ever again.

- It's not putting up with sin

God forgives, but he doesn't put up with sin. If someone is beating you up, although it's hard, you should try to forgive him. This doesn't mean that you shouldn't call the police, since what he's doing is wrong and illegal.

And forgiving certainly doesn't mean that you let the person do it again. You can forgive but at the same time put a stop to abuse by removing yourself from the situation or calling in the appropriate authority.

- It's not seeking revenge

Get the person with Romans 12:19 to stand up and read the passage.

When you forgive, although you are letting the person off your hook, you are not letting them off God's hook. The situation doesn't necessarily change but you are free.

Forgiveness is to set a prisoner free and then realise that you were the prisoner! It's primarily an issue between you and God. God loves you and wants you to be free from the past, that's why he commands us to forgive. It's got very little to do with the person that hurt you.

Forgiveness is for our own benefit. It is not about who was right or wrong but about clearing the rubbish out of our lives and leaving it there.

Lead straight into the discussion, either in smaller groups or altogether.

Discussion:

- Would you say that you have been forgiven a little or a lot by God?

- Do you ever think that your sins aren't as 'bad' as other people's?

- Do you think it's necessary to remember hurts from the past in order to truly forgive?

- Who continues to suffer when there's no forgiveness; the person who has hurt someone or the person who has been hurt?

- Has this session changed what you think about forgiveness or not?

- Next time someone offends or hurts you, will you be quicker to forgive? Why / why not?

 RESPONSE

Leader's Note: The best place for the young people to do the actual forgiving is during the Steps To Freedom In Christ Away Day/Weekend which should be the next session of the course. However, we don't want to rob them of the opportunity of making a response to what God has said to them in this session if they want to. Select whichever of these alternatives seems appropriate:

Either:

Get together as many bricks or rocks as you have people in your group and hand them out. Ask everyone to stand, holding the brick in their hands

Many of us will have unforgiveness in our hearts, burdening us and stopping us from growing.

We're going to have a moment of silence now. Ask the Holy Spirit to remind you of anyone you need to forgive [leave pause].

If you are ready to make a choice now to forgive those people that God has brought to mind, you can do that now quietly in your own heart using the prayer on page 41 of the Youth Guide 15-18.

Great feeling of freedom, isn't it!

Or:

We're going to have a moment of silence now. Ask the Holy Spirit to remind you of anyone you need to forgive [leave pause].

If you are ready to make a choice to forgive those people when we go through The Steps To Freedom next time, tell God now.

As a symbol of letting go of these people that we have been connected to through unforgiveness, you can now put your brick down on the floor. (Or drop it in a bucket of water.)

Leader's note: you may need a bit of extra time on this bit as there could be all sorts of thoughts and emotions welling up in different members of the group. Allow space for tears and make sure there are enough leaders around if anyone needs added support or care.

Closing prayer:

Lord, thank you that you have heard the cries of our hearts today and that you have enabled us to make a choice to forgive people for what they have done to us. As we drop these bricks down we thank you that this is the end of these issues and we can know true forgiveness in You, Amen.

⭐ AND THERE'S MORE!

Refer the young people to the questions on page 40 of the Youth Guide 15-18:

- Does unforgiveness give us freedom or tie us to the person who caused the pain? Why?

- Why is forgiveness firstly between you and God?

- Is it you or the other person who is damaged more by unforgiveness?

- We are forgiven by God. If we don't forgive, what does that say about how much we value God's gift of forgiveness to us?

Suggest that they answer these at home as a way of making sure they have understood the main points of this session.

❓ CLOSING QUESTION

Ask them to consider before next time the question on page 41 of the Youth Guide 15-18:

'Have you grown as a Christian as quickly as you wanted? If not, what do you think is in the way?'

THE STEPS TO FREEDOM IN CHRIST

'Submit yourselves, then, to God. Resist the devil, and he will flee from you.'

James 4:7

STEPS TO FREEDOM IN CHRIST
CORE

PREPARATION
The Steps To Freedom In Christ concludes Part C of Freedom In Christ For Young People and is the part of the course where young people will be invited to repent of past issues.

The third book in The Freedom In Christ Discipleship Series, Break Free, Stay Free (Monarch 2008), corresponds to Part C of the course. Read pages 56 - 98 for the material that relates to The Steps To Freedom.

KEY VERSE
James 4:7 – 'Submit yourselves, then, to God. Resist the devil, and he will flee from you.'

AIM
To lead the young people through a process of repentance to resolve their personal and spiritual conflicts so that they take hold of their freedom in Christ, become aware of lies that they have been believing, and can go on to take steps to renew their mind.

KEY TRUTH
Christ has set us free (Galatians 5:1), but we will not experience that freedom without genuine repentance which involves not only saying sorry to God, but also resisting the devil and turning our back on lies that we have believed.

OVERVIEW
The Steps To Freedom In Christ are an integral part of the course. Please do not be tempted to miss them out and make every effort to encourage your young people to be there. It is envisaged that they take place on an Away Day or Weekend which could, if desired, also include one or more of Sessions 8, 9 and 10.

INTRODUCTION
The Steps To Freedom In Christ are a really exciting part of this course! There is no need to feel daunted about leading your group through. You will discover that this is a kind, gentle, straightforward process that is really effective in helping Christians take hold of the freedom that Christ has won for them.

First, we are going to consider the general principles behind The Steps To Freedom In Christ. Then we will look at the practicalities of leading your group through.

THE IMPORTANCE OF 'THE STEPS'
We live in a world where there is so much stuff that can hold us back if we let it, and the temptations for young people grow every day. It is so tough being a young person today.

The Steps to Freedom in Christ is about young people standing firm in their relationship with God. It is a 'step by step' approach in which they look - with the help of the Holy Spirit - at seven different areas of their lives where they may have messed up. When he shows them, the areas they need to address, they then choose to say three things to God:

1. I am sorry for the things I have done wrong here.

2. I am going to turn my back on this rubbish

3. I am going to follow your way and believe the truth about who I am and how you want me to live.

We have looked in this course a couple of times at Ephesians 4:26-27, which talks about not giving the devil a foothold – a point of influence in our lives. When we get turn our back on the rubbish and choose to follow God, we get rid of this foothold. This then in turn helps us see and believe the truth of all God is and what he thinks of us.

Although your young people have hopefully already been impacted and changed simply by hearing the truth of who they now are in Christ, the reality is that, if the devil has footholds in our lives because of where we mess up, the teaching will not have lasting impact.

However, imagine the potential of a generation of young people sold out for God and not held back by any of the rubbish! That is why the Steps is such an important part of this course.

HOW DO THE STEPS WORK?
The process is based on James 4:7: "Submit to God. Resist the devil and he will flee from you."

During each step, you start by having time and space to ask the Holy Spirit to show you anything that you have done or believe that is wrong. You then say sorry, turn your back on it and commit to following God in that area.

Having done this, right at the end of the process you command the enemy to leave your presence.

It is a kind and gentle process. You are in control and the outcome is in your hands. It's just between you and God.

It is not a magic formula - the Steps themselves don't set anyone free, but Jesus does!

BECOMING AWARE OF LIES
During The Steps To Freedom process, the young people might become aware of lies they have been believing. Encourage them to write these down. The next session teaches them how to deal with them. This is crucial because, although they will close the doors to the enemy by repenting, if they do not get rid of the lies they believe and deal with them. then they will inevitably return to the area in which they messed up before and open the door again.

A WAY OF LIFE
What we are doing here is not a one-off process. We are really trying to teach the young people a way of life. When they mess up in the future, we want them to know straightaway how to deal with it: to say sorry; turn their back on it; and commit to following God. They then need to deal with any lies that led them to mess up.

PRACTICAL CONSIDERATIONS

VENUE
It is recommended that you hold this session in pleasant surroundings, away from your church if possible. There are some great Christian activity and retreat centres around (contact YFC for suggestions if you need them), or you could even borrow another church's premises. The room you use should be large enough for participants to have some degree of privacy. It is helpful if people can spread out. It may help to have some music playing in the background during the Steps so that people can pray out loud without

feeling that others are listening. Some groups like really loud music so that they can shout out to God without anyone else hearing!

TIMING
You can download some sample timetables from the website. Suffice to say that you need to allow three hours at least for the Steps process. You can, of course, take breaks during that time but don't let the young people get too distracted by other things during those breaks to the extent that the prayerful atmosphere is lost.

Note that, depending on the time available, you can plan to combine one or more of Sessions 8, 9 and 10 with a Steps To Freedom Away Day/Weekend.

PRAYER
Although you will find the process gentle and, at times, almost 'matter-of-fact', don't forget that a huge amount of spiritual business is being done.

The more prayer you put in beforehand, the better. You can download a prayer strategy from the website. Try to recruit some people from your church who will pray for you well in advance of the day.

We also recommend you make a declaration when you get to the venue before the young people arrive. The enemy will want to disrupt the day as much as possible but, of course, his ability to do that is limited as long as you submit to God and resist him. A possible declaration is below:

"We have a right to be in this place at this time and God is going to do amazing things today. If anything has gone on in here that has given the enemy any kind of right, we take that right away now by the authority we have in Jesus Christ. We command every enemy of the Lord Jesus to leave this place now and stay away while we are here!"

OVERVIEW OF THE PROCESS
Each participant will need a copy of the Youth Guide, a pencil or pen and a separate sheet of paper for Step 3. There will be an introduction to each part of the process (either using the DVD or given by you directly).

The group will then pray together out loud the prayers written in the Youth Guide. Then each person will spend some time alone with God. Nobody will be embarrassed or asked to share anything with the group or another person. It is solely an encounter with God. It is helpful to explain to the group that some may get in touch with real pain, and tears are understandable and acceptable.

People will at times benefit from individual attention during the Steps that they find difficult (most usually Steps 1, 3 and 6). Plan to have a reasonable number of leaders available whose role is to walk around and help those who are struggling (one for every ten people would be a good starting point). Leaders should themselves have been through the Steps To Freedom In Christ.

Some people will have very little to deal with on some steps, whereas others may have a lot. Suggest that those who do not have much on a particular step spend time praying for those who do: that the Holy Spirit will reveal everything that needs to be revealed; and that Satan's attempts to interfere in the process will be ineffective.

CHILD PROTECTION ISSUES
We recommend strongly that you ensure that you get consent from parents for their children to attend the Away Day/Weekend and to go through the Steps. You can download some sample consent forms and cover letters from our website.

You are running this process with the support and under the authority of your church. Make sure that church leaders are aware of what it is, when and where it is taking place and that you do it in accordance with whatever guidelines and processes have already been established by the church.

Make sure especially that you and members of your team are well-acquainted with your church's Child Protection Policy. It is possible that an issue may arise where you need to notify the relevant authorities so it's important that you know in advance what to do.

THOSE WHO STRUGGLE

You may occasionally find that some young people are carrying too much 'baggage' to process the Steps in a group environment.

If someone is really struggling, reassure them that that's perfectly OK. It just means they have a lot to deal with or a particularly big issue. Suggest that they do what they can during the Away Day/Weekend but that they don't have to worry about completing everything.

If they and their parents are willing, you will then want to arrange to take them through the Steps individually at a later date (but as soon as possible). An individual Steps session will give them more time to process the parts they find difficult and they will be encouraged through the bits they find hard by leaders who can remind them of the truth. You will find that they experience a great freedom!

Make sure that you have worked out in advance with your church leaders some sensible guidelines for arranging an individual Steps session, for example:

- Ensure you have parental consent.

- Make sure there are always two leaders present, one to lead the appointment and one to pray (not only spiritually sensible but also sensible from a Child Protection point of view).

- A female should have female leaders and a male should have male leaders.

Note, of course, that some young people may just struggle with sitting still for more than a minute or two. Taking regular breaks will help but do make sure that they do not disrupt others, removing them from the room if necessary.

FURTHER INFORMATION

If you would like to know more about leading people through individual Steps To Freedom In Christ appointments, you could attend a "Helping Others Find Freedom In Christ" day, run regularly by Freedom In Christ and also available on DVD.

Freedom In Christ Ministries is always happy to answer questions from leaders about the Steps process and how best to approach it.

GO FOR IT!

STEPS TO FREEDOM IN CHRIST
11-14

The Steps can take place in a large or small group setting and the Youth Guide 11-14 (pages 59-79) will lead you through clearly and steadily. You can introduce each step using the text in the Youth Guide or use the introduction to each step on the DVD.

The process is straightforward and self-explanatory. Give the young people time and space to listen to the Holy Spirit in the relevant sections and encourage them to pray the prayers out loud and really do some business with God.

🔍 STARTING POINT

Get the young people to spread out as much as possible. Emphasise that this is a time and space for them to reflect just for them and God - not to help out their friends! Make sure they are comfortable – the process may take a couple of hours so use bean bags, comfortable chairs or whatever you have.

INTRODUCTION

Say:

Welcome to The Steps to Freedom In Christ. This time is just space for you to spend with God and sort out any stuff that is holding you back in your life. All you need is yourself, a copy of the Youth Guide, a pen and another bit of paper.

◉ DVD CHAPTER 1

Play chapter 1 of the Steps DVD Session or summarise 'The Steps To Freedom In Christ', pages 60-61 of the Youth Guide 11-14.

* Lead the group through the opening prayer and declaration.

The Youth Guide clearly marks the format for each step. Use it to lead the group through the prayers, questions and times of space where the young people invite the Holy Spirit to speak to them. Give the young people time and space to listen to the Holy Spirit in the relevant sections – a few minutes in each as necessary. Don't rush.

Encourage them to pray the prayers out loud even if it is just a whisper to add conviction and speak to the spiritual world around them.

STEP 1: FAKE V REAL

◉ DVD CHAPTER 2

Play chapter 2 of the Steps DVD or summarise 'Fake v Real' in the Youth Guide.

* Invite the young people to pray the opening prayer.

* Ask the young people to spend some time marking the relevant boxes and answering the questions.

* Invite the young people to pray the prayer for each box they marked/thing they wrote down.

* Ask the young people to spend some time answering the questions about negative thoughts.

* Invite the young people to pray the prayer for each thing they wrote down.

* Invite the young people to pray the prayer asking God to show them the things that have become more important than God in their lives.

* Invite the young people to pray the prayer for each box they marked.

You have completed Step One – well done!

STEP 2: LIES V TRUTH

 DVD CHAPTER 3

Play chapter 3 of the Steps DVD or summarise 'Lies v Truth' in the Youth Guide.

- Invite the young people to pray the opening prayer.

- Ask the young people to spend some time marking the relevant boxes.

- Invite the young people to pray the prayer for each box they marked.

- Ask the young people to look up the Bible verses next to the lie that they have turned their back on and read it.

- Ask the young people to spend some time marking the relevant boxes about how we can mislead ourselves.

- Invite the young people to pray the prayer for each box they marked.

- Ask the young people to spend some time marking the relevant boxes about how we can try and protect ourselves.

- Invite the young people to pray the prayer for each box they marked.

- Invite the young people to read aloud as a group the truth declaration.

Great – you are through Step 2!

STEP 3: BITTERNESS V FORGIVENESS

 DVD CHAPTER 4

Play chapter 4 of the Steps DVD or summarise 'Bitterness v Forgiveness' in the Youth Guide.

- Invite the young people to pray the opening prayer.

- Ask the young people to write down on a separate piece of paper the names of those people who came to mind. Make sure you leave enough time for this.

- Invite the young people to pray the prayer for each person they wrote down.

- Invite the young people to pray the prayer for healing.

- Invite the young people to read aloud as a group the statements about who God really is.

You are through Step 3.

STEP 4: REBELLION V OBEDIENCE

DVD CHAPTER 5

Play chapter 5 of the Steps DVD or summarise 'Rebellion v Obedience' in the Youth Guide.

- Invite the young people to pray the opening prayer.

- Ask the young people to spend some time marking the relevant boxes.

- Invite the young people to pray the prayer for each box they marked.

You are through Step 4.

STEP 5: PRIDE V HUMILITY

◉ DVD CHAPTER 6

Play chapter 6 of the Steps DVD or summarise 'Pride v Humility' in the Youth Guide.

- Invite the young people to pray the opening prayer.

- Ask the young people to spend some time marking the relevant boxes.

- Invite the young people to pray the prayer for each box they marked.

- Invite the young people to pray the prayer about the wrong ways we look at people.

- Ask the young people to spend some time answering the questions about particular people they have been prejudiced against.

- Invite the young people to pray the prayer for each group or person they wrote down.

Well done – you are through Step 5!

STEP 6: IMPRISONMENT V FREEDOM

◉ DVD CHAPTER 7

Play chapter 7 of the Steps DVD or summarise 'Imprisonment v Freedom' in the Youth Guide.

- Invite the young people to pray the opening prayer.

- Ask the young people to spend some time marking the relevant boxes.

- Invite the young people to pray the prayer for each box they marked.

- Invite the young people to pray the prayer thanking God for forgiving them and committing to following him wholeheartedly

Well done – one step to go!

STEP 7: CURSES V BLESSINGS

◉ DVD CHAPTER 8

Play chapter 8 of the Steps DVD or summarise 'Curses v Blessings' in the Youth Guide.

- Invite the young people to pray the opening prayer.

- Ask the young people to spend some time answering the question.

- Invite the young people to pray the prayer for each thing that came to mind.

Well done – you are through Step 7!

CONCLUSION

◉ DVD CHAPTER 9

Play chapter 9 - Conclusion - of the Steps DVD or summarise the conclusion to The Steps To Freedom in the Youth Guide 15-18.

- Summarise the section about how to stay free.

- Invite the young people to pray the final prayer.

- Invite the young people to turn to pages 8 and 9 and say the truths out loud as a group to conclude the session.

Say something like:

You might feel on cloud nine right now — or you might just feel tired! Remember that the point of this process was not to get a good feeling but to claim your freedom in Christ. If you have honestly dealt with everything the Holy Spirit has shown you today, then you have claimed your freedom. Now you need to concentrate on walking in it.

God may well show you more areas you need to deal with in the next few days, weeks, months and years — but you now know what to do. Wherever you are, it's easy simply to turn your back on wrong things and move on.

The next session (Session 10) will help you deal with any lies that you have found you have been believing. In the meantime remember the truth about what God thinks about you and keep going!

Leader's Note: after the Steps process, there may be particular issues that have surfaced as a result. Do allow time and space after the Steps for young people to talk to you about these.

STEPS TO FREEDOM IN CHRIST
15-18

The Steps can take place in a large or small group setting and the Youth Guide 15-18 (pages 59-79) will lead you through clearly and steadily. You can introduce each step using the text in the Youth Guide or use the introduction to each step on the DVD.

The process is straightforward and self-explanatory. Give the young people time and space to listen to the Holy Spirit in the relevant sections and encourage them to pray the prayers out loud and really do some business with God.

🔍 STARTING POINT

Get the young people to spread out as much as possible. Emphasise that this is a time and space for them to reflect for just them and God - not to help out their friends! Make sure they are comfortable – the process may take a couple of hours so use bean bags, comfy chairs or whatever you have.

INTRODUCTION

Say:

Welcome to The Steps to Freedom In Christ. This time is just space for you to spend with God and sort out any stuff that is holding you back in your life. All you need is yourself, a copy of the Youth Guide, a pen and another bit of paper.

◉ DVD CHAPTER 1

Play chapter 1 of the Steps DVD Session or summarise 'The Steps To Freedom In Christ', pages 60-61 of the Youth Guide 15-18.

Lead the group through the opening prayer and declaration.

The Youth Guide clearly marks the format for each step. Use it to lead the group through the prayers, questions and times of space where the young people invite the Holy Spirit to speak to them. Give the young people time and space to listen to the Holy Spirit in the relevant sections – a few minutes in each as necessary.

Encourage them to pray the prayers out loud even if it is just a whisper to add conviction and speak to the spiritual world around them.

STEP 1: FAKE V REAL

◉ DVD CHAPTER 2

Play chapter 2 of the Steps DVD or summarise 'Fake v Real' in the Youth Guide.

- Invite the young people to pray the opening prayer.

- Ask the young people to spend some time marking the relevant boxes and answering the questions.

- Invite the young people to pray the prayer for each box they marked/thing they wrote down.

- Ask the young people to spend some time answering the questions about spiritual experiences.

- Invite the young people to pray the prayer for each thing they wrote down.

- Ask the young people to spend some time answering the questions about negative thoughts.

- Invite the young people to pray the prayer for each thing they wrote down.

- Invite the young people to pray the prayer asking God to show them the things that have become more important than God in their lives.

- Invite the young people to pray the prayer for each box they marked.

You have completed Step One – well done!

STEP 2: LIES V TRUTH

◉ DVD CHAPTER 3

Play chapter 3 of the Steps DVD or summarise 'Lies v Truth' in the Youth Guide.

- Invite the young people to pray the opening prayer.

- Ask the young people to spend some time marking the relevant boxes.

- Invite the young people to pray the prayer for each box they marked.

- Ask the young people to look up the Bible verses next to the lie that they have turned their back on and read it.

- Ask the young people to spend some time marking the relevant boxes about how we can mislead ourselves.

- Invite the young people to pray the prayer for each box they marked.

- Ask the young people to spend some time marking the relevant boxes about how we can try and protect ourselves.

- Invite the young people to pray the prayer for each box they marked.

- Invite the young people to read aloud as a group the truth declaration.

Great – you are through Step 2!

STEP 3: BITTERNESS V FORGIVENESS

◉ DVD CHAPTER 4

Play chapter 4 of the Steps DVD or summarise 'Bitterness v Forgiveness' in the Youth Guide.

- Invite the young people to pray the opening prayer.

- Ask the young people to write down on a separate piece of paper the names of those people who came to mind. Allow plenty of time for this.

- Invite the young people to pray the prayer for each person they wrote down.

- Invite the young people to pray the prayer for healing.

- Invite the young people to read aloud as a group the statements about who God really is.

You are through Step 3.

STEP 4: REBELLION V OBEDIENCE

⊚ DVD CHAPTER 5

Play chapter 5 of the Steps DVD or summarise 'Rebellion v Obedience' in the Youth Guide.

- Invite the young people to pray the opening prayer.
- Ask the young people to spend some time marking the relevant boxes.
- Invite the young people to pray the prayer for each box they marked.

You are through Step 4.

STEP 5: PRIDE V HUMILITY

⊚ DVD CHAPTER 6

Play chapter 6 of the Steps DVD or summarise 'Pride v Humility' in the Youth Guide.

- Invite the young people to pray the opening prayer.
- Ask the young people to spend some time marking the relevant boxes.
- Invite the young people to pray the prayer for each box they marked.
- Invite the young people to pray the prayer about the wrong ways we look at people.
- Ask the young people to spend some time answering the questions about particular people they have been prejudiced against.
- Invite the young people to pray the prayer for each group or person they wrote down.

Well done – you are through Step 5!

STEP 6: IMPRISONMENT V FREEDOM

⊚ DVD CHAPTER 7

Play chapter 7 of the Steps DVD or summarise 'Imprisonment v Freedom' in the Youth Guide.

- Invite the young people to pray the opening prayer.
- Ask the young people to spend some time marking the relevant boxes.
- Invite the young people to pray the prayer for each box they marked.

Sexual Sin

Summarise the section on sexual sin.

- Invite the young people to pray the prayer asking the Holy Spirit to reveal any sexual sin.

- Invite the young people to pray the prayer for each person they wrote down.

- Invite the young people to pray the prayer asking the Holy Spirit to reveal any sexual abuse.

- Invite the young people to pray the prayer for each abusive situation and person they wrote down.

Draw the attention of the young people to the box at the bottom of page 77 in the Youth Guide 15-18 which refers to some additional prayers that are available (to you - not them directly) via our website. Find an appropriate way of letting those who need those prayers get hold of them without having to reveal to everyone else what the issues are. Make sure that you have checked what prayers are available in advance of the session and have downloaded them.

- Invite the young people to pray the prayer thanking God for making them clean.

- Invite the young people to pray the prayer thanking God for forgiving them and committing to following him wholeheartedly.

Well done – one step to go!

STEP 7: CURSES V BLESSINGS

⊚ DVD CHAPTER 8

Play chapter 8 of the Steps DVD or summarise 'Curses v Blessings' in the Youth Guide.

- Invite the young people to pray the opening prayer.

- Ask the young people to spend some time answering the question.

- Invite the young people to pray the prayer for each thing that came to mind.

Well done – you are through Step 7!

CONCLUSION

Summarise the section about how to stay free.

- Invite the young people to pray the final prayer.

- Invite the young people to turn to pages 8 and 9 and say the truths out loud as a group to conclude the session.

⊚ DVD CHAPTER 9

Play chapter 9 - Conclusion - of the Steps DVD or summarise the conclusion to The Steps To Freedom in the Youth Guide 15-18.

Say something like:

You might feel on cloud nine right now — or you might just feel tired! Remember that the point of this process was not to get a good feeling but to claim your freedom in Christ. If you have honestly dealt with everything the Holy Spirit has shown you today, then you have claimed your freedom. Now you need to concentrate on walking in it.

God may well show you more areas you need to deal with in the next few days, weeks, months and years — but you now know what to do. Wherever you are, it's easy simply to turn your back on wrong things and move on.

The next session (Session 10) will help you deal with any lies that you have found you have been believing. In the meantime remember the truth about what God thinks about you and keep going!

Leader's Note: after the Steps process, there may be particular issues that have surfaced as a result. Do allow time and space after the Steps for young people to talk to you about these. Remember that there are some additional prayers for specific issues including eating disorders and abortion available in the Additional Resources section of the website.

SESSION TEN:
TRUTH = FREEDOM

'But solid food is for the mature, who by
constant use have trained themselves to
distinguish good from evil.'

Hebrews 5:14

TRUTH = FREEDOM CORE

PREPARATION

This is the first of four sessions in Part D, the final part of Freedom In Christ For Young People. It is a particularly important session and rounds off the core teaching on the course by giving a concrete strategy - 'Stronghold-Busting' - for renewing the mind.

The accompanying material for this session is at the end of the third book in The Freedom In Christ Discipleship Series, Break Free, Stay Free (Monarch 2008), on pages 99-110.

KEY VERSE

Hebrews 5:14 – 'But solid food is for the mature, who by constant use have trained themselves to distinguish good from evil.'

AIM

To help people understand that taking hold of their freedom in Christ is not a one-off experience – it needs to become a way of life – and to provide the group with tools to help them to do just that.

KEY TRUTH

Our success in continuing to walk in freedom and grow in maturity depends on the extent to which we continue to renew our minds and train ourselves to distinguish good from evil.

OVERVIEW

If we dealt honestly with everything the Holy Spirit showed us during The Steps To Freedom In Christ, we have taken hold of the freedom that Christ won for us. Walking in freedom needs to become a way of life. In this session we look at strategies for renewing our mind and resisting Satan's attack. We will learn how to deal with faulty ways of thinking that were uncovered during The Steps To Freedom In Christ process.

INTRODUCTION

In this session we're going to find out about some more things that might stop us from growing spiritually, and also what we can do about them. We will be introducing the young people to a key strategy for renewing their minds that we call 'Stronghold-Busting'.

If you went to a restaurant and fancied, say, steak with green beans and new potatoes but discovered two options for that on the menu, 'normal' or 'liquidised', which would you choose?

Well, since you're not exactly a baby, you'd probably go for 'normal'. You know how to chew and your body is able to digest what you chew. For a baby, however, a normal steak would be a disastrous dinner choice; if the baby didn't choke on it on the way down, it would certainly come straight back up as soon as his stomach realised it wasn't grown up enough to deal with it.

Just as we expect to mature physically as we grow up, we should mature expect to mature spiritually as we grow as Christians. Unfortunately, a lot of Christians have grown old, but never matured.

Paul found this problem in the church in Corinth:

'Brothers and sisters, I could not address you as spiritual but as worldly – mere infants in Christ. I gave you milk, not solid food, for you were not yet ready for it. Indeed, you are still not ready. You are still worldly. For since there is jealousy and quarrelling among you, are you not worldly?' (1 Corinthians 3:1-3)

The Corinthians kept repeating the same sins over and over again – Paul mentions jealousy and quarrelling specifically here – and their behaviour showed they had a long way to go before they could be considered mature Christians.

Now, new Christians are not expected to be mature at once, just like babies aren't expected to eat steak. But the Christians in Corinth had been Christians for some time, yet still hadn't matured. We want to do everything we can to ensure that your young people don't stay stuck as spiritual babies but go on to become mature, fruitful Christians as quickly as possible.

BARRIERS TO MATURITY

- **Not taking hold of your freedom in Christ**

You will hopefully know by now that you already have everything to be able to be truly free and to live a godly life. Maturity, however, is something that takes a little time to develop. But we can't mature if we haven't first taken hold of that freedom.

This was the Corinthians' problem: no matter how much they wanted to mature, until they got rid of the sin issue - that jealousy and quarrelling - they weren't able to. Try as hard as you like to mature but if you are walking around with lots of footholds of the enemy still in place, it's just not going to happen.

- **Not taking personal responsibility**

Paul couldn't fix the Corinthians' problem himself. What they needed to do was confess what they'd done wrong, say sorry to God for it, submit themselves to Jesus and resist the devil - just as we did in The Steps To Freedom In Christ. They had to do that for themselves. Paul could only point them towards the truth.

We need other people around us to support, encourage and love us. But at the end of the day, only I can be responsible for my own relationship with God. Do you know that there is only one person that can stop you becoming the becoming the person God wants you to be? Yes, you've guessed it. You!

- **Not knowing the basic truths**

The writer to the Hebrews had encountered a similar problem as Paul, and writes:

'Though by this time you ought to be teachers, you need someone to teach you the elementary truths of God's word all over again. You need milk, not solid food! Anyone who lives on milk, being still an infant, is not acquainted with the teaching about righteousness. But solid food is for the mature, who by constant use have trained themselves to distinguish good from evil.' (Hebrews 5:12-14)

The Hebrews weren't stuck in sin like the Corinthians were, but they struggled to grasp the most fundamental truths. Maturity isn't just about being able to give the textbook answer to questions like 'Has God accepted you?' but to really feel and know the truth in our hearts.

- **Faulty thinking**

The writer goes on:

'Therefore let us leave the elementary teachings about Christ and go on to maturity, not laying again the foundation of repentance from acts that lead to death, and of faith in God, instruction about baptisms, the laying on of hands, the resurrection of the dead and eternal judgement.' (Hebrews 6:1-2)

To stop ourselves from faulty thinking we need to know the truth so well that we recognise fakes when we see them.

STRATEGIES FOR GROWTH

- **Uncovering lies**

How do you think a Christian can be transformed?

There's a verse in the Bible that gives us a definitive answer. Romans 12:2 says, "Be transformed by the renewing of your mind".

That's something we've mentioned quite a lot in the course so far. It's so important that we understand that this is what needs to happen if we want to grow so that we don't go chasing other things we think might help. If we focus on renewing our minds - replacing lies with truth - we will be transformed. God says so!

The first step in renewing your mind is to work out which parts of your thinking need to be changed, what lies we have been believing. A lie in this context is anything you've been believing that is not in line with what God says in his Word.

Hopefully most of your group will have been realising lies they have been believing as we've gone through the course and might already have done some work on them using the lists of Biblical truth from the first three sessions perhaps. In addition, they are likely to have become aware of lies during The Steps To Freedom. One way of uncovering possible lies is to get them to look back at the words they said after 'which made me feel' in the forgiveness prayer in Step 3 when they told God what people who hurt them made them feel like. Did they see the same word pop up again and again (eg. stupid, useless, dirty)? This is quite likely to show up a lie.

It's also possible to spot lies if you find that you struggle with fear. Behind a fear there's always a lie. For example, if you're scared of Satan, you have probably believed the lie that he's more powerful than you. We know that's a lie, because 1 John 4:4 says: 'He who is in us is greater than the one who is in the world.'

- **Dealing with lies**

So how do you renew your mind? It's all very well uncovering a particular lie but that on its own does not get rid of it. The whole point of a lie is that it feels very true!

Renewing the mind is not an instant thing. It takes a bit of time but we have an important strategy to share with the young people that will help them enormously if they are prepared to give it a go. We call it 'Stronghold-Busting' and it has four stages:

1. Find out a lie that you have believed (something that goes against what God says about you in the Bible).

2. Find as many Bible verses as you can that tell the truth and write them down. You might find a concordance, www.biblegateway.com or a helpful pastor useful at this point.

3. Write a prayer or declaration looking a bit like this:

    I refuse to believe the lie that...

    I declare the truth that...

4. Finally, read the Bible verses and say the prayer / declaration out loud every day for 40 days.

Why 40 days? Well, once you've dealt with any foothold of the enemy, a lie is basically just a habit, just a way of thinking that you do automatically. It takes about 40 days to break a habit.

If you miss a day or two along the way, that's OK - don't get too legalistic about it - but do persevere until the end.

Health Warning! We guarantee that any Stronghold-Buster will feel like a complete waste of time for most of those 40 days. In a way, that's the point! There would be no need to do one if the lie didn't feel true. However, as you grit your teeth day after day and make a conscious decision to believe God's Word rather than your feelings, eventually the stronghold will crumble and your thinking will change permanently. You will be transformed!

You may need to encourage your young people quite a lot over the 40 day period that they are doing a Stronghold-Buster. Tell them it's only to be expected that it feels like a complete waste of time and that nothing is changing but assure them that, if they stick with it, they will see transformation. Paul likens the Christian life to a race (Philippians 3:13-15), where you have to keep running, keep persevering to reach the goal.

We have put a couple of sample Stronghold-Busters on page 244 and you can download some from our website. However, don't just hand them out to your young people. An important part of the process is if they do their own thinking in putting it together rather than simply take someone else's ready-made solution.

QUESTIONS TO THINK ABOUT AS YOU PREPARE:

1. Have you ever seen an adult behave like a baby? What was it like?

2. Have you matured as a Christian as quickly as you would like? What are some of the things that have hindered you?

3. What kind of truths do you think are important to know to be able to grow?

4. What practical steps are you going to take to maintain your freedom and continually renew your mind?

STRONGHOLD-BUSTER EXAMPLES

ALWAYS FEELING ALONE

Deuteronomy 31:6 - Be strong and courageous. Do not be afraid or terrified because of them, for the LORD your God goes with you; he will never leave you nor forsake you.

Isaiah - 46:4 Even to your old age and grey hairs I am he, I am he who will sustain you. I have made you and I will carry you; I will sustain you and I will rescue you.

Jeremiah 29:11 - "For I know the plans I have for you," declares the LORD, "plans to prosper you and not to harm you, plans to give you hope and a future."

Romans 7:37-38 - For I am convinced that neither death nor life, neither angels nor demons, neither the present nor the future, nor any powers, neither height nor depth, nor anything else in all creation, will be able to separate us from the love of God that is in Christ Jesus our Lord.

Dear Heavenly Father

I refuse to believe the lie that I am abandoned and forgotten and will be left on my own.

I declare the truth that you love me, that you have plans to give me a hope and a future and that absolutely nothing can separate me from your love.

In Jesus' name. Amen

FEELING IRRESISTIBLY DRAWN TO INTERNET PORN

Romans 6:11-14 - In the same way, count yourselves dead to sin but alive to God in Christ Jesus. Therefore do not let sin reign in your mortal body so that you obey its evil desires. Do not offer the parts of your body to sin, as instruments of wickedness, but rather offer yourselves to God, as those who have been brought from death to life; and offer the parts of your body to him as instruments of righteousness. For sin shall not be your master, because you are not under law, but under grace.

1 Corinthians 6:19 - Do you not know that your body is a temple of the Holy Spirit?

1 Corinthians 10:13 - No temptation has seized you except what is common to man. And God is faithful; he will not let you be tempted beyond what you can bear. But when you are tempted, he will also provide a way out so that you can stand up under it.

Galatians 5:16 - So I say, live by the Spirit, and you will not gratify the desires of the flesh.

Galatians 5:22 - But the fruit of the Spirit is love, joy, peace, patience, kindness, goodness, faithfulness, gentleness and self-control.

I refuse to believe the lie that I cannot resist the temptation to look at internet porn.

I declare the truth that God will always provide a way out when I am tempted and I will choose to take it.

I declare the truth that if I live by the Spirit - and I choose to do that - I will not gratify the desires of the flesh and the fruit of the Spirit, including self-control, will grow in me.

I count myself dead to sin and refuse to let sin reign in my body or be my master. Today and every day I give my body to God to be used only for what is right and declare that the power of sin is broken in me. My body is a temple of the Holy Spirit.

TRUTH = FREEDOM 11-14

PRAYER AND DECLARATION

Encourage everyone to join together in saying the following prayer and declaration. You can download the PowerPoint slides with the words for these from the website.

It would be good to suggest that the young people stand up and speak out the declaration clearly and confidently to the heavenly realms. They could shout it out and use appropriate actions!

PRAYER

❝ Lord, please help us to keep growing in you and growing closer to you every day. Help us to meet with you in this time together and to take away from it all that you want to say to us, Amen.

DECLARATION: IN A CLEAR, CONFIDENT TONE!

> **"** We command all evil to leave this place right now. You have no right to be here! We are Children of God and you can't touch us! Our minds will be peaceful places just for us and the Lord Jesus.

STARTING POINT

In order to recap on the last session and the Steps To Freedom In Christ, you might like simply to ask whether one or two people have anything to share following the Steps. What happened during the session? Have they experienced a greater level of freedom?

INTRODUCTORY ACTIVITIES

CRAWLATHON

Set up a track around your venue using masking tape.

Try and make it as long and varied as possible.

Get two volunteers and ask them to race each other in the track – crawling like a baby. Award a prize (and possibly sticking plasters) to the winner.

Leader's Note: you may want to get hold of some gloves and knee pads to prevent injuries or carpet burns. Also make sure you only choose people wearing trousers or shorts.

BABY FOOD

Buy four different (but of equal size) jars of baby food. Choose some really yucky flavours. Pick four volunteers who must compete in finishing their jar first. Don't forget to check for food allergies. Or simply set up some of the other leaders.

DVD CHAPTER 1

Play Session 10, chapter 1 – 'Playtime' – of the accompanying DVD.

Explain:

As we'll see later on in this session, there are certain things that we should just stop doing as we get older – eating baby food is one of those things!

WORSHIP ACTIVITY

Provide everyone with slips of paper (around 2 by 10 cm) and pens, and ask the young people to write on the slips things that have held them back from God in the past.

Give them a few minutes to do this and then stick the slips together into a paper chain. Stand in a circle, holding the chain in your hands.

Read out loud Galatians 5:1 and Romans 8:1-2, as you all break the chain.

Pray:

Father God, we thank you for the freedom that we have in Christ. Thank you that we don't have to be bound by these things anymore. Amen.

INTRODUCTION TO SESSION

Today we're going to find out about some more things that might stop us from growing spiritually, and also what we can do about them.

MOVIE CLIP

Video clip: The Incredibles (PG)

Chapter: 30

Start clip: 01:39:00

End clip: 01:41:17

As most of the Incredible family return from their adventure, it turns out that little Jack-Jack isn't just your average baby.

Explain:

Jack-Jack surprised everyone by not behaving like an ordinary baby – some people surprise us by not acting like ordinary teenagers or adults, but just like babies!

Sometimes this is true in our spiritual lives as well, and this can really cause problems.

Prepare beforehand a baby's beaker with milk in and a plate with a cooked piece of meat on it. Alternatively show a photo of each item.

Ask the young people to turn to the person next to them and answer these questions:

- If you came to a restaurant and these were the two options on the menu, which would you choose?

- What do you think you'd be expected to choose? Why?

Explain:

Well, since you're not exactly a baby, you'd probably be expected to choose the solid food; you're mature enough to cope with the meat, you know how to chew and your body is able to digest it.

For a baby, however, steak would be a disastrous dinner choice. If the baby didn't choke on it on the way down, it would certainly return straight back up when his stomach realised it wasn't grown up enough to deal with it.

Just like we should mature physically as we grow up, we should mature spiritually as we grow as Christians. Unfortunately, a lot of Christians have grown old, but never matured.

⊙ DVD CHAPTER 2

Play Session 10, chapter 2 – 'Strongholds' – of the accompanying DVD.

Paul found this problem in the church in Corinth:

'Brothers and sisters, I could not address you as spiritual but as worldly – mere infants in Christ. I gave you milk, not solid food, for you were not yet ready for it. Indeed, you are still not ready. You are still worldly. For since there is jealousy and quarrelling among you, are you not worldly?'

(1 Corinthians 3:1-3)

As the Corinthians kept doing the same sins over and over again – Paul mentions jealousy and quarrelling specifically here – they showed that they had quite a long way to go before they could be considered mature Christians.

Get hold of a baby picture of a leader and show your group.

Aaaah..... wasn't he/she cute?

BABY BEHAVING!
Divide the group into teams.

Give each team a leader, a towel for a nappy, and dummy.

See which team can dress their leader as a baby quickest, or the best within a limited time.

Do you think these babies are cute too?

Grown-ups who act like babies aren't cute any more.

BARRIERS TO GROWTH
In order for us to stop acting like spiritual babies, setting our systems up to be able to swallow some steak, we need to find out what the main barriers are to growing up:

• Not taking hold of your freedom in Christ

It's important to realise that Jesus has set us free, and to choose to live in a way that reflects that.

If you've gone through this course, you have all the tools to do that.

• Not taking personal responsibility

What the Corinthians needed to do was to confess and say sorry for what they'd done wrong, submit to Jesus and to resist the devil.

They had to do that themselves; Paul could only point out the truth to them but not actually do it for them.

- Not knowing basic truths

The writer to the Hebrews had encountered a similar problem as Paul, and writes:

'Though by this time you ought to be teachers, you need someone to teach you the elementary truths of God's word all over again. You need milk, not solid food! Anyone who lives on milk, being still an infant, is not acquainted with the teaching about righteousness. But solid food is for the mature, who by constant use have trained themselves to distinguish good from evil.' (Hebrews 5:12 -14)

The Hebrews weren't stuck in sin like the Corinthians were, but they had struggled to grasp the most fundamental truths.

- Not thinking straight

The writer goes on:

'Therefore let us leave the elementary teachings about Christ and go on to maturity, not laying again the foundation of repentance from acts that lead to death, and of faith in God, instruction about baptisms, the laying on of hands, the resurrection of the dead and eternal judgement.' (Hebrews 6:1-2)

To stop ourselves from thinking in a faulty way, we need to know the truth so well that we recognise lies as they come along.

THE MAIN POINT

STRATEGIES FOR GROWTH

UNCOVERING LIES
Game - Get into teams of three.

Each team must comes up with a statements about each of the team members, two of which are true and one false.

Each team member reads out a statement and the other teams have to vote on which is the false one.

◉ DVD CHAPTER 3

Play Session 10, chapter 3 – 'Breaking Strongholds' – of the accompanying DVD.

Explain:

Part of maturing as a Christian is about hunting down the lies that we have been believing, and destroying them with God's truth! Paul says in Romans that we have to be transformed by the renewing of our minds (Romans 12:1). We need to get rid of the old stuff and fill our minds with the truth about who we are and who God is.

You might have uncovered a few lies during 'The Steps To Freedom In Christ'. They're especially easy to spot in Step 3 (Forgiveness) when you tell God how people who hurt you made you feel. Did you see the same word pop up again and again (eg. stupid, useless, dirty)? This is probably a lie you've believed about yourself.

It's also possible to spot lies if you find that you struggle with fear. Behind a fear there's always a lie. For example, if you're scared of Satan, you have probably believed the lie that he's more powerful than you.

We know that's a lie, because 1 John 4:4 says: 'He who is in us is greater than the one who is in the world.'

DEALING WITH LIES

We're going to learn a powerful way of renewing our minds called 'Stronghold-Busting.'

This is how to do it:

1. Find out a lie that you have believed (something that goes against what God says about you in the Bible).

2. Find as many Bible verses as you can that tell the truth and write them down. You might find a concordance, www.biblegateway.com or a youth leader or pastor useful at this point.

3. Write a prayer or declaration looking a bit like this:

    I turn my back on the lie that...

    I declare the truth that...

4. Finally, read the Bible verses and say the prayer / declaration every day for 40 days (this is based on psychologists telling us that it takes 6 weeks to break a habit). Don't get too obsessive about it, it's OK to miss one or two days, but try to persevere until the end.

If you have done your own Stronghold-Buster and are happy to share it and your experience of using it, do that now.

RESPONSE

Let them know that the four stages of Stronghold-Busting are written on page 43 of the Youth Guide 11-14 in the Challenge section.

Divide the young people into two or three groups and give them each a different lie to work on. You could ask people to share lies they have come to realise they have believed. Alternatively you could use the sample lies on page 244 (but don't let them see the sample Stronghold-Busters!) or use common lies such as 'I need to look great to feel good about myself', 'I am useless', 'I can never do anything right'. They may need help in finding appropriate Bible verses so be prepared with some tools such as a concordance, Bible software or the Internet.

Bring them back together and let them share what they have come up with. Encourage them to do the Challenge section at home on a lie that they have been believing. Encourage them to ask you and other leaders for help in finding appropriate 'truth verses'.

TAKING A LONG-TERM VIEW

Remember to do your Stronghold-Buster for 40 days because, once you've dealt with any foothold of the enemy in the Steps To Freedom, a lie is basically just a habit, just a way of thinking that you do automatically. It takes about 40 days to break a habit.

If you miss a day or two along the way, that's OK but do persevere until the end.

Health Warning! I guarantee that your Stronghold-Buster will feel like a complete waste of time for most of those 40 days. In a way, that's the point!

There would be no need to do one if the lie didn't feel true.

However, as you grit your teeth day after day and make a conscious decision to believe God's Word rather than your feelings, eventually the stronghold will crumble and your thinking will change permanently.

You will be transformed.

So, don't get discouraged if you don't think it's working to begin with.

And don't think you're going to 'bust' a long list of strongholds all at once. Deal with one properly before you move on to the next.

Paul likens the Christian life to a race (Philippians 3:13-15), where you have to keep running, keep persevering to reach your goal. If you do keep running, you will get there.

OTHER PRACTICAL STEPS

Ask other people around you to help.

Maybe you have a friend who can text you now and then to see how you're getting on with a certain stronghold.

Or you might have a mature Christian friend who can support you all the way.

Finally, once you've finished this course, it might be a good idea to do the teaching again.

The second time around you're more likely to be able to connect with the truth on a different level.

You might not do the whole course, it could just be useful to go through your notes.

👥 SMALL GROUPS & PRAYER FOCUS

- Have you ever seen an adult behave like a baby? What was it like?

- Have you matured as a Christian as quickly as you would like? What are some of the things that have hindered you?

- What kind of truths do you think are important to know to be able to grow?

- What practical steps are you going to take to maintain your freedom and continually renew your mind?

AND THERE'S MORE!

Draw the group's attention to the questions on page 44 of the Youth Guide 11-14:

- What is a 'spiritually mature' person like?

- Why does God want us to keep growing as Christians and not stay as babies?

- What kind of thing stops us growing up as a Christian?

- Why is it a good idea to ask a mature Christian to support and pray for you?

Note: might you be able to make connections with mature Christians in your church who will support and pray for the young people?

? CLOSING QUESTION

Ask the group to consider this question before the next session (it's on page 45 of the Youth Guide 11-14):

When another Christian does something wrong to you, what would be a good way for you to respond?

TRUTH = FREEDOM 15-18

 ## PRAYER AND DECLARATION

Encourage everyone to join together in saying the following prayer and declaration. You can download the PowerPoint slides with the words for these from the website.

It would be good to suggest that the young people stand up and speak out the declaration clearly and confidently to the heavenly realms. They could shout it out and use appropriate actions!

PRAYER

❝ Lord, please help us to keep growing in you and growing closer to you every day. Help us to meet with you in this time together and to take away from it all that you want to say to us, Amen.

DECLARATION: IN A CLEAR, CONFIDENT TONE!

❝ We command all evil to leave this place right now. You have no right to be here! We are Children of God and you can't touch us! Our minds will be peaceful places for just us and the Lord Jesus.

Q STARTING POINT

Over the welcome drinks encourage the group to talk about school stories and funny memories. Have they had any embarrassing incidents?

In order to recap on the last session and the Steps To Freedom In Christ, you might like simply to ask whether one or two people have anything to share following the Steps. What happened during the session? Have they experienced a greater level of freedom?

DVD CHAPTER 1

Play Session 10, chapter 1 – 'Playtime' – of the accompanying DVD.

Ask the group:

What has changed in your life?

What has changed since starting this course?

SOAPBOX

Share an embarrassing incident or story from your school days. This has all been quite serious – can you make them laugh with an old memory? How are you different now? Have you matured? Does the group think that you would be guilty of behaving like that again?

DVD CHAPTER 2

Play Session 10, chapter 2 – 'Strongholds' – of the accompanying DVD.

Paul found this problem in the church in Corinth:

'Brothers and sisters, I could not address you as spiritual but as worldly – mere infants in Christ. I gave you milk, not solid food, for you were not yet ready for it. Indeed, you are still not ready. You are still worldly. For since there is jealousy and quarrelling among you, are you not worldly?'

(1 Corinthians 3:1-3)

As the Corinthians kept repeating the same sins over and over again – Paul mentions jealousy and quarrelling specifically here – they showed that they had quite a long way to go before they could be considered mature Christians.

New Christians are not expected to be mature at once, just like babies aren't expected to be eating steak. But the Christians in Corinth had been Christians for some time, but still hadn't matured.

Get hold of a baby picture of a leader and show your group.

Aaaah.... wasn't he/she cute?

Or

Try getting hold of a few leaders' baby pictures and encourage the group to guess who's who!

BARRIERS TO GROWTH

Leader's Note: before the session try getting some of the young people to lead the next section, discuss what might be the best way – in pairs, small groups, altogether? Try not to suggest problems with their ideas straight away, but helpfully steer them to think through any issues that might arise with that style.

Here are some of the things that stop us growing as Christians:

• Not taking hold of your freedom in Christ

You will hopefully know by now that you already have everything you need to be truly free and to live a godly life. Maturity, however, is something that takes a little time to develop. But we can't be mature if we haven't first taken hold of that freedom.

This was the Corinthians' problem: no matter how much they wanted to mature, until they could get rid of their jealousy and stop quarrelling, they weren't able to.

• Not taking personal responsibility

Paul couldn't fix the Corinthians' problem himself. What they needed to do was confess what they'd done wrong, say sorry to God for it, submit themselves to Jesus and resist the devil. They had to do that themselves; Paul could only point out the truth.

We need other people around us to support, encourage and love us. But at the end of the day, only I can be responsible for my own relationship with God. In reality, it's only you who can stop yourself from becoming the person God wants you to be.

• Not knowing the basic truths

The writer to the Hebrews had encountered a similar problem as Paul, and writes:

'Though by this time you ought to be teachers, you need someone to teach you the elementary truths of God's word all over again. You need milk, not solid food! Anyone who lives on milk, being still an infant, is not acquainted with the teaching about righteousness. But solid food is for the mature, who by constant use have trained themselves to distinguish good from evil.' (Hebrews 5:12-14)

The Hebrews weren't stuck in sin like the Corinthians were, but they struggled to grasp the most fundamental truths. Maturity isn't just about being able to give the textbook answer to questions like 'Has God accepted you?' but to really feel and know the truth in our hearts.

• Faulty thinking

The writer goes on:

'Therefore let us leave the elementary teachings about Christ and go on to maturity, not laying again the foundation of repentance from acts that lead to death, and of faith in God, instruction about baptisms, the laying on of hands, the resurrection of the dead and eternal judgement.' (Hebrews 6:1-2)

To stop ourselves from faulty thinking we need to know the truth so well that we recognise fakes when we see them.

Read out the points on page 42 of the Youth Guide 15-18:

- When we first become a Christian, we are a spiritual baby but we need to grow up and become mature.

- We need to take responsibility for what we believe and learn God's truth so that we can uncover any lies we have fallen for.

- It is about dealing with busting strongholds properly, one at a time, not all at once!

DISCUSSION

Have you ever seen an adult behave like a baby? What was it like?

Have you matured as a Christian as quickly as you would like? What are some of the things that have hindered you?

What kind of truths do you think are important to know to be able to grow?

What practical steps are you going to take to maintain your freedom and continually renew your mind?

WORSHIP ACTIVITY

Provide everyone with slips of paper (around 2 by 10 cm) and pens, and ask the young people to write down the things that have held them back from God in the past.

Give them a few minutes to do this and then stick the slips together into a paper chain. Stand in a circle, holding the chain in your hands.

Read out loud Galatians 5:1, Romans 8:1-2, as you all break the chain.

Pray:

Father God, we thank you for the freedom that we have in Christ. Thank you that we don't have to be bound by these things any more. Amen.

THE MAIN POINT

DVD CHAPTER 3

Play Session 10, chapter 3 – 'Breaking Strongholds' – of the accompanying DVD.

Explain:

Part of maturing as a Christian is about hunting down the lies that we have been believing and destroying them with God's truth! Paul says in Romans that we have to be transformed by the renewing of our minds (Romans 12:1). We get rid of the old stuff and fill our minds with the truth about who we are and who God is.

You might have uncovered a few lies during 'The Steps To Freedom In Christ'. They're especially easy to spot in Step 3 (Forgiveness) when you tell God how people who hurt you made you feel.

Did you see the same word pop up again and again (eg. stupid, useless, dirty)? This is probably a lie you've believed about yourself.

It's also possible to spot lies if you find that you struggle with fear. Behind a fear there's often a lie. For example, if you're scared of Satan, you have probably believed the lie that he's more powerful than you.

We know that's a lie, because 1 John 4:4 says:

'He who is in us is greater than the one who is in the world.'

DEALING WITH LIES

We're going to learn a powerful way of renewing our minds called 'Stronghold-Busting.'

This is how to do it:

1. Find out a lie that you have believed (something that goes against what God says about you in the Bible).

2. Find as many Bible verses as you can that tell the truth and write them down. You might find a concordance, www.biblegateway.com or a youth leader or pastor useful at this point.

3. Write a prayer or declaration looking a bit like this:

    I turn my back on the lie that...

    I declare the truth that...

4. Finally, read the Bible verses and say the prayer / declaration every day for 40 days (this is based on psychologists telling us that it takes 6 weeks to break a habit). Don't get too obsessive about it, it's OK to miss one or two days, but try to persevere until the end.

If you have done your own Stronghold-Buster and are happy to share it and your experience of using it, do that now.

Let them know that the four stages of Stronghold-Busting are written on page 45 of the Youth Guide 15-18 in the Challenge section.

Divide the group into pairs.

Thank God first for revealing the lie and leading you towards the truth. Then do some Stronghold-Busting on a lie that one of you realises you have believed. Follow the four stages.

They may need help in finding appropriate Bible verses so be prepared with some tools such as a concordance, Bible software or the Internet.

Bring them back together and let one or two share what they have come up with. Encourage them to do the Challenge section at home on a lie that they have been believing. Encourage them to ask you and other leaders for help in finding appropriate 'truth verses' if they struggle to find them.

TAKING A LONG-TERM VIEW
Remember to do your Stronghold-Buster for 40 days because, once you've dealt with any foothold

of the enemy in the Steps To Freedom, a lie is basically just a habit, just a way of thinking that you do automatically. It takes about 40 days to break a habit.

If you miss a day or two along the way, that's OK but do persevere until the end.

Health Warning! I guarantee that your Stronghold-Buster will feel like a complete waste of time for most of those 40 days. In a way, that's the point!

There would be no need to do one if the lie didn't feel true.

However, as you grit your teeth day after day and make a conscious decision to believe God's Word rather than your feelings, eventually the stronghold will crumble and your thinking will change permanently.

You will be transformed.

So, don't get discouraged if you don't think it's working to begin with.

And don't think you're going to 'bust' a long list of strongholds all at once. Deal with one properly before you move on to the next.

Paul likens the Christian life to a race (Philippians 3:13-15), where you have to keep running, keep persevering to reach your goal. If you do keep running, you will get there.

OTHER PRACTICAL STEPS
Ask other people around you to help.

Maybe you have a friend who can text you now and then to see how you're getting on with a certain stronghold.

Or you might have a mature Christian friend who can support you all the way.

Finally, once you've finished this course, it might be a good idea to do the teaching again.

The second time around you're more likely to be able to connect with the truth on a different level.

You might not do the whole course, it could just be useful to go through your notes.

 # AND THERE'S MORE!

Direct the group's attention to page 44 of the Youth Guide 15-18 and read the questions in the 'What's it to me?' section. Suggest that they complete their answers at home.

*   How can you take responsibility for growing in your faith so that you become spiritually mature?

*   What can stop us and what can help us grow as a Christian?

*   God always wants to help us grow and become more like Jesus. How do we know what he is like? How do we become more like him?

? CLOSING QUESTION

Ask the young people to think about this question for next week (on page 45 of the Youth Guide 15-18):

When another Christian does something wrong to you, what would be a good way for you to respond?

SESSION ELEVEN:
LOVING OTHERS

'Jesus replied: "Love the Lord your God with all your heart and with all your soul and with all your mind." This is the first and greatest commandment. And the second is like it: "Love your neighbour as yourself." All the Law and the Prophets hang on these two commandments.'

Matthew 22:37-40

LOVING OTHERS CORE

PREPARATION

This is the second of four sessions in Part D, the final part of Freedom In Christ For Young People. Having taken hold of our freedom In Christ, we need to keep learning, following and growing as a Christian. and in these next three sessions we will look at how to stand firm, relate to others and aim to become more like Jesus.

The accompanying material for this session is in the fourth book in The Freedom In Christ Discipleship Series, The You God Planned (Monarch 2008), pages 77-92.

KEY VERSE

Matthew 22:37-40 – 'Jesus replied: "Love the Lord your God with all your heart and with all your soul and with all your mind." This is the first and greatest commandment. And the second is like it: "Love your neighbour as yourself." All the Law and the Prophets hang on these two commandments.'

AIM

To understand our roles and responsibilities in relation to other people so that we can grow together in Christ.

KEY TRUTH

As disciples of Christ, we must assume responsibility for our own character and seek to meet the needs of others, rather that the other way round.

OVERVIEW

Jesus' great commandment says we are to love the Lord our God with all our heart, soul and mind, and to love our neighbour as ourselves. That sums up the whole Biblical message. We are called to love God and love one another. We cannot have a righteous relationship with God to the exclusion of others. A right relationship with God will lead to a right relationship with our neighbours. In this session we will consider rights, responsibilities, judgment, discipline, accountability and the needs of others.

INTRODUCTION

God has created us to be in relationship with one another, and he has also given us direction in his Word for how to 'do' relationships. Today we're exploring how best to be a good friend, son, daughter, sister, brother etc.

Everyone knows that Christians are supposed to love other people - Jesus said that the most important commandment is that we're to love God and 'love your neighbour as yourself' (Matthew 22:40) - and everyone who's a Christian knows how hard it is...

In this session, we're going to think about how it's possible for someone who is free in Christ to relate well to others; to show them grace and love. If we try to do this before we are really walking in freedom, it can amount to trying - and usually failing! - to obey a set of rules. But now we are free to make good choices.

The first important thing to remember is that how we relate to others is, just like the rest of our lives, built on the foundation of who we are in Christ and what he has done for us.

- 'We love because he first loved us' (1 John 4:19).

- We give freely because we have received freely (Matthew 10:8).

- We are merciful because he has been merciful to us (Luke 6:36).

- We forgive in the same way that Jesus has forgiven us (Ephesians 4:32).

RESPONSIBILITIES

If you listen to a couple having an argument, they often attack the other person's **character** ('You're so selfish') while looking out for their own **needs** ('You are never around when I need you'). Is that how relationships are supposed to work?

Consider the following two passages:

Who are you to judge someone else's servant? To his own master he stands or falls. And he will stand, for the Lord is able to make him stand (Romans 14:4).

Are we to tell people to sort out their character flaws? No, that's not our responsibility. We are not to judge. Each person is responsible before God for their own character. If we try to play the role of the Holy Spirit by pointing out someone else's character faults, it won't work because we are not God.

Do nothing out of selfish ambition or vain conceit, but in humility consider others better than yourselves. Each of you should look not only to your own interests, but also to the interests of others. Your attitude should be the same as that of Christ Jesus. (Philippians 2:3-5).

Where we do have a responsibility towards others before God, it is to meet their needs. So our responsibilities are for **our own character** and to meet **others' needs**. Spend a few minutes thinking about that. What do others need from you?

SPIRITUAL SELF-AWARENESS

We're often really good at spotting other people's sins or bad habits, whilst being completely blind to our own. When we do that, it's often a sign that we are not living that closely to God.

Just look in the Bible at how people react when they get close to God.

In Isaiah 6:1 we read, "In the year that King Uzziah died, I saw the Lord seated on a throne, high and exalted, and the train of his robe filled the temple."

What was the result of this amazing experience of such a close encounter with God? Did Isaiah cry out, 'Woe to me, because my mother is a bad woman'? No! What he actually said was, "Woe to me! I am ruined! For I am a man of unclean lips."

In Luke 5 Peter had been fishing all night without success when Jesus told him to put his nets in a specific place and he started catching fish after fish. Peter suddenly realised just who Jesus was. Did he say, "Go away from me Lord, I have a sinful wife"? No! What Peter did say was, "I am a sinful man".

When we get close to God, we don't become aware of how sinful other people are, but we see ourselves in the bright light of the holiness of God. If we have a period of our life when we're lukewarm towards God, we tend to spot – and point out – other people's sin rather than our own. If you find yourself doing that, have a good look at your own relationship with God.

IT'S NOT ABOUT RIGHTS

Every relationship we have contains both rights to receive and responsibilities to give – but where should we put the emphasis? Satan will tempt us to focus on rights.

You might get angry with your mother, because you think it's your right to receive the newest trainers - but what about your responsibility to honour and love your mother? Or you might fall out with your best friend because you think it's your right that he or she should be there for you all the time - but what about your responsibility to support and care for your friend?

We shouldn't focus on our 'rights', but on our responsibilities, otherwise the relationship will break down sooner or later.

So, in our relationships we shouldn't focus on what we deserve, but on what we can give.

WHAT ABOUT WHEN OTHERS DO WRONG?

What should we do if another Christian keeps sinning? Should we ignore it? Or should we confront them?

In Matthew 7:1 Jesus tells us very clearly that we are not to judge another person. Remember that judging is to do with their character. It is the role of the Holy Spirit to convict them of sin.

The Bible does say, however, that we should help each other within the church by disciplining each other (Galatians 6:1). What's the difference? Well, discipline is not about someone's character, it's about their behaviour. If we personally see another Christian sinning, the Bible tells us to help that person in their relationship with God.

Suppose I catch a friend telling an obvious lie, and I confront them. I could say, "You're a liar!" but actually that would be judgment because I have maligned their character. It would be much better to say, "You have just said something untrue," which simply calls attention to sinful behaviour that I have personally observed.

If the difference between the two phrases seems too subtle, take some time to think it through: the first phrase implies that he has the identity of a liar, that his character is that of a liar. In short it implies that deep down inside he is bad and leaves little hope that he could change. The second phrase says nothing about his identity or character. It just calls out a behaviour issue. It leaves plenty of hope for the future. In fact, perhaps even better would be to say, "You're not a liar. So why did you just tell a lie?" The truth is that this is a child of God who has just acted out of character. Helping him realise that it's acting out of character gives real hope for positive change.

Calling somebody "a liar", "stupid", "clumsy", "proud", or "evil" is an attack on character. It leaves people with no way forward and no resolution because they can't instantly change their character.

If, on the other hand, you point out someone's sinful behaviour to them, you are giving them something that they can work with: "You are right, what I just said wasn't true, and I am sorry I said it, will you forgive me?" That puts an end to the issue there and then, but attacking another person's character can cause lasting damage.

The purpose of this process is never to judge or condemn someone, but to restore them to Christ. It's not your responsibility to force a person to repent. It's between that person and God.

DISCIPLINE AND PUNISHMENT

We need to know the difference between these two things.

God has let the punishment that we deserved fall on Jesus, and how he judges us at the end of the day will depend also on our relationship with Christ. God does discipline us, though. Like any loving father would (Hebrews 12:5-11), he gives us the possibility to ask for forgiveness and to change.

Punishment and judgement look to the past whereas discipline is about looking to the future and moving on with God. It is a positive thing if done in the right way.

Why not pause at this point and read Hebrews 12:1-11.

- Why does God discipline us?

- What is the end result of God's discipline?

- Why is discipline so painful?

SHOULD WE EXPRESS OUR NEEDS?

We all have needs to be accepted and loved – remember the first session about Adam and his needs for security, acceptance and significance? So what should we do if we're in a friendship where those needs aren't met?

Think about these two scenarios:

Two lads always go to watch their football team on a Saturday afternoon. One of the lads starts going out with a girl whom he has fancied for ages but she always plays hockey on a Saturday at the same time and wants her boyfriend to watch her. The other friend suddenly has no one to go to the football with. How does he feel? What should he do? Would a girl react in the same way?

Two girls arrange to meet up for coffee once a week. One of them decides she is too busy and keeps coming up with excuses or promises to be there and stands the other one up. How does the other friend feel? What should she do? Would a boy react in the same way?

It is really important in these scenarios that we do two things.

1. Be honest about how we feel – say this is what you did, without exaggerating, and how it made you feel.

2. Don't be critical of the person – especially their character – don't use phrases like, 'you're so ......' but rather, 'when you did this it made me feel ....'

The main point to focus on from today's session is what we can give in a friendship rather than what we deserve to receive.

QUESTIONS TO PONDER AS YOU PREPARE:

1. What should we do if someone judges us? Should we get defensive?

2. What should we do if we're in a relationship or friendship where our needs aren't met?

3. If we want someone to love us, what should we do? If we need a friend, what should we do?

LOVING OTHERS 11-14

PRAYER AND DECLARATION

Encourage everyone to join together in saying the following prayer and declaration. You can download the PowerPoint slides with the words for these from the website.

It would be good to suggest that the young people stand up and speak out the declaration clearly and confidently to the heavenly realms. They could shout it out and use appropriate actions!

PRAYER

❝ Thank you Father that you have given me other people to relate to. Help me to understand how to do that in a way that reflects you. In Jesus' name, Amen.

DECLARATION: IN A CLEAR, CONFIDENT TONE!

❝ We belong to Jesus Christ. We instruct any and all evil to leave our presence now in Jesus' name.

STARTING POINT

Start by giving a short summary of the previous session. A good resource for this is the Overview found in the Core of the previous session.

You could ask one or two to share how they are getting along with stronghold-busters. Encourage them to keep going with these. Remind them that, even though it probably feels like a waste of time sometimes, they will eventually see a breakthrough.

INTRODUCTORY ACTIVITIES

BACK-TO-BACK
Get two people to sit on the floor, back to back.

They have to stand straight up without using their hands.

If they manage it, add another person and keep doing so until it's not working anymore.

How many can you manage?

Explain:

You couldn't have done that by yourselves; we are created by God to need each other!

FRIENDS LIKE THESE
Get two people out the front who claim to be good friends or even going out. Send one out of the room and ask the other one the following questions:

What is your friend's favourite food?

What is your friend's favourite colour?

What is your friend's most embarrassing moment?

If your friend were a superhero who would they be?

Then get the friend back in the room and ask them what the actual answers are – give them a point/ prize for each correct answer. If you have time, play the game again with another couple.

WORSHIP ACTIVITY

Provide pens and a few sticky notes for everyone.

Encourage the group to think of the people that have meant the most to them, and then write it on a note in the following format (you might what to write one first as a model):

Dear God – THANK YOU SO MUCH for my mother - because she has always been there for me. Bob

Or

Jenny – Because she is such a great best friend. Dave

Ask everyone to stick the notes on a wall (or a floor, or a table) where everyone can see, then get people to pray 'thank you' prayers, all out loud at the same time (eg 'Father God, I thank you for Bob's mother, that she's always been there for him, Amen.' or 'Dear God, thank you that Jenny is such a great friend to Dave. Amen.')

It is important that the focus of this activity is thanking God for our friends, not just thanking them!

INTRODUCTION TO SESSION
Since God made us to be in relationship with one another, he has also shown us how to do it. That's what we're looking into today.

 ## DVD CHAPTER 1

Play Session 11, chapter 1 – 'People, People, People' – of the accompanying DVD.

Explain

Everyone knows that Christians are supposed to love other people - Jesus said the most important commandment is that we're to love God and

'love your neighbour as yourself' (Matthew 22:40).

And everyone who is a Christian knows how hard it is. We can only do it because of what Jesus has done for us:

'We love because he first loved us' (1 John 4:19)

THE MAIN POINT

 ## DVD CHAPTER 2

Play Session 11, chapter 2 – 'Setting Them Straight' – of the accompanying DVD.

The Bible has many practical tips for how to relate to each other.

Here are four 'guidelines' for healthy relationships and there is an action for each one to be repeated as you progress through them as memory aids.

1. I should not point out other people's faults ACTION – point in front of you.

Game – hand out post-its and get young people to write one positive thing about the person on their right and stick the post it to their head.

Prime a leader sitting next to another leader to write a really negative comment on their post it.

Then ask each person to take the note off their head and read it out.

Ask the leader who had the negative note on their head to say how they felt.

Explain that when your character is attacked, it can be really hurtful.

If you listen to a couple having an argument, they often attack the other person's character ('You're so selfish') while looking out for their own needs ('You are never around when I need you'). Is that how relationships are supposed to work?

Get a young person to stand up and read Romans 14:4.

Are we to tell people to sort out their character flaws? No, that's not our responsibility. It's between that person and God.

Get another young person to stand up and read Philippians 2:3-5.

According to this verse, what are our responsibilities towards others?

It's to meet their needs.

So our responsibilities are for **our own character** and to meet **others' needs**. If we try and play the role of the Holy Spirit by pointing out someone else's faults, it won't work, because we are not God.

2. I should not look out for my rights in a relationship ACTION – put hand over eyebrows as if shielding your eyes to look into the distance.

Give one of the group members a box of sweets/chocolates.

Explain that they are theirs and they do not have to give them away but can do so if they want to.

Ask group members if they think they deserve a sweet – why should they all be given to one person?

Ask the person with the sweets how many they are going to give away and would they give all of them away?

Explain that in our relationships we shouldn't focus on what we deserve, but on what we can give.

In some ways, every relationship we are in has both rights and responsibilities – but where should we put the emphasis? Satan will tempt us to focus on rights.

You might get angry with your mother, because you think it's your right to receive the newest trainers.

But what about your responsibility to honour and love your mother?

Or you might fall out with your best friend because you think it's your right that he or she should be there for you all the time.

But what about your responsibility to support and care for your friend?

DISCUSSION
Divide into groups of 4-6 and discuss the following questions:

- What is your responsibility towards other people?

- How do you want to be treated by others?

3. I should not criticise other Christians, but I can help them ACTION – wag your finger as if telling someone off.

So, we know that we're not to play the role of the Holy Spirit by pointing out other people's sin; but what should we do if another Christian keeps messing up? Should we ignore it? Or should we confront them?

In Matthew 7:1 Jesus tells us very clearly that we are not to judge another person. Judging has something to do with who that person is, their character.

🎞 TV CLIP

Illustrate with a clip from a TV talent show (you can probably find one on the Internet) in which the judges criticise awful singing. Point out the way this makes the person being judged feel.

The Bible does say, however, that we should help each other within the church by disciplining each other (Galatians 6:1).

This is not about a person's character, but about their behaviour, it is about lovingly confronting a Christian if they keep messing up. Leader's Note: refer to the information on page 264 of the Core section if you find you need more details here.

Explain that the Galatians verse says they need to be restored gently.

Illustration:

To demonstrate this pass an egg round the group and say this is done as gently as we are able so that we can really sensitively help others.

4. I should stay calm when others get on my nerves ACTION – motion your hands up and down at the side of your body as if signalling calm in the room.

If someone starts pointing out all our faults, it can be difficult to not get angry and defensive. But we should make Jesus our model in this:

'When they hurled their insults at him, he did not retaliate; when he suffered, he made no threats. Instead, he entrusted himself to him who judges justly.'

(1 Peter 2:23)

Those who criticise you are either immature or hurting, and being aggressive and retaliating will only feed their anger.

⊙ DVD CHAPTER 3

Play Session 11, chapter 3 – 'Responsibility To Love?' – of the accompanying DVD.

Explain

By learning to be humble like Jesus, we may get a chance instead to serve the person who criticises us, and lead them closer to God. If we come in anger, we only invoke more anger, but if we, like Jesus, come in humility and acceptance, the other person receives a chance to soften their heart.

DISCUSSION – ARE YOU A GOOD FRIEND?
Place a large piece of paper in the middle of the group and ask them to write down - what do you think makes a good friend?

Ask the young people to rate themselves out of ten as to how good a friend they think they are – Depending on your group either allow them to do this quietly in their head or out loud.

ACTION RECAP – go through the actions again to recap on the points you have looked at today.

Recap again the main point from today's session: we need to focus on what we can give in a friendship rather than what we deserve.

RESPONSE

Give the young people a postcard. Put on some quiet music.

We're going to respond by using these postcards.

God wants us to have good relationships with the people around us.

In a moment's silence, think about a friend whom you want to encourage and write them a note thanking them for being your friend.

You might need to apologise for focusing on what you deserve rather than what you can give. Focus on the positives and encourage them as a child of God just like you.

If you can remember some of the truths about you we are in Christ encourage your friend with those.

Pray

Father, help us to be good friends and to focus on what we can give in a friendship rather than what we deserve. Amen

SMALL GROUPS & PRAYER FOCUS

* What should we do if someone criticises us? How should we react?

* What should we do if we don't think we're getting what we deserve in a friendship?

* What needs do we all have as people and friends?

⭐ AND THERE'S MORE!

Draw the group's attention to the questions on page 48 of the Youth Guide 11-14 and suggest they complete them at home:

- If God loves us no matter what, how does this make it easier to love others?

- How does it feel when someone points out your faults?

- Why is it better to focus on your responsibilities in a relationship, rather than on your rights?

- How can we build other people up?

Encourage the group to keep going with their stronghold-busters. Even though it probably feels like a waste of time sometimes, they will eventually see a breakthrough.

? CLOSING QUESTION

The question to consider before next week is on page 49 of the Youth Guide 11-14:

'What are your goals for the rest of your life? How can you be sure that you want the same thing as God for your life?'

LOVING OTHERS 15-18

PRAYER AND DECLARATION

Encourage everyone to join together in saying the following prayer and declaration. You can download the PowerPoint slides with the words for these from the website.

It would be good to suggest that the young people stand up and speak out the declaration clearly and confidently to the heavenly realms. They could shout it out and use appropriate actions!

PRAYER

" Thank you Father that you have given me other people to relate to. Help me to understand how to do that in a way that reflects you. In Jesus' name, Amen.

DECLARATION: IN A CLEAR, CONFIDENT TONE!

" We belong to Jesus Christ. We instruct any and all evil to leave our presence now in Jesus' name.

STARTING POINT

Start by giving a short summary of the previous session. A good resource for this is the Overview found in the Core of the previous session.

You could ask one or two to share how they are getting along with stronghold-busters. Encourage them to keep going with these. Remind them that , even though it probably feels like a waste of time sometimes, they will eventually see a breakthrough.

Since God made us to be in relationship with one another he has also shown us how to do it. That's what we're looking into today.

⊙ DVD CHAPTER 1

Play Session 11, chapter 1 – 'People, People, People' – of the accompanying DVD.

Explain:

Everyone knows that Christians are supposed to love other people - Jesus said the most important commandment is that we're to love God and

'love your neighbour as yourself' (Matthew 22:40).

And everyone who is a Christian knows how hard it is. We can only do it because of what Jesus has done for us:

- We love because he first loved us (1 John 4:19).

- We give freely because we have received freely (Matthew 10:8).

- We are merciful because he has been merciful to us (Luke 6:36).

- We forgive in the same way that Jesus has forgiven us (Ephesians 4:32).

⌂ SOAPBOX

Some people are easy to love, others are not. The challenge with family is that you are stuck with them no matter how well you get on together!

Give an example of a family member's behaviour that irritated you (keep the person anonymous and the story quite light).

E.g. a sibling who would always steal the best bed when you went on holiday or your cousin's irritating laugh.

Everyone is different but God calls us to love them all. The thing that annoys us is probably more to do with us than it is to do with them. Try to look through God's eyes – he loves no matter what.

⊙ DVD CHAPTER 2

Play Session 11, chapter 2 – 'Setting Them Straight' – of the accompanying DVD.

The Bible has many practical tips for how to relate to each other.

Here are four 'guidelines' for healthy relationships:

I SHOULD NOT POINT OUT OTHER PEOPLE'S FAULTS

If you listen to a couple having an argument, they often attack the other person's character ('You're so selfish') while looking out for their own needs ('You are never around when I need you'). Is that how relationships are supposed to work?

Get a young person to stand up and read Romans 14:4.

Are we to tell people to sort out their character flaws? No, that's not our responsibility. It's between that person and God.

Get another young person to stand up and read Philippians 2:3-5.

According to this passage, what are our responsibilities towards others?

It's to meet their needs.

So our responsibilities are for **our own character** and to meet **others' needs**. If we try and play the role of the Holy Spirit by pointing out someone else's faults, it won't work, because we are not God.

I SHOULD NOT LOOK OUT FOR MY RIGHTS IN A RELATIONSHIP

Explain that in our relationships we shouldn't focus on what we deserve, but on what we can give.

Every relationship we are in has both rights and responsibilities – but where should we put the emphasis? Satan will tempt us to focus on rights.

You might get angry with your mother, because you think it's your right to stay out as long as you want with your mates.

But what about your responsibility to honour and love your mother?

Or you might fall out with your best friend because you think it's your right that he or she should be there for you all the time.

But what about your responsibility to support and care for your friend?

Discussion:

Divide into groups of 4-6 and discuss the following questions:

- What is your responsibility towards other people?
- How do you want to be treated by others?

I SHOULD NOT CRITICISE OTHER CHRISTIANS, BUT I CAN HELP THEM

So, we know that we're not to play the role of the Holy Spirit by pointing out other people's sin; but what should we do if another Christian keeps messing up? Should we ignore it? Or should we confront them?

In Matthew 7:1 Jesus tells us very clearly that we are not to judge another person. Judging has something to do with who that person is; their character.

The Bible does say, however, that we should help each other within the church by disciplining each other (Galatians 6:1).

This is not about a person's character, but about their behaviour, it is about lovingly confronting a

Christian if they keep messing up.

Explain that the Galatians verse says that they need to be 'restored gently'.

To demonstrate this, pass an egg around the group saying that we need to do it as gently as we are able so that we can really sensitively help others.

I SHOULD STAY CALM WHEN OTHERS GET ON MY NERVES

If someone starts pointing out all our faults, it can be difficult not to get angry and defensive. But we should make Jesus our model in this:

'When they hurled their insults at him, he did not retaliate; when he suffered, he made no threats. Instead, he entrusted himself to him who judges justly.' (1 Peter 2:23)

Those who criticise you are either immature or hurting, and being aggressive and retaliating will only feed their anger.

 # WORSHIP ACTIVITY

Provide pens and a few sticky notes for everyone.

Encourage the group to think of the people that have meant the most to them, and then write it on a note in the following format (you might want to write one first as a model):

Dear God – THANK YOU SO MUCH for my mother - Because she has always been there for me. Bob

Or

Jenny – Because she is such a great best friend. Dave

Ask everyone to stick the notes on a wall (or a floor, or a table) where everyone can see, then get people to pray 'thank you' prayers, all out loud at the same time (eg. 'Father God, I thank you for Bob's mother, that she's always been there for him, Amen.' or 'Dear God, thank you that Jenny is such a great friend to Dave. Amen.')

It is important that the focus of this activity is thanking God for our friends, not just thanking them!

At this point, review the What's the point? section on page 46 of the Youth Guide 15-18 which says:

- Staying close to God and having a good relationship with him should lead to good relationships with others.

- We have two main responsibilities: making sure we do what is right and helping meet others' needs.

- When others are struggling with sin, look to build them up with love and acceptance when helping them walk in truth.

 # DVD CHAPTER 3

Play Session 11, chapter 3 – 'Responsibility To Love?' – of the accompanying DVD.

Explain

By learning to be humble like Jesus, we may get a chance instead to serve the person who criticises us, and lead them closer to God. If we come in anger, we only invoke more anger, but if we, like Jesus, come in humility and acceptance, the other person receives a chance to soften their heart.

SMALL GROUPS

EITHER:

Refer the young people to page 48 of the Youth Guide 15-18 and get them to run through the questions there:

- Does the fact that God loves us no matter what we do make it easier to love other people? Why? Why not?

- Why do we naturally focus on our rights in a relationship? How would the relationship change if we focused instead on our responsibilities?

- Why does God discipline us and how does it make us better Christians?

- What's the difference between judging someone and disciplining them?

OR: (if you would prefer them to do those questions at home)

- What should we do if someone criticises us? How should we react?

- What should we do if we don't think we're getting what we deserve in a friendship?

- What needs do we all have as people and friends?

RESPONSE

Give the young people a postcard. Put on some quiet music.

We're going to respond by using these postcards.

God wants us to have good relationships with the people around us.

In a moment's silence, think about a friend whom you want to encourage and write them a note thanking them for being your friend.

You might need to apologise for focusing on what you deserve rather than what you can give. Focus on the positives and encourage them as a child of God just like you.

If you can remember some of the truths about who we are in Christ, encourage your friend with those.

Pray

Father, help us to be good friends and to focus on what we can give in a friendship rather than what we deserve. Amen

AND THERE'S MORE!

Draw the group's attention to page 49 of the Youth Guide 11-18:

Challenge: Encourage at least two people every day this week either by saying something that builds them up or giving them something unconditionally. Take a special interest in those who seem to be on the edge of things.

Think: Healthy relationships are made up of rights and responsibilities. It can be really easy to focus on our rights. Think about your responsibilities as a Christian to your friends, parents and teachers.

Encourage the group to keep going with their stronghold-busters. Even though it probably feels like a waste of time sometimes, they will eventually see a breakthrough.

? CLOSING QUESTION

The question for next week is on page 49 of the Youth Guide 15-18:

'What are your goals for the rest of your life? How can you be sure that you want the same thing as God for your life?'

SESSION TWELVE:
WHERE ARE YOU GOING?

'The goal of this command is love, which comes from a pure heart and a good conscience and a sincere faith.'

1 Timothy 1:5

WHERE ARE YOU GOING? CORE

PREPARATION

This is the third of four sessions in Part D, the final part of Freedom In Christ For Young People. The accompanying material for this session is in the fourth book in The Freedom In Christ Discipleship Series, The You God Planned (Monarch 2008), pages 13-55.

KEY VERSE

1 Timothy 1:5 – 'The goal of this command is love, which comes from a pure heart and a good conscience and a sincere faith.'

AIM

To understand how faith relates to the goals and desires we have for our lives so that we can live a life of genuine freedom in Christ and become the person God created us to be.

KEY TRUTH

Nothing and no one can keep us from being the person God created us to be.

OVERVIEW

It is important that we understand the difference between godly goals and godly desires, and see that there is no godly goal for our lives that we cannot achieve in Christ. Our godly desires on the other hand may or may not be achieved. Their outcome is beyond our control and we must resist the temptation to base our value on achieving them. God's goal for our lives is that we become more like Christ, and bringing our own goals in line with that will enable us to live a life of true freedom.

INTRODUCTION

In this session, we want to help the young people understand what God's overriding goal for their life is. We then want them to evaluate any goal they have to see if it ties in with God's overall goal for them.

It might be helpful at this point to say exactly what we mean by 'goal'. All of us spend our lives working for the things that we have come to believe will make us happy and fulfilled. These are our goals.

We are specifically referring to those things we have come to believe are fundamental to our sense of who we are and what we achieve in our lives, those results by which we measure our very selves.

It is possible, of course, to have other objectives – such as getting up earlier or staying awake during the talk at church – but if we fail to achieve them, we will probably just shrug our shoulders and resolve to try harder in future.

We are not talking about those things but about the big things we have come to believe are fundamental to our sense of fulfilment and achievement in life which, if we don't achieve them, leave us feeling inadequate or thinking we are failures.

GOD'S GOAL FOR OUR LIVES

What characteristics would a goal from a loving, caring God have?

First of all, it would be achievable. Would God ever say in effect, "I have something for you to do. I know you won't be able to do it, but give it your best shot." That's ridiculous! It's like saying to someone, "I want you to cut the grass. Unfortunately, it's covered with rubble, the mower doesn't work and there's no fuel. But try your best anyway." God does not work like that.

To put it another way, no God-given goal for your life need ever be impossible, uncertain, or blocked – God would not do that to you. You can become the person God intends.

Secondly, God's goal for your life cannot be dependent on other people. If it were, they may choose not to co-operate and it would not be a goal that we could definitely achieve. God is absolutely fair and would not ask us to do something that was not completely within our ability to do.

Similarly, it cannot be dependent on circumstances. We cannot control or influence the circumstances of our life that much. If our goal were dependent on them, we could never be certain that it would be fulfilled.

So what is God's goal for our lives? Actually it's not about what we **do**. It's all about what we are **like**. Above all, God wants us to develop in character. To put it another way, he wants us to become more and more like Jesus. That's it!

Circumstances may go against us. Perhaps we fail a crucial exam. That can be tough but what a great opportunity to grow in perseverance. People may go against us. Perhaps our friends fall out with us. What a great opportunity to grow in love towards them.

Maybe that sounds just a little bit trite! However, think about it. Why could Paul say that he actually rejoices in his sufferings (Romans 5:3)? Was he some kind of masochist? No, look at the verse in its context:

'Not only so, but we also rejoice in our sufferings, because we know that suffering produces perseverance; perseverance, character; and character, hope' (Romans 5:3-4).

He rejoices because they actually help him towards God's goal for him, growing in character and therefore becoming more like Jesus.

FEELINGS CAN HIGHLIGHT WRONG GOALS

We looked in Session 8 at how negative emotions can help us by showing us that we're living our lives by the wrong goals.

If we have an experience or are in a relationship that ends up making us feel angry, anxious or depressed, it might well be because we're working towards a goal that's wrong for us, based on something we believe that's wrong.

Let's see how that works. Can you remember a time when you were younger that all your friends were allowed to do something and you weren't? Maybe it was going to a concert in a dodgy part of town. Perhaps this had become so important that it felt as if your whole life depended on going and you decided to have one last go at persuading your parents to relent.

How did you feel as you waited to talk to them? Well, when a goal we have is uncertain, we feel anxious.

What about when you asked them really nicely with your best pleading eyes and they still said no very firmly. How did you feel then? Did you thank them for caring so deeply for you? No - you exploded in a fit of anger! When a goal we have is blocked, we feel angry.

Finally, when your angry tantrum didn't achieve a change of mind and you realised that there was no way you were going to get to the concert, how did you feel then? Depressed, because your goal had become impossible, completely out of reach.

BLOCKED GOALS LEAD TO ANGER

When we want to achieve a particular goal and something gets in the way, we get angry. That emotion may well be flagging up to you a goal that is not in line with God's goal for your life. Because, remember, God's goal for your life cannot be blocked.

So, if your mother's goal is to have a happy and loving family; anyone in your family has the potential to block the goal and make her angry. Or if you have a good, spiritual goal, like 'My goal is that everyone in my school / work becomes Christians,' who has the potential to block that goal? Every single person in your school / work! If you have goals that are dependent on others, you'll end up fed up and disillusioned if you don't achieve the goal.

The anger you feel when a goal is blocked can be a good signpost for you – maybe you should aim for a slightly different goal?

UNCERTAIN GOALS LEAD TO ANXIETY

If you feel anxious, it's likely to be because you have an uncertain goals. So, for example, if you've come to believe that your sense of worth or well-being is dependent on having enough money in the bank, you'll end up anxious, because there are no guarantees that you'll be able to ever make enough money or that stock market crash won't wipe out what you do have. No God-given goal is uncertain.

IMPOSSIBLE GOALS LEAD TO DEPRESSION

Sometimes, when we discover that a goal, that might have been uncertain and made us anxious, is definitely not going to be achieved, we can get depressed. Depression can sometimes have physical causes but if not, it's often rooted in a sense of hopelessness and helplessness.

Imagine that you had a best friend who wasn't a Christian, and you made it your life goal to help him or her become a Christian. As the years go past, and nothing happens, you might start believing that you're a bad friend and a useless Christian, and eventually you might even get depressed.

But at the end of the day you can't convert someone, only God can. Wanting your friends to become Christians is good and right, but not if it's a goal that you base your self-worth on!

The thing is, most of us don't even know what our goals are. We've just kind of unconsciously developed them. When we feel anxious, angry or depressed, those seemingly negative emotions are doing us a real favour in prompting us to look inside and work out what we have been believing that is not in line with God's Word.

Stop and think about it;

- Do you agree that emotions can show whether your goals are in line with God's will?

- How do you tend to react to blocked goals? Do you remember a time when you didn't get what you wanted? How did that make you feel?

- If we believe that our self-worth depends on a wrong goal, how can we change that before we get depressed?

- How should we respond when one of our goals is blocked?

TURNING BAD GOALS INTO GOOD GOALS

If God gave you a goal for your life, would anyone be able to block it? No. Would it be uncertain? No. Would it be impossible? No.

We need to know the difference between a godly 'goal' and a godly 'desire'.

A godly goal is any specific aim that reflects God's purpose for your life and does not depend on people or circumstances beyond your ability or right to control, for example, becoming more self-controlled.

A godly desire is any specific result that depends on the cooperation of other people, the success of events or circumstances which you have no right or ability to control, for example, someone becoming a Christian.

We have to be aware that many of our desires in life won't be met. But there's no need for that to affect our sense of who we are. When we don't get what we desire we might be disappointed, but we don't need to get depressed.

If we choose goals that are to do with what we are like not what we do, we will avoid lots of unnecessary anger, anxiety and depression. So, in our example of your non-Christian friend, you could change your goal to 'I want to be the best and most caring friend that I can be' – only you can affect the outcome of that!

NOBODY CAN STOP YOU
God's goal for you is to be the person that he made you to be. He wants you to become more and more like Jesus in character. Who can stop you achieving that? Nobody. Apart from you!

QUESTIONS TO THINK ABOUT AS YOU PREPARE

1. What's the difference between a goal and a desire?

2. What do you think is God's goal for your life? Can anyone or anything block it?

3. How do you feel about the fact than nothing can keep you from being the person God created you to be?

WHERE ARE YOU GOING? 11-14

LEADER'S PREPARATION

Pray together:

> Father God, in this session call us all to follow you more; to head for the goal you have for our lives. Amen.

YOU MAY NEED

Two buckets or bins and ping pong balls or scrunched up paper

Accompanying DVD / DVD player / TV / projector

Paper and pens

Blindfold

Goal keeper gloves

Bibles

Small group questions

PRAYER AND DECLARATION

Encourage everyone to join together in saying the following prayer and declaration. You can download the PowerPoint slides with the words for these from the website.

It would be good to suggest that the young people stand up and speak out the declaration clearly and confidently to the heavenly realms. They could shout it out and use appropriate actions!

PRAYER

> Father, please help me to realise that you have purposes and plans for my life so that I can truly live in your freedom. In Jesus' name, Amen.

DECLARATION: IN A CLEAR, CONFIDENT TONE!

> Jesus is my closest friend. He doesn't have any time for you enemies of his. He doesn't want you hanging about bothering me, and trying to distract and irritate me. So I tell all evil to leave!

🔍 STARTING POINT

Start by giving a short summary of the previous session. A good resource for this is the Overview found in the Core of the previous session.

INTRODUCTORY ACTIVITIES

PING PONG BUCKET BALL

- Split the group into two teams.

- Get two buckets or bins and put them at one end of the room.

- A couple of metres away from them mark a line with some gaffer/masking tape.

- Give each team at least three ping pong balls.

- From the line the two teams must bounce/throw the balls into the buckets.

- Award one point if a ball bounces in the bucket and bounces out again and three points if it stays in there.

Alternatively use scrunched-up balls of newspaper or, if you have the facility, have a basketball shooting competition. The point of the game is that the players are shooting for a goal.

Leave the game set up for the purposes of the talk.

⊙ DVD CHAPTER 1

Play Session 12, chapter 1 – 'When I Grow Up...' – of the accompanying DVD.

Ask the group:

- In your wildest dreams, what would you love to achieve in your life?

- Where would you love to be?

- What would you love to be doing?

- What do you think God wants to see you become? Just imagine...

- How are you going to get there?

- What are you going to aim for?

Explain:

We were trying to hit a goal in our game and today is all about goals in our lives – how do we even know that we're aiming for the right goals?

WORSHIP ACTIVITY

Give everyone a slip of paper and a pen, and ask them to write one line of worship to God.

When everyone is done, put all the slips of paper in a hat, mix them and pass the hat around.

Let the young people pick one slip at a time and read it out loud. Encourage everyone to respond in some way to the line (eg. say amen, woop woop, clap etc.) and then pass the hat on.

INTRODUCTION TO SESSION

We're going to try to find out what God's goal for our lives is.

We all have goals in our lives, places we want to reach. But the question is whether they're just our good ideas or whether they're from God.

God's goal for us is not so much what we **do** but what we are **like**.

He wants us to become more and more like Jesus.

THE MAIN POINT

DVD CHAPTER 2

Play Session 12, chapter 2 – 'God's Goal' – of the accompanying DVD.

FEELINGS CAN HIGHLIGHT WRONG GOALS

The main point of today's session is that God's goal for us is to become more like Jesus. So to emphasise this whenever I ask the question, 'What's God's goal for us?' You say/shout, 'To become more like Jesus.'

Sometimes we set goals in our lives without really being aware of it, we just aim for what money and fame – stuff the world says will make us happy. However, these goals will not make us happy long term if they are not in line with what God wants for us.

So, how do we know if we're heading the wrong way?

Remember how we talked a few sessions ago about emotions, and how they can be warning signs to show that something is wrong. Well, if we have an experience or are in a relationship that ends up making us feel angry, anxious or fed up, it might be because we're working towards a goal that's wrong for us, based on something we believe that's wrong.

Here's some examples:

• Blocked goals lead to anger

Get the buckets and the ping pong balls out again. Ask a volunteer to play the game again but this time appoint a 'goalkeeper' whose job it is to block the bucket – this should hopefully be quite easy and make it really difficult for the player to score in the goal.

Ask the player how this made them feel – hopefully anger is the relevant emotion!

When we want to get somewhere, and someone else stops you, it's easy to get angry as demonstrated by this game. The anger you feel when a goal is blocked can be a good signpost for you – maybe the goal you are aiming for is a wrong one. Because no goal that God has for you can be blocked.

- Uncertain goals lead to anxiety

Play the bucket and ping pong ball game again. This time blindfold a different volunteer and tell them you are going to move the goal.

Then get the player to try and play without telling them where the goal has moved to. Ask the player how this made them feel – hopefully this time anxiety is the relevant emotion!

If you feel anxious, it might be because some of your goals are uncertain; there are no guarantees that you will be able to reach them.

- Impossible goals lead to being fed up and depressed

Play the bucket and ping pong ball game one more time. This time get someone to try and score in the bucket but turn the bucket upside down making the game impossible.

Let the player try for a while! Then ask the player how this made them feel – hopefully this time being fed up/frustration is the relevant emotion!

Sometimes, when we discover that a goal, that might have been uncertain and made us anxious, is impossible, we can get totally fed up and depressed.

Imagine that you had a best friend who wasn't a Christian, and you made it your life goal to help them come to know Jesus.

If nothing happens, you might start believing that you're a bad friend and a useless Christian, and get totally fed up. But it's not your choice whether your friend becomes a Christian or not!

TURNING BAD GOALS INTO GOOD GOALS
If God gave you a goal for your life, would anyone be able to block it? No. Would it be uncertain? No. Would it be impossible? No.

If God gives us a goal there will be no one who will be able to stop us achieving that goal – He loves us and would not give us something that's too difficult for us.

This is why God's only goal for us is to become more like Jesus. What's God's goal for us? To become more like Jesus.

THE DIFFERENCE BETWEEN A 'GOAL' AND A 'DESIRE'
A godly desire is something good that we would like to happen, but we have no power over whether it happens or not – other people can get in the way.

When we don't get what we desire we might get disappointed, but we shouldn't need to get too fed up.

It is absolutely brilliant to have dreams about what you can do with your life so long as we make sure we know these are desires and not goals and when other people get in the way of them we don't get too angry, anxious or fed up.

A godly goal is one that God has set in place for you, and it only depends on you whether you can reach it or not. What's God's goal for us? To become more like Jesus.

If we change our goals to be in line with God's will, we will avoid lots of unnecessary anger, anxiety and upset.

So, in our example of your non-Christian friend, you could change your goal to 'I want to be the best and most caring friend that I can be' – like Jesus – only you can affect the outcome of that!

◉ DVD CHAPTER 3

Play Session 12, chapter 3 – 'Aiming Right' – of the accompanying DVD.

GOD'S GOAL FOR OUR LIVES
What's God's goal for us? To become more like Jesus.

God's goal for us is to be the person that he made us to be; he wants us to become like Jesus. Nobody, apart from yourself, can stop you from getting there, but every day will be a struggle against the world, the flesh (remember that?) and the devil.

God's goal for our life is to do with our character – what we are **like** – rather than what we **do**.

When we run into difficulties, we shouldn't run away (where we'll bump into the same problem again sooner or later), but we should work through them and end up better people ourselves.

That is how we grow and become more like Jesus.

↗ RESPONSE

DISCUSSION
If we are to become more like Jesus with our lives, it is important that we know what he is like.

So, what is Jesus like?

Hand out pieces of paper and ask the young people to write down the characteristic of Jesus that they would most like to develop in their own lives. Encourage the young people to write God's goal for their lives at the bottom of the sheet of paper.

Then put the bucket used for the game in the middle of the room, screw up the bits of paper and shoot them into the goal as a sign of saying that our goal is to become more like Jesus.

Review the points on page 51 of the Youth Guide 11-14 which say:

- God's main goal for you is that you grow to be more like Jesus.

- You are the only one who can stop yourself achieving this.

- We need to put our hope in God and in his plan for our lives.

Pray:

Lord, we bring all these emotions and goals before you. We're sorry when we've reacted in ways that aren't honouring to you. We're sorry when we've lived with goals which might have been good desires, but aren't your goals for our lives. Thank you that you forgive us. Help us to

know, and live by, your goal for our lives. Amen

 ## SMALL GROUPS & PRAYER FOCUS

- What's the difference between a goal and a desire?

- What do you think is God's goal for your life? Can anyone or anything block it?

- How do you feel about the fact than nothing can keep you from being the person God created you to be?

 ## AND THERE'S MORE!

Direct the young people's attention to the questions on page 52 of their Youth Guide 15-18:

- Goals that seem uncertain, blocked or impossible make us feel anxious, angry and really discouraged. Can you see this in your life?

- Write down some of your goals that are probably not right then ask God to show you the truth about them.

- Where should you put your sense of worth – in your goals or in God? Why?

- When hard times come along why should we not run away?

Suggest that they spend some time at home consider these and also the Challenge and Think sections on page 51:

Challenge: Think about the thing you most want to become or do in your life. Becoming more like Jesus and following him is more important than that. Tell God that following him and his plans are more important than your own.

Think: How much do you listen to what the world says your goals should be – looking good, having money, owning the latest gadgets, having a girlfriend/ boyfriend - what does God say?

? CLOSING QUESTION

This is on page 53 of the Youth Guide 15-18:

If you discover that your goals for your life are different from God's – would you be willing to change?

Encourage the group to keep going with their stronghold-busters. Even though it probably feels like a waste of time sometimes, they will eventually see a breakthrough.

WHERE ARE YOU GOING? 15-18

LEADER'S PREPARATION

Pray together:

> Father God, in this session call us all to follow you more; to head for the goal you have for our lives. Amen.

YOU MAY NEED

Accompanying DVD / DVD player / TV / projector

Bucket/ bin

Paper

Pens

Hat

Bibles

PRAYER AND DECLARATION

Encourage everyone to join together in saying the following prayer and declaration. You can download the PowerPoint slides with the words for these from the website.

It would be good to suggest that the young people stand up and speak out the declaration clearly and confidently to the heavenly realms. They could shout it out and use appropriate actions!

PRAYER

> Father, please help me to realise that you have purposes and plans for my life so that I can truly live in your freedom. In Jesus' name, Amen.

DECLARATION: IN A CLEAR, CONFIDENT TONE!

> Jesus is my closest friend. He doesn't have any time for you enemies of his. He doesn't want you hanging about bothering me, and trying to distract and irritate me. So I tell all evil to leave!

STARTING POINT

Start by giving a short summary of the previous session. A good resource for this is the Overview found in the Core of the previous session.

Over the welcome drinks ask the group;

- In your wildest dreams, what would you love to achieve in your life?

- Where would you love to be?

- What would you love to be doing?

- What do you think God wants to see you become? Just imagine?

- How are you going to get there?

- What are you going to aim for?

DVD CHAPTER 1

Play Session 12, chapter 1 – 'When I Grow Up...' - of the accompanying DVD.

SOAPBOX

Share a personal story about what you wanted to achieve, be or do.

Explain:

Today we're going to look into how that works and we're going to find out about God's goal for our lives.

We all have goals in our lives, places we want to reach. But the question is whether they're our best ideas or whether they're from God.

FEELINGS CAN HIGHLIGHT WRONG GOALS

The main point of today's session is that God's goal for us is to become more like Jesus. So to emphasise this whenever I ask the question, 'What's God's goal for us?' You say/shout, 'To become more like Jesus.'

Sometimes we set goals in our lives without really being aware of it, we just aim for what money and fame – stuff the world says will make us happy. However, these goals will not make us happy long term if they are not in line with what God wants for us.

DVD CHAPTER 2

Play Session 12, chapter 2 – 'God's Goal' – of the accompanying DVD.

What you aim for in life depends on what you believe.

Ever played darts? Think about it; the further away you move the more important it becomes that your aim is good! As a new Christian, your aim might not be great but if you never learn to throw straight, to aim for the right goals, you could end up miles away from where you ought to be!

WHAT IS SUCCESS FOR A CHRISTIAN?

It's important to aim right, turn to the person next to you and answer these questions.

In twelve months time, where would you have wanted to get to in your Christian life?

What would you call a success?

The answer is not what we do, but what we are like – it's about being more like Jesus.

Leader's Note: get your leaders to lead this section in small groups, so have as many groups as you have leaders. Encourage them to use relevant personal stories. If it is normally only you leading the session, ask a couple of guests to come along and help out for one night. Try to ensure the leaders get the information before the session so they can prepare.

FEELINGS CAN HIGHLIGHT WRONG GOALS

Remember how we talked a few sessions ago about emotions, and how they can be warning signs to show that something is wrong. Well, if we have an experience or are in a relationship that ends up making us feel angry, anxious or depressed, it might be because we're working towards a goal that's wrong for us, based on something we believe that's wrong. God wants what is best for us and has given us these feelings to let us know that we may be aiming for the wrong thing.

Warning!

However, sometimes we can feel like we are struggling but it is God's way of moulding us and shaping us through a challenging experience. Be wary of making decisions solely based on feelings.

BLOCKED GOALS LEAD TO ANGER

When we want to get somewhere, and someone else stops you, it's easy to get angry. Unfortunately, some goals we might have are quite easily blocked.

So, if your mother's goal is to have a happy and loving family; anyone in your family has the potential to block the goal and make her angry. Or if you have a good, spiritual goal, like 'My goal is that everyone in my school / work becomes Christians,' who has the potential to block that goal? Every single person in your school / work! If you have goals that are dependent on others, you'll end up fed up and disillusioned if you don't achieve the goal.

The anger you feel when a goal is blocked can be a good signpost for you – maybe you should aim for a slightly different goal?

UNCERTAIN GOALS LEAD TO ANXIETY

It's not just anger that highlights a wrong goal, anxiety does too. If you feel anxious, it's because some of your goals are uncertain; there are no guarantees that you will be able to reach them. So, for example, if you've come to believe that your sense of worth or well-being is dependent on making lots of money, you'll end up anxious, because there are no guarantees that you'll ever be able to make enough money. We need a goal that is certain.

IMPOSSIBLE GOALS LEAD TO DEPRESSION

Sometimes, when we discover that a goal, that might have been uncertain and made us anxious, is impossible, we can get depressed. Depression can depend on physical and chemical reasons in our body, but if not, it's often rooted in a sense of hopelessness and helplessness.

Imagine that you had a best friend who wasn't a Christian, and you made it your life goal to help him or her become a Christian. As the years go past, and nothing happens, you might start believing that you're a bad friend and a useless Christian, and eventually you might even get depressed.

But at the end of the day you can't convert someone, only God can. Wanting your friends to become Christians is good and right, but not if it's a goal that you base your self-worth on!

DISCUSSION
- Do you agree that emotions can show whether your goals are in line with God's will?

- How do you tend to react to blocked goals? Do you remember a time when you didn't get what you wanted? How did that make you feel?

- If we believe that our self-worth depends on a wrong goal, how can we change that before we get depressed?

- How should we respond when one of our goals is blocked?

TURNING BAD GOALS INTO GOOD GOALS
If God gave you a goal for your life, would anyone be able to block it? No. Would it be uncertain? No. Would it be impossible? No.

God had a goal that seemed impossible for a young girl name Mary. An angel told her that although she was a virgin, she would have a son, and that he would be the Saviour of the world. When she wondered at this, the angel said: 'For nothing is impossible with God.' (Luke 1:37)

We need to understand what God's goal for our life is and then say with Mary: 'I am the Lord's servant. May it be to me as you have said.'

No God-given goal can be dependent on people or circumstances that we have no right or ability to control.

Altogether - Bring the groups back together, discuss their thoughts and lead into the next section.

THE DIFFERENCE BETWEEN A 'GOAL' AND A 'DESIRE'
We need to know the difference between a godly 'goal' and a godly 'desire'.

A godly goal is any specific aim that reflects God's purpose for your life and does not depend on people or circumstances beyond your ability or right to control. E.g. becoming more self controlled.

We only have the ability and right to control ourselves, so if we cooperate with God, his goal for our life will be reached.

A godly desire is any specific result that depends on the cooperation of other people, the success of events or circumstances which you have no right or ability to control. E.g. someone becoming a Christian.

We have to be aware that many of our desires in life won't be met, and that shouldn't affect our sense of who we are. When we don't get what we desire we might get disappointed, but we shouldn't need to get depressed.

If we identify our goals to be only ones that we and God can influence, we will avoid lots of unnecessary anger, anxiety and depression. So, in our example of your non-Christian friend, you could change your goal to 'I want to be the best and most caring friend that I can be' – only you can affect the outcome of that!

⬆ WORSHIP ACTIVITY

Give everyone a slip of paper and a pen, and ask them to write one line of worship to God.

When everyone is done; put all the slips of paper in a hat, mix them and pass the hat around.

Let the young people pick one slip at a time, read it out loud, encourage everyone to respond in some way to the line (eg. amen, woop woop, clap etc) and then pass the hat on.

◎ DVD CHAPTER 3

Play Session 12, chapter 3 – 'Aiming Right' - of the accompanying DVD.

GOD'S GOAL FOR OUR LIVES
What's God's goal for us? To become more like Jesus.

God's goal for us is to be the person that he made us to be; he wants us to become like Jesus. Nobody, apart from yourself, can stop you from getting there, but every day will be a struggle against the world, the flesh (remember that?) and the devil.

God's goal for our life is to do with our character – what we are like – rather than what we do.

When we run into difficulties, we shouldn't run away (where we'll bump into the same problem again sooner or later), but we should work through them and end up better people ourselves.

That is how we grow and become more like Jesus.

Review the points on page 50 of the Youth Guide 15-18:

*   God's main goal for you is that you become more and more like Jesus.

*   The only person who can stop you achieving this is you!

*   God doesn't want us to live in despair but has a plan for our lives that we can fulfil no matter what our circumstances.

DISCUSSION
*   What's the difference between a goal and a desire?

*   What do you think is God's goal for your life? Can anyone or anything block it?

*   How do you feel about the fact than nothing can keep you from being the person God created you to be?

↗ RESPONSE

If we are to become more like Jesus with our lives, it is important that we know what he is like.

Ask: 'What is Jesus like?'

Then hand out pieces of paper and ask the young people to write down the characteristic of Jesus that they would most like to develop in their own lives.

Then put a bucket or bin in the middle of the room, screw up the bits of paper and shoot them into the goal as a sign of saying that our goal is to become more like Jesus.

Pray:

Lord, we bring all these emotions and goals before you. We're sorry when we've reacted in ways that aren't honouring to you. We're sorry when we've lived with goals which might have been good desires, but aren't your goals for our lives. Thank you that you forgive us. Help us to know, and live by, your goal for our lives. Amen

Encourage the young people to write God's goal for their lives at the bottom of the sheet of paper.

 # AND THERE'S MORE!

Point out the Challenge and Think sections on page 53 of the Youth Guide 15-18:

Challenge: Are there any goals you have that feel really important to achieve in order to feel good about yourself? Are these in line with God's main goal for you of becoming more like Jesus? Write them down and ask God to help you to begin to aim for his goal for your life.

Think: Do you get angry, anxious or discouraged when you think of what you want to achieve in life and maybe even feel like a failure? God does not want us to feel like this. He has given us a goal that is achievable!

CLOSING QUESTION

The question for next week is on page 53 of the Youth Guide 15-18:

If you find out that your goals are not the same as God's goals for your life – would you be willing to change them? How easily could you change what you believe?

Encourage them to keep going with their stronghold-busters. Even though it probably feels like a waste of time sometimes, they will eventually see a breakthrough.

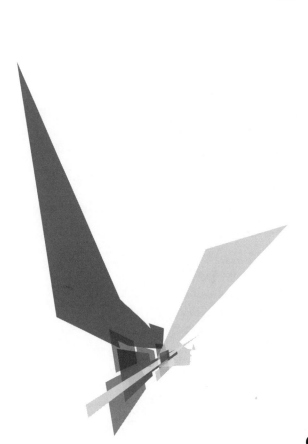

SESSION THIRTEEN:
KEEPING GOING

'I have learned to be content whatever the circumstances. I know what it is to be in need, and I know what it is to have plenty. I have learned the secret of being content in any and every situation, whether well fed or hungry, whether living in plenty or in want. I can do everything through him who gives me strength.'

Philippians 4:11-13

KEEPING GOING CORE

INTRODUCTION

This is our last session, and we are going to finish off by gathering some great ideas for how to stay on the right path, to live our lives free in Christ.

In this last session, we're going to think about eight key areas of our lives and look briefly at what God says is true about them. As you prepare, take some time to consider these things yourself. After each one, pause and ask yourself, 'Do you agree? Why?'

First, however, why not have a go at completing a short series of questions that we will ask the young people to consider too (it's part of the downloadable material for this session). Please spend a few minutes looking at these – rate yourself from 1 (very low) to 5 (very high) on each one and answer the "I would be more" question.

		1	2	3	4	5	
1.	How successful am I?	1	2	3	4	5	I would be more successful if...
2.	How significant am I?	1	2	3	4	5	I would be more significant if...
3.	How fulfilled am I?	1	2	3	4	5	I would be more fulfilled if...
4.	How satisfied am I?	1	2	3	4	5	I would be more satisfied if...
5.	How happy am I?	1	2	3	4	5	I would be happier if...

6. How much fun am I having?	1	2	3	4	5	I would have more fun if...
7. How secure am I?	1	2	3	4	5	I would be more secure if...
8. How peaceful am I?	1	2	3	4	5	I would have more peace if...

We would be fascinated to know what you put there. Did any youth leader score themselves a 5 on every question do you think?. In fact, do you think it could be right for a Christian to score a 5 on every question?

Well, does God want you to be successful? Does He want you to feel secure? One thing's for sure. He certainly hasn't called you to be a miserable, unfulfilled, insignificant failure!

It all comes down to how you define the meaning of 'success', 'significance' and so on. What we want the young people to know is this: if they believe what God says about these eight key areas (use his true definition), there's no reason whatsoever why they should not be hitting '5's - if not all the time, at least much of the time. Their answers (and yours!) to the questions, incidentally, will show what they currently believe 'success', 'significance' etc. mean - and that might well not be in line with God's definition of them.

So let's look at them briefly.

1) WE'RE SUCCESSFUL IF WE HAVE THE RIGHT GOAL
What are your goals for life? How likely do you think you are to achieve those goals?

It's perfectly possible to be a complete failure in the eyes of the world and be successful in the eyes of God. You can also be a success in this world, and a complete failure for all eternity. If your goal is to be a pop star, you might not look very successful in your own eyes. But if your goal is God's goal for your life; to become more like Jesus, you are probably already a success!

2) SIGNIFICANT ACTIVITIES HAVE ETERNAL VALUE
What lasts for eternity? The world thinks that the final of a major sporting event is significant when it happens, but does anyone really care in 25 years time, even less in eternity? You might think that a certain band that you listen to is really significant, but where will that band be in 20 years from now?

On the other hands, we can seriously underestimate the significance of some of the things we do; 'I just help with the children's work.' That's amazingly significant! You're teaching truth to children who are themselves hugely important to God and might go on to change the world. Wow! What a privilege!

There are no insignificant children of God, and there are no insignificant tasks in the kingdom of God.

3) WE'RE FULFILLED WHEN WE SERVE OTHERS
Peter wrote: 'Each one should use whatever gift he has received to serve others, faithfully administering God's grace in its various forms' (1 Peter 4:10). Fulfilment is discovering our own uniqueness in Christ and using our gifts and talents to build others up and glorify God.

The world tells us that we need to have lots of stuff, be famous, have the perfect boyfriend or girlfriend, in order to be fulfilled. God tells us to be the person that he has made us to be, and to serve other people. That's what will make us fulfilled.

4) WE'RE SATISFIED WHEN WE LIVE A QUALITY LIFE
Jesus said: 'Blessed are those who hunger and thirst for righteousness, for they will be filled' (Matthew 5:6). The only way to be satisfied is to live a righteous life.

What causes you to be dissatisfied with something? It's the quality of something, the quality of the relationship or the quality of the food you're trying to eat. Satisfaction is not about having lots of relationships, but good quality ones.

5) WE'RE HAPPY WHEN WE WANT WHAT WE HAVE

Adverts tell us that we will only be happy when we have a better mobile, trendier clothes or the newest trainers. It's all about having what we want. Yet so many people have all these things, but are not happy. True happiness is wanting what you have. By focusing on what you don't have, you will inevitably become unhappy. Turn that around, however, and, as Paul wrote:

'Godliness with contentment is great gain. For we brought nothing into the world, and we can take nothing out of it. But if we have food and clothing, we will be content with that.' (1 Timothy 6:6-8)

We already have everything we need to make us happy for eternity: Christ and the fantastic spiritual life he gave us.

6) WE HAVE FUN WHEN WE ENJOY LIFE MOMENT BY MOMENT

The best way to have fun is to stop trying to be cool. Some people solve this by drinking alcohol ot taking drugs which lessen their inhibitions. And they end up decidedly uncool!

We don't need to do drink or take drugs to stop our inhibitions holding us back. We can just relax, and know our worth in Christ – we don't need to try to impress anyone. Stop caring about what people might say, start caring about what God will say and have fun!

7) WE ARE SECURE WHEN WE FOCUS ON ETERNAL VALUES

We can't find security in things that won't last (our looks, our talents, friends or family), but it has to be based on things that are eternal. Jesus said that no one can snatch us out of his hand (John 10:27-29). Paul declared that nothing can separate us from the love of God in Christ (Romans 8:35-39).

How much more secure can you get than that?

8) WE FIND GOD'S PEACE INSIDE NOT OUTSIDE

We already have peace **with** God (Romans 5:1). The peace **of** God is something we need to grab hold of every day inside ourselves. It doesn't come from things outside of us – money, insurance policies, alarm systems – but God puts it in our hearts.

'My peace I give you. I do not give to you as the world gives. Do not let your hearts be troubled and do not be afraid.' (John 14:27)

TODAY IS THE FIRST DAY OF THE REST OF YOUR LIFE

Walking by faith means making a decision to believe what God says is true and to live in the power of the Holy Spirit. Are you doing that in these eight crucial areas?

This session might have shown you a couple of areas where you need to decide to believe things differently. Remember that God's goal for you is to make you like Jesus – it's about your character, what you're **like** rather than what you **do**.

As you lead this sessions, we suggest that you give it a celebratory feel. It would be great to hear stories of how God has changed the young people's lives during the course. But then start to look ahead:

- What are they going to do with their new-found freedom?

- How can they direct their lives to meeting the needs of others?

- What opportunities are there for them to get involved with significant activities (those whose results will last for eternity)?

KEEPING GOING 11-14

LEADER'S PREPARATION

Pray together:

❝ Father God, thank you for everything you have done in me and all the young people during this course. Please help today to be a fantastic first day of the rest of our lives. Amen.

YOU MAY NEED

'What do I believe?' questionnaire (downloadable) and pens

Large plan / bricks / binoculars

Accompanying DVD / DVD player / TV / projector

Basketball hoop / money / washing up bowl & brush

Some fine food and some economy food

Party poppers / Life jacket or float

Bibles

Large sheets of paper / flipchart and marker pens

Small group questions

 ## PRAYER AND DECLARATION

Encourage everyone to join together in saying the following prayer and declaration. You can download the PowerPoint slides with the words for these from the website.

It would be good to suggest that the young people stand up and speak out the declaration clearly and confidently to the heavenly realms. They could shout it out and use appropriate actions!

PRAYER

❝ Father, help us to walk away at the end of the session today with a deeper understanding of who we are in you and a stronger ability to walk on your path, ultimately being changed to be more and more like Jesus, Amen.

DECLARATION: IN A CLEAR, CONFIDENT TONE!

❝ Jesus is the king of the world and the king of my life. He holds all authority in his hands and stamps his enemies under his feet. All his enemies - be gone now in Jesus' name!

YOU NEVER KNOW, IT MIGHT JUST WORK!

As this is the final session, why not do something a little different? When Jesus talked about the Kingdom of God, he often talked of celebrations and feasts. Why not throw a a party to celebrate the end of the course and what God has done in the young people's lives?

There are two ways you could run this final session. You could run it like the other sessions and the material for this follows.

On the other hand, you could do something like this:

- Prepare by decorating your venue or having a social activity (see the Launch Session, pages 24 - 26, for ideas - do something different to your launch session).

- Play the game in the Starting Point below or your favourite game from the course so far.

- Have a party! Eat the snacks you have prepared. Allow the young people space to chat.

- Bring the group together and ask them to share together two things in pairs: 1. The main thing they have learned from the course, 2. One way in which they will live their life differently.

- Have a feedback session in which people can share the same things with the whole group. You may want to encourage the group to cheer loudly - to celebrate! You could have some party poppers to let off at appropriate moments.

- Watch the DVD for this session - we suggest you run it all the way through in one go.

- In the same pairs, ask them to share one thing that they want to do to show God's love to those around them and one challenge that they are still facing.

- Encourage them to pray for each other about the things they have talked about.

🔍 STARTING POINT

WHAT DO I BELIEVE?
Hand out the 'What do I believe?' questionnaire and spend five minutes or so in silence as everyone gets a chance to complete it.

BALANCING ACT
Get hold of a large plank and balance it on a couple of bricks at each end (don't make it too high!). See who can walk down the plank the fastest (use a stop watch), but with the added twist that they must look the wrong way through a pair of binoculars as they do so.

Leader's Note: Make sure you risk assess this activity before you decide to do it.

Explain

Well done to those of you who stayed on the plank. With some tips we look at today, it shouldn't be quite as hard to stay on the path of life.

⬆ WORSHIP ACTIVITY

Put the list below (downloadable) up onto a big screen. Ask the young people to reflect on what God has done in their lives throughout this course, and let them choose one statement that best describes their situation.

Teach the group the line from 1 Chronicles 16:34 (The Message):

'Give thanks to God – he is good and his love never quits.'

Stand in a circle and let one person at a time read out 'their' statement. Between each person read the Bible verse out loud together.

Statements:

- God has made me grow.

- I know better now that God loves me.

- God has met me.

- God has changed my life.

- I know that God has accepted me.

- I have found freedom in Jesus.

- God has changed the direction of my life.

- I have been saved by God.

- I know now that I don't have anything to be scared of.

- God has made me a better person.

- I love God so much more now.

INTRODUCTION TO SESSION

Give a short summary of the previous session. A good resource for this is the Overview found in the Core of the previous session.

This is our last session, and we're going to finish off by picking up some great ideas for how to live our lives free in Christ.

◉ DVD CHAPTER 1

Play Session 13, chapter 1 – 'Focusing On Success?' – of the accompanying DVD.

Ask the group:

- What does success mean to you?

- Maybe getting amazing grades in your exams?

- Getting a great job?

- Having loads of money?

- Getting the girl or getting the guy?

- Getting through one day to the next?

STATIONS

Set up eight stations around your venue and move from station to station as you go through the different points. Leaders's Note: have some appropriate props at each station - some are suggested below.

After each station, discuss 'Do you agree? Why? Why not?'

I'm not going to ask you to share what you wrote in the questionnaire earlier, but here's a question for you: Do you think anyone here ticked a 5 for every section? If they did, do you think they're a bit mad ?

OVERVIEW

In this last session, as we're learning to stay on the right path, I'm going to take you on a walk to show you that we should be able to tick 5 for each of them, if not all the time at least much of it.

It all depends on what you see as the meaning of the different things. Does 'success' mean the same thing to you as it means to God? If it doesn't we might need to do some more renewing of our minds.

1) WE'RE SUCCESSFUL IF WE HAVE THE RIGHT GOAL

Gather the group around the basket ball hoop (or something similar). Let the young people take a few shots at the hoop. Ask how successful they think they were at this.

It's perfectly possible to be a complete failure in the eyes of the world and be successful in the eyes of God. You can also be a success in this world, and a complete failure for all eternity. If your goal is to be a pop star, you might not look very successful in your own eyes.

But if your goal is God's goal for your life; to become more like Jesus; it doesn't matter if you can't sing or dance, you can be a success.

Discuss in small groups or all together: Do you agree? Why? Why not?

2) WE'RE SIGNIFICANT BECAUSE OF OUR ETERNAL VALUE

What lasts for eternity? The world thinks that a major sporting event [choose one that appeals to your group] is significant when it happens, but does anyone really care in 25 years time, even less in eternity?

You might think that a certain band that you listen to is really significant, but where will that band be in 20 years from now?

We might think that what we do isn't really significant: 'I just help with the young children at church'. That's amazingly significant! You're teaching truth to 5-year olds (who are very significant to God) and you're freeing up parents (again very significant) to worship. There are no insignificant children of God, and there are no insignificant tasks in the kingdom of God.

Discuss in small groups or all together: Do you agree? Why? Why not?

3) WE'RE FULFILLED WHEN WE SERVE OTHERS

Get out the washing up bowl and brush. Encourage some of the young people to do some washing up! If you served refreshments earlier, this is a good way to get the plates and cups cleaned!

Peter wrote:

'Each one should use whatever gift he has received to serve others, faithfully administering God's grace in its various forms' (1 Peter 4:10).

Fulfilment is discovering our own uniqueness in Christ and using our gifts and talents to build others up and glorify God.

The world tells us that we need to have lots of stuff, be famous or have the perfect boyfriend or girlfriend in order to be fulfilled. God tells us to be the person that he has made us to be, and to serve other people. That's what will make us fulfilled.

Discuss in small groups or all together: Do you agree? Why? Why not?

4) WE'RE SATISFIED WHEN WE LIVE A QUALITY LIFE

Have some top of the range food and some cheaper food ready. Share it all out and then let the young people eat it.

Jesus said:

'Blessed are those who hunger and thirst for righteousness, for they will be filled' (Matthew 5:6).

The only way to be satisfied is to live a righteous life.

What causes you to be dissatisfied with something? It's the quality of something, the quality of the relationship or the quality of the food you're trying to eat. Satisfaction is not about having lots of relationship, but good quality ones.

Discuss in small groups or all together: Do you agree? Why? Why not?

5) WE'RE HAPPY WHEN WE WANT WHAT WE HAVE

Have some advertisements for desirable items on show.

Adverts tell us that we will only be happy when we have a better phone, trendier clothes or the newest trainers. It's all about having what we want. Yet so many people have all these things, but are not happy.

True happiness is wanting what you have. By focusing on what you don't have, you will inevitably become unhappy. Paul wrote:

'Godliness with contentment is great gain. For we brought nothing into the world, and we can take nothing out of it. But if we have food and clothing, we will be content with that.' (1 Timothy 6:6-8)

We already have everything we need to make us happy for eternity: Christ and eternal life.

Discuss in small groups or all together: Do you agree? Why? Why not?

Ask the group what they have that really makes them happy.

6) WE HAVE FUN WHEN WE ENJOY LIFE MOMENT BY MOMENT

Share out some party poppers and let your group members let them off.

The best way to have fun is to stop trying to be cool. To do that we have to get rid of our inhibitions. Some people do that by drinking too much or taking drugs – and they certainly end up decidedly uncool!

We don't have to do that. We can just relax, and know our worth in Christ – we don't need to try to impress anyone. Stop caring what people might say, start caring about what God will say and have fun!

Discuss in small groups or all together: Do you agree? Why? Why not?

7) WE ARE SECURE WHEN WE FOCUS ON ETERNAL VALUES
You could gather round a clock to emphasise that this is about things that last over time.

We can't find security in things that won't last (our looks, our talents, friends or family), but it has to be based on things that are eternal. Jesus said that no one can snatch us out of his hand (John 10:27-29).

Paul declared that nothing can separate us from the love of God in Christ (Romans 8:35-39). How much more secure can you get than that?

Discuss in small groups or all together: Do you agree? Why? Why not?

8) WE FIND GOD'S PEACE INSIDE NOT OUTSIDE
Use one of the young people as a prop - the peace of God is inside them!

We already have peace **with** God (Romans 5:1). The peace **of** God is something we need to grab hold of every day inside ourselves. It doesn't come from things outside of us – money, insurance policies, alarm systems – but God puts it in our hearts.

'My peace I give you. I do not give to you as the world gives. Do not let your hearts be troubled and do not be afraid.' (John 14:27)

Discuss in small groups or all together: Do you agree? Why? Why not?

◉ DVD CHAPTER 2

Play Session 13, chapter 2 – 'Serving God' – of the accompanying DVD.

Explain: Today is the first day of the rest of your life.

Walking by faith means making a decision to believe what God says is true - particularly about these eight important areas - to choose every day to live in the power of the Holy Spirit.

This session might have showed you a couple of areas where you need to decide to believe things differently. Remember that God's goal for you is to make you like Jesus – it's about your character, what you're **like**, rather than what you **do**.

↗ RESPONSE

Make a large board or piece of paper, where the top quarter is filled with the words:

'We're following God's goal for our lives.'

Hand out the illustration of the outline of a person (downloadable) and cut out a few more than you have people in your group.

Ask your group to spend some time quietly thinking about whether they're ready to say to God that they want to follow his goal for their life.

If they feel that they are, they may write their name on a cut-out-person or draw their features on it and then stick it up on the board.

Pray:

Father, we stand together as a small part of the Body of Christ, and we say that we want to follow you – properly! We want to follow your goal for our lives, we want to become more like Jesus. Amen.

DVD CHAPTER 3

Play Session 13, chapter 3 – 'Freedom In Christ' – of the accompanying DVD.

SMALL GROUPS & PRAYER FOCUS

Spend some time in small groups considering these questions:

*   What am I going to do with my new-found freedom?

*   What will I do to meet the needs of others?

*   What opportunities are there for me to get involved with significant activities (those whose results will last for eternity)?

Then pray for one another, saying thank you to God for what he is doing in each of your lives, and asking him to continue doing it.

AND THERE'S MORE!

Remind the young people of the three lists of Biblical truth from the first three sessions and suggest that they keep referring to them.

Encourage them to keep going with their stronghold-busters. Even though it probably feels like a waste of time sometimes, they will eventually see a breakthrough.

Refer them to the question on page 55 of the Youth Guide 11-14:

*   How are you going to keep living in freedom and growing as a Christian?

KEEPING GOING 15-18

YOU NEVER KNOW, IT MIGHT JUST WORK!

As this is the final session, why not do something a little different? When Jesus talked about the Kingdom of God, he often talked of celebrations and feasts. Why not throw a party to celebrate the end of the course and what God has done in the young people's lives?

There are two ways you could run this final session. You could run it like the other sessions and the material for this follows.

On the other hand, you could do something like this:

- Prepare by decorating your venue or having a social activity (see the Launch Session, pages 24 - 26, for ideas - do something different to your launch session).

- Prepare something extra special to eat and drink this week.

- Do the Worship Activity below on page 312.

- Bring the group together and ask them to share together two things in pairs: 1. The main thing they have learned from the course, 2. One way in which they will live their life differently.

- Get a large ball such as a beach ball and have the group throw it one to another. When someone catches the ball, they have to share a highlight from the course. Encourage a round of applause after each person who shares.

- Watch the DVD for this session - we suggest you run it all the way through in one go.

- In the same pairs, ask the young people to share one thing that they want to do to show God's love to those around them and one challenge that they are still facing.

- Encourage them to pray for each other about the things they have talked about.

PRAYER AND DECLARATION

Encourage everyone to join together in saying the following prayer and declaration. You can download the PowerPoint slides with the words for these from the website.

It would be good to suggest that the young people stand up and speak out the declaration clearly and confidently to the heavenly realms. They could shout it out and use appropriate actions!

PRAYER

Father, help us to walk away at the end of the session today with a deeper understanding of who we are in you and a stronger ability to walk on your path, ultimately being changed to be more and more like Jesus, Amen.

DECLARATION: IN A CLEAR, CONFIDENT TONE!

Jesus is the king of the world and the king of my life. He holds all authority in his hands and stamps his enemies under his feet. All his enemies - be gone now in Jesus' name!

STARTING POINT

Over the welcome drinks ask the group:

What does success mean to you?

- Maybe getting amazing grades in your exams?

- Getting a great job?

- Having loads of money?

- Getting the girl or getting the guy?

- Getting through one day to the next?

Give a short summary of the previous session. A good resource for this is the Overview found in the Core of the previous session.

This is our last session, and we're going to finish off by picking up some great ideas for how to live our lives free in Christ.

DVD CHAPTER 1

Play Session 13, chapter 1 – 'Focusing On Success?' of the accompanying DVD.

⌂ SOAPBOX

Leader's Note: Ask eight young people or a mixture of leaders and young people to take one of the eight truths each and present it / lead discussion on it to the group. If you have a large group give them the paragraphs before the evening. Alternatively give them out on the night and allow 10 minutes' preparation time. Make sure you telephone / go round the people you have asked to encourage them and ensure they understand what they are supposed to be doing. You could show them the 11-14s session plan and the various props associated with the eight areas there to help with creative ideas.

WHAT DO I BELIEVE?

Hand out the 'What do I believe?' questionnaire (downloadable) and spend five minutes or so in silence as everyone gets a chance to complete it.

I'm not going to ask you to share what you put down but here's a question for you: Do you think anyone here ticked a 5 for every section? If they did, do you think they're a bit mad ?

In this last session, as we're learning to stay on the right path. We're going to look briefly at the eight areas on the questionnaire. Maybe by the end you'll see that it could be possible to put a 5 down - even for you! - if not all the time at least much of it.

It all depends on what you see as the meaning of the different things. Does 'success' mean the same thing to you as it means to God? If it doesn't we might need to do some more renewing of our minds.

Hand over to the people who are going to lead on the eight areas.

1) WE'RE SUCCESSFUL IF WE HAVE THE RIGHT GOAL

It's perfectly possible to be a complete failure in the eyes of the world and be successful in the eyes of God. You can also be a success in this world, and a complete failure for all eternity. If your goal is to be a pop star, you might not look very successful in your own eyes.

But if your goal is God's goal for your life; to become more like Jesus; it doesn't matter if you can't sing or dance, you can be a success.

Do you agree? Why? Why not?

2) WE'RE SIGNIFICANT BECAUSE OF OUR ETERNAL VALUE

What lasts for eternity? The world thinks that a major sporting event [choose one that appeals to your group] is significant when it happens, but does anyone really care in 25 years time, even less in eternity?

You might think that a certain band that you listen to is really significant, but where will that band be in 20 years from now?

We might think that what we do isn't really significant: 'I just help with the young children at church'. That's amazingly significant! You're teaching truth to 5-year olds (who are very significant to God) and you're freeing up parents (again very significant) to worship. There are no insignificant children of God, and there are no insignificant tasks in the kingdom of God.

Do you agree? Why? Why not?

3) WE'RE FULFILLED WHEN WE SERVE OTHERS

Peter wrote:

'Each one should use whatever gift he has received to serve others, faithfully administering God's grace in its various forms' (1 Peter 4:10).

Fulfilment is discovering our own uniqueness in Christ and using our gifts and talents to build others up and glorify God.

The world tells us that we need to have lots of stuff, be famous or have the perfect boyfriend or girlfriend in order to be fulfilled. God tells us to be the person that he has made us to be, and to serve other people. That's what will make us fulfilled.

Why? Why not?

4) WE'RE SATISFIED WHEN WE LIVE A QUALITY LIFE
Jesus said:

'Blessed are those who hunger and thirst for righteousness, for they will be filled' (Matthew 5:6).

The only way to be satisfied is to live a righteous life.

What causes you to be dissatisfied with something? It's the quality of something, the quality of the relationship or the quality of the food you're trying to eat. Satisfaction is not about having lots of relationship, but good quality ones.

Do you agree? Why? Why not?

5) WE'RE HAPPY WHEN WE WANT WHAT WE HAVE
Adverts tell us that we will only be happy when we have a better phone, trendier clothes or the newest trainers. It's all about having what we want. Yet so many people have all these things, but are not happy.

True happiness is wanting what you have. By focusing on what you don't have, you will inevitably become unhappy. Paul wrote:

'Godliness with contentment is great gain. For we brought nothing into the world, and we can take nothing out of it. But if we have food and clothing, we will be content with that.' (1 Timothy 6:6-8)

We already have everything we need to make us happy for eternity: Christ and eternal life.

Do you agree? Why? Why not?

6) WE HAVE FUN WHEN WE ENJOY LIFE MOMENT BY MOMENT
The best way to have fun is to stop trying to be cool. To do that we have to get rid of our inhibitions. Some people do that by drinking too much or taking drugs – and they certainly end up decidedly uncool!

We don't have to do that. We can just relax, and know our worth in Christ – we don't need to try to impress anyone. Stop caring what people might say, start caring about what God will say and have fun!

Do you agree? Why? Why not?

7) WE ARE SECURE WHEN WE FOCUS ON ETERNAL VALUES

We can't find security in things that won't last (our looks, our talents, friends or family), but it has to be based on things that are eternal. Jesus said that no one can snatch us out of his hand (John 10:27-29).

Paul declared that nothing can separate us from the love of God in Christ (Romans 8:35-39). How much more secure can you get than that?

Do you agree? Why? Why not?

8) WE FIND GOD'S PEACE INSIDE NOT OUTSIDE

We already have peace **with** God (Romans 5:1). The peace **of** God is something we need to grab hold of every day inside ourselves. It doesn't come from things outside of us – money, insurance policies, alarm systems – but God puts it in our hearts.

'My peace I give you. I do not give to you as the world gives. Do not let your hearts be troubled and do not be afraid.' (John 14:27)

Do you agree? Why? Why not?

 # DVD CHAPTER 2

Play Session 13, chapter 2 – 'Serving God' – of the accompanying DVD.

TODAY IS THE FIRST DAY OF THE REST OF YOUR LIFE

Walking by faith means making a decision to believe what God says is true - particularly about these eight important areas - and to choose every day to live in the power of the Holy Spirit.

This session might have showed you a couple of areas where you need to decide to believe things differently. Remember that God's goal for you is to make you like Jesus – it's about your character, what you're **like**, rather than what you **do**.

 # WORSHIP ACTIVITY

Put the list below up on a big screen:

Ask the young people to reflect on what God has done in their lives throughout this course, and let them choose one statement that best describes their situation.

Teach the group the line from 1 Chronicles 16:34 (The Message):

'Give thanks to God – he is good and his love never quits.'

Stand in a circle and let one person at a time read out 'their' statement. Between each person read the Bible verse out loud together.

Statements:

- God has made me grow.

- I know better now that God loves me.

- God has met me.

- God has changed my life.

- I know that God has accepted me.

- I have found freedom in Jesus.

- God has changed the direction of my life.

- I have been saved by God.

- I know now that I don't have anything to be scared of.

- God has made me a better person.

- I love God so much more now.

Review the items under 'What's the point?' on page 54 of the Youth Guide 15-18:

- Becoming more like Jesus will involve a choice every day to throw out wrong beliefs and exchange them for the truth.

- God is intimately concerned with your life and has plans to give you a hope and a future.

- Don't try to be like someone else! Be the unique person that God has designed you to be.

↗ RESPONSE

Make a large board or piece of paper, where the top quarter is filled with the words:

'We're following God's goal for our lives.'

Hand out the illustration of the outline of a person (downloadable) and cut out a few more than you have people in your group.

Ask your group to spend some time quietly thinking about whether they're ready to say to God that they want to follow his goal for their life.

If they feel that they are, they may write their name on a cut-out-person or draw their features on it and then stick it up on the board.

Pray:

Father, we stand together as a small part of the Body of Christ, and we say that we want to follow you – properly! We want to follow your goal for our lives, we want to become more like Jesus. Amen.

⊙ DVD CHAPTER 3

Play Session 13, chapter 3 – 'Freedom In Christ' of the accompanying DVD.

👥 SMALL GROUPS & PRAYER FOCUS

Spend some time in small groups considering these questions:

• What am I going to do with my new-found freedom?

• What will I do to meet the needs of others?

• What opportunities are there for me to get involved with significant activities (those whose results will last for eternity)?

Then pray for one another, saying thank you to God for what he is doing in each of your lives, and asking him to continue doing it.

⭐ AND THERE'S MORE!

Remind the young people of the three lists of Biblical truth from the first three sessions and suggest that they keep referring to them.

Encourage them to keep going with their stronghold-busters. Even though it probably feels like a waste of time sometimes, they will eventually see a breakthrough.

Refer them to the 'Challenge' on page 57 of the Youth Guide 15-18:

'Think about the thing that has most stood out to you during this course, the most important thing you have discovered, and tell someone else this week.'

ADDITIONAL INFORMATION

ABOUT YOUTH FOR CHRIST

British Youth for Christ was started in 1946 by Billy Graham, and now, 60 years later YFC remains committed to evangelism and discipleship of young people.

Our mission is to "take the good news relevantly to every young person in Britain".

We seek to achieve this through day-to-day contact and working in partnership with individuals, churches and Christian agencies across the country.

Around 80% of our work is done in schools, and we have year-out teams who communicate through sports and creative arts, working with local YFC centres to demonstrate the love of God to thousands of young people each week.

The work of Youth for Christ is far reaching:

- It touches young offenders in prison, schools, youth groups, churches and summer holiday camps

- It provides resources like Freedom In Christ for Young People to youth group leaders around the country.

- We have almost 70 local centres across the country – from the Shetlands in the north of Scotland, down to the Isle of Wight, and across to Wales.

Freedom In Christ for Young People builds on and complements our existing youth resources including:

- Mettle

- Rock Solid

- The Art of Connecting.

Find out more at **www.yfc.co.uk**

Youth for Christ

ABOUT FREEDOM IN CHRIST

Freedom In Christ Ministries (FICM) was founded in the USA in 1988 by Dr. Neil T. Anderson, author of best-selling books such as Victory Over The Darkness and The Bondage Breaker. Well over four million copies have been sold worldwide.

It now has offices and representatives in many countries. The UK office was started by Steve and Zoë Goss in 1999. See the next page for more details of the USA office. For contact details in other countries, please consult our international website at www.ficminternational.org.

The mission of FICM is to equip the Church worldwide, enabling it to establish its people, marriages and ministries alive and free in Christ through genuine repentance and faith in God.

FICM IN THE UK:

- The Freedom In Christ Discipleship Course (upon which Freedom In Christ For Young People is based) was written specifically for UK church leaders in order to help them make fruitful disciples (not just converts). Well over 100,000 have used it in the UK. It is often used as a follow-on to Christian basics courses such as Alpha and Christianity Explored.

- FICM runs conferences and training for leaders and provides opportunities for them to experience the Steps To Freedom.

- We are always happy to offer advice to leaders and youth leaders on general discipleship and how to help those struggling with deeper issues.

- Ask us for our full colour catalogue of, books, DVDs and CDs with resources for churches and individuals as well as areas such as fear, depression and addiction. You can also see full details on our website including a range for young people.

- If you are using Freedom In Christ materials to help others, you will benefit from joining the Freedom Fellowship. You will receive a binder containing helpful documents and tips and receive regular news, and encouragement. Open to anyone involved in helping others take hold of their freedom (cost: £20 per year).

HOW CAN WE SERVE YOU?

Our role in life is to support church leaders and youth leaders. For details of any of the above, or if there is any other way we can help you, feel free to contact us. See our website at www.ficm.org.uk, e-mail us at info@ficm.org.uk, or write to us at: Freedom In Christ Ministries, PO Box 2842, Reading RG2 9RT, UK.

INTERNATIONAL WEBSITE DETAILS
For a complete list go to www.ficminternational.org

Canada:	www.ficm.ca
South Africa:	www.ficmsa.co.za
UK:	www.ficm.orfg.uk
USA:	www.ficm.org

FREEDOM IN CHRIST

MESSAGE TO AMERICAN YOUTH PASTORS AND LEADERS

Youth in America today are fully immersed in a culture of postmodernism that steals true joy, kills faith and destroys true hope in the living God and in our Lord Jesus Christ. That's why we are pleased to bring you Freedom in Christ for Young People, a joint venture of Freedom in Christ Ministries (FICM) and Youth for Christ (YFC). Developed in Britain with much collaboration over here in the States, this project provides a warm bath of grace and truth that can truly liberate and transform the hearts of young people.

The video portions, with British presenters, Nathan Iles and Kate John, are simple and engaging. Filmed on-site around the United Kingdom (UK), the sequences are short in duration and powerful in content. Nathan's accent is a little stronger than Kate's but your young people will enjoy his straightforward approach as well as Kate's kind, compassionate heart. You may even find your youth listening more attentively because of their accents.

The Youth Guides are simple, clear, interactive and colorful, with separate age-appropriate guides for 11-14 and 15-18 year olds. The Leader's Guide is thorough and comprehensive. We have worked hard to avoid language and cultural matters that would confuse or distract American kids. You will notice a few spelling differences in words like 'neighbour', 'armour', 'recognise, 'defence'. The spelling differences even provide a bit of international flavor (flavour?) to the material and you and your young people will easily get used to them. Over here in America, we have designed a website where you can register for access to:

- PowerPoint presentations of the Freedom in Christ for Young People teaching sessions
- Additional teaching resources for use during the sessions
- A glossary of British terms used by Nathan and Kate during the video portions, so you can prepare your young people for what they will hear before they watch the videos
- Creative ideas from other youth leaders using the Freedom in Christ for Young People material to make the sessions more fun and learning more interactive

You will also be able to connect with a team of youth leaders experienced in helping young people discover freedom in Christ. They can answer questions and even help you learn to minister to hurting youth through training in how to use The Steps to Freedom in Christ one-to-one. It's all at: **www. generationfreedom.org/fic4youngpeople**

I commend this resource to you as Jesus-centered, biblically accurate, youth-culturally relevant, and life-transforming. Based on the Biblically balanced best-selling books by FICM founder, Dr. Neil Anderson, **Victory Over the Darkness** and **The Bondage Breaker**, and the DVD series "The Freedom in Christ Small Group Bible Study" (an adult discipleship study), Freedom in Christ for Young People is well-worth the investment.

One of the most exciting elements of this project is the development of two, brand new versions of The Steps to Freedom in Christ, one for middle schoolers and one for high school students. As a father of both, I am thrilled with how powerful these tools will be.

We trust that as you pray, prepare and present the Freedom in Christ for Young People material, you will be personally encouraged and genuinely excited in your ministry. We look forward to "meeting" you at www. generationfreedom.org/fic4youngpeople

Rich Miller (President, FICM-USA)

THE FREEDOM IN CHRIST DISCIPLESHIP BOOK SERIES

These four books by Steve Goss are highly recommended to those leading the course. Available from Freedom In Christ Ministries or Christian bookshops.

- **Each book corresponds to a part of Freedom In Christ For Young People**
- **Highly recommended to youth leaders for background information**
- **Concise, straightforward and quick to read**

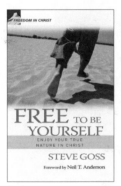

FREE TO BE YOURSELF
ENJOY YOUR TRUE NATURE IN CHRIST
Many Christians act as they think a Christian should act – and find that they simply can't keep it up. They either drop out or burn out. True fruitfulness comes from realising that we became someone completely new the moment we became Christians. Corresponds to sessions 1 to 3 of Freedom In Christ For Young People.

WIN THE DAILY BATTLE
RESIST AND STAND FIRM IN GOD'S STRENGTH
If you are a Christian you are in a raging battle, whether you like it or not. Your only choice is to stand and fight or to become a casualty. Arrayed against you are the world, the devil and the flesh. They seem formidable. However, once you understand just who you are in Christ and how your enemies work, you can expect to emerge victorious from every skirmish with them. Corresponds to sessions 4 to 7 of Freedom In Christ For Young People.

BREAK FREE, STAY FREE
DON'T LET THE PAST HOLD YOU BACK
Every Christian has a past. It can hold us back big-time. Those of us carrying a lot of "stuff" know that only too well. But even those who have had a relatively trouble-free existence thus far will benefit from understanding how to identify, and resolve, past sin and negative influences that stop us moving on. Corresponds to sessions 8 to 10 (part) of Freedom In Christ For Young People.

THE YOU GOD PLANNED
DON'T LET ANYTHING OR ANYONE HOLD YOU BACK
Once we have claimed our freedom in Christ, how do we remain in it and become the people God is calling us to be? How do we know what God is calling us to be anyway? Are the goals we have for our lives in line with his goals? How can we stop other people getting in the way of our growth to fruitfulness? And how do we avoid getting in their way? Corresponds to sessions 10 (part) to 13 of Freedom In Christ For Young People.

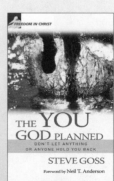

FREEDOM IN CHRIST
FOR YOUNG PEOPLE

"IT IS FOR FREEDOM THAT CHRIST HAS SET US FREE!"

GALATIANS 5:1